CATHOLIC DIOCESES, LEGAL SYSTEMS, AND CORPORATE ACCOUNTABILITY

This book explores how different legal systems handle a particularly difficult type of corporate wrongdoing: Catholic dioceses' responsibility for child sexual abuse.

Usually, when people think about corporate wrongdoing, they think about tax fraud, insider trading, and similar 'white-collar' crime. As corporations, dioceses' responsibility for child sexual abuse exists separately from that of individual perpetrators, and this corporate responsibility is the focus of this book.

Through an analysis of cases involving dioceses that have significant documented histories of priests abusing children, this book illustrates how criminal law, canon law, tort law, bankruptcy law and an Australian Royal Commission have responded (or why they have not). The cases involve the Diocese of Ballarat, in Victoria, Australia, and the Diocese of Gallup, in northern Arizona and New Mexico, in the United States. Each diocese faced similar claims in a diverse field of legal systems, so very different legal systems were handling, in essence, the same cases in dissimilar contexts.

Employing a novel interdisciplinary approach, the book traces the theories, purposes, doctrines, procedures, and logistics of engaging with these different legal systems – evaluating what they can and cannot do. Revitalising theories of responsive law, the book demonstrates that it is possible for legal systems to better hold not just Catholic dioceses, but corporations more generally, to account for wrongdoing, but we may need to rethink how those systems are structured.

Catholic Dioceses, Legal Systems, and Corporate Accountability

Meredith Edelman

•HART•

OXFORD • LONDON • NEW YORK • NEW DELHI • SYDNEY

HART PUBLISHING

Bloomsbury Publishing Plc

Kemp House, Chawley Park, Cumnor Hill, Oxford, OX2 9PH, UK

1385 Broadway, New York, NY 10018, USA

Bloomsbury Publishing Ireland Limited, 29 Earlsfort Terrace, Dublin 2, D02 AY28, Ireland

HART PUBLISHING, the Hart/Stag logo, BLOOMSBURY and the Diana logo are trademarks of Bloomsbury Publishing Plc

First published in Great Britain 2025

A catalogue record for this book is available from the British Library.

A catalogue record for this book is available from the Library of Congress.

Library of Congress Control Number: 2025945686

ISBN: HB: 978-1-50998-207-3
ePDF: 978-1-50998-209-7
ePub: 978-1-50998-208-0

Typeset by Compuscript Ltd, Shannon

For product safety related questions contact productsafety@bloomsbury.com

To find out more about our authors and books visit www.hartpublishing.co.uk. Here you will find extracts, author information, details of forthcoming events and the option to sign up for our newsletters.

PREFACE

There is a wealth of research describing and lamenting the Roman Catholic Church's responsibility for sexual and other kinds of abuse, as well as the difficulties and outcomes of legal processes involving these religious organisations. The literature on this problem reveals significant unaddressed or under-addressed accountability of Catholic organisations, and raises serious questions about whether legal systems are failing to hold wrongdoers accountable. Often, this literature then turns to specific ways that systems could change in order to better respond to victims of child sexual abuse or prevent it happening in the first place. Some reforms have been implemented, and many people have received compensation who otherwise might not have.

But another deep well of literature finds similarly unaddressed or under-addressed accountability of powerful corporations across many domains. Scholars from a range of disciplines point to corporate activity and the limited punishments that corporations face for law-breaking as creating or contributing to the many serious problems facing humanity in the contemporary era.

I take seriously the conclusions reached about the unaddressed accountability of Catholic, as well as other religious, secular and public, organisations that have and continue to turn a blind eye to child abuse. I also take seriously the unaddressed accountability of business corporations around the world for other damaging forms of wrongdoing. This book takes Catholic dioceses' responsibility for child sexual abuse as a case study to consider whether the problem lies in the legal systems, regardless of the nature of the underlying wrong.

Catholic dioceses' responsibility for child sexual abuse may not be the kind of wrong that, for many people, would come to mind when thinking about corporate wrongdoing in the abstract. Corporate wrongdoing tends to be thought of as having to do with defective products, environmental pollution or destruction, misleading advertisements, fraud, tax evasion, securities law violations or anti-competitive conduct. This book starts from the premise that there are more similarities than differences between dioceses' responsibility for abuse and other kinds of corporate wrongs.

Consider how many schools, childcare facilities, hospitals, sporting teams and other kinds of organisations have been identified as responsible for sexual, physical, emotional and other forms of abuse of vulnerable people. Between private military companies, private prisons and the work cultures that enable the likes of Harvey Weinstein, Roger Ailes and George Tyndall, it should not be difficult to imagine the magnitude of corporate responsibility for violence. Other, more 'typical' types of corporate wrongs like pollution, dangerous working conditions and dangerous products cause serious damage to life, health and wellbeing around the world. Diocesan responsibility for child sexual abuse is a complex issue, but in its complexity, it brings to the fore issues that impact the capacity of legal systems to hold corporations accountable for any kind of wrongdoing. This book seeks to explore these issues through the example of two Catholic dioceses which each faced multiple kinds of legal processes.

The literature on the problem of abuse in institutional contexts and on the legal disputes arising from it tends to focus on specific rules – arguing for or measuring the effects of changes to statutes of limitation, for example. Others focus on the outcomes of processes – how they impacted stakeholders, how they changed perceptions, or how they changed law or policy to make it easier to file lawsuits. They tend to argue for social change to prevent child sexual abuse, or for specific changes to law or policy to make it easier to access existing legal systems in order to seek the forms of accountability available.

This book challenges the premise that existing systems are even reasonably fit for the purpose of holding an organisation accountable for serious wrongdoing. Could it be that the systems themselves are standing in the way of dioceses actually being held responsible, and they similarly stand in the way of corporate accountability for harmful products, deaths of workers, damaged ecosystems, tax evasion, fraud and war crimes? By comparing multiple systems tasked with addressing the same problem, this book challenges readers to critically assess how well our legal systems respond to corporate wrongdoing. Catholic dioceses and child sexual abuse are the focus of the legal processes, but the focus of the book is the legal processes themselves.

Why did I choose Catholic dioceses as a case study? From a methodological standpoint, the Church holds unique social, legal and political positions around the world. Between the Church's social positioning and years of advocacy by Survivors and lawyers, there is keen public interest in and condemnation of clerical child sexual abuse. Survivors' quests for justice have been pursued in a variety of ways around the world, including lawsuits, inquiries, royal commissions and independent investigations. This web of legal battlegrounds where cases involving clerical child sexual abuse are presented creates a unique opportunity for empirical analysis of different types of legal systems.

By illustrating how different legal systems handle cases involving the same kind of wrong by the same kind of corporation, this book can distinguish between more and less responsive characteristics of legal systems. Systems like canon law and Chapter 11 bankruptcy, which few people might think should be involved in a legal matter involving child sexual abuse, nonetheless have been involved in a significant number of cases. Tort and criminal law are the systems that most would consider appropriate for handling these cases, but even those whose cases result in a conviction, agreed settlement or finding in their favour rarely have good things to say about the processes. The Australian Royal Commission into Institutional Responses to Child Sexual Abuse was created specifically to address the widespread concern that the Church, like other powerful institutions, was evading accountability for serious wrongdoing, but an Act of Parliament was required to implement its recommendations.

Readers who have chosen this book because of their interest in legal, historical or sociological matters specifically relevant to child sexual abuse and the Catholic Church may find my methodology and conclusions different from most literature in that space, but may nevertheless find the book useful. Observations about the differences between dioceses, how social differences between victims can impact whether they receive redress, and why Survivor advocacy has been so critical to the redress that has been achieved will likely resonate with those readers. They may find that the chapter on canon law helps contextualise their observations of how different Catholic leaders have responded to allegations of abuse, or that comparing so many different systems of law handling the problem gives them a different perspective on these processes.

Over the course of the decade since I began work on the research that informs this book, I have had the privilege to meet, and have benefited from speaking with, many people who have played critical roles in achieving justice for Survivors of child sexual abuse. Lawyers, journalists, activists and others work tirelessly to ensure people who were harmed as children have their voices heard. In this process, I have learned a great deal about the lifelong impact of abuse, and the difficulty of pursuing any kind of justice for Survivors. I owe a deep debt of gratitude to the brave people who spoke with me, and to the brave Survivors who they work with.

Given my gratitude to the people on whose stories my research depends, I want to acknowledge I do not feel adequate to the task of drawing specific conclusions about what justice should look like for those impacted by clerical child sexual abuse. I believe that those most impacted in a given case of corporate wrongdoing should have an active role in deciding what justice should look like for them. The scandal of child sexual abuse in the Church is much more than an example of corporate wrongdoing, but this book uses the legal proceedings arising from the scandal as a way to learn about corporate accountability. Its findings call for the reimagining of corporate accountability processes in order to better hear and respond to the perspectives, needs and interests of those harmed by corporations, especially those from marginalised communities. Survivors' hard-fought battles for justice against Catholic organisations, across so many different legal fora, have enabled a comparison of the fora themselves which ultimately points to a better way of dealing with corporate wrongdoing of all kinds.

This book is dedicated to the Survivors whose fortitude in their quest for justice serves as inspiration and the professionals who commit their careers to help traumatised people seek recourse. I offer it in the hope that different kinds of legal systems could better account for trauma and social power, meet the human need to be vindicated after being wronged, and find better ways to respond to corporate wrongdoing.

I would also like to express my deepest thanks to my family, and to the many colleagues, teachers and friends whose wisdom, feedback, support and kindness have enriched my life personally, intellectually and professionally. Without the lessons I learned from you, this this book would never have been possible. An incomplete list: Kathryn Henne, John and Valerie Braithwaite, Kim-Marie Spence, Irina Herrschner, Wenting Cheng, Carolyn Sutherland, Catrina Denvir, Marie-Eve Loiselle, Deb Cleland, Veronica Taylor, Sarah Bloom-Raskin, Scott Risner, Kate Ogg, Kurt Ramlo, Emily Rodgers, Teshia Jn Baptiste, Ann Lawrence, Van Durrer, Lovee Sarenas, Gillian Brown, Mary Dudziak, Brian Rothschild, Ron Garet, Sabiha Kazi, Kelly Sherrieb, Michael Birkel, Mary Garman, Judy Peterson and Beverly Greis. Early in my career, I had the privilege of working for two federal judges, the Honorable Philip R Martinez and the Honorable Richard M Neiter. Both were intellectual giants from whom I learned a great deal about the workings of law. More importantly, both men were kind, principled, generous and deeply committed to an inclusive ideal of justice. They both reminded me of my father, who spent most of his long career as a lawyer representing vulnerable and marginalised children.

> Spare Me the sound of your hymns,
> And let Me not hear the music of your lutes,
> But let justice well up like water,
> Righteousness like an unfailing stream.
>
> – Amos 5:23–24 *NJPS Tanakh*

Meredith Edelman
16 May 2025

TABLE OF CONTENTS

GLOSSARY

Introduction

This book engages with literature across a range of disciplines and subjects. Each of these disciplines and subjects has a vocabulary and a set of terms not widely used in other contexts. Other terms I use have political or social meanings that require explanation, and so it is useful to provide a list here of defined terms. This section is intended to explain a few important terms, and, where necessary, explain or reflect on the defined term's meaning. The Glossary may be used as a reference resource, as usage may not otherwise be defined in the text. Terms are listed in the lower case unless they are meant to be understood as acronyms or proper nouns.

Definitions

ACBC

Australian Catholic Bishops Conference.

CDF

Instituted in 1542 by Pope Paul III as the *Sacred Roman and Universal Inquisition*, the oldest Congregation, or department, in the Roman Curia was, from 1965, known as the Congregation for the Doctrine of the Faith or the Sacred Congregation for the Doctrine of the Faith. In 2022, the name was changed to Dicastery for the Doctrine of the Faith, after significant reforms implemented by Pope Francis, discussed in chapter four. I will continue to use the now-outdated acronym 'CDF', to reflect the name that was in use during the time I conducted research for this book, and when most sources I relied on were written.

CLAN

Care Leavers Australia Network.

plans of reorganization

Although this book generally follows OSCOLA conventions and English spelling, references to plans of reorganization and similar topics of corporate reorganization will reflect the American convention, as it is a term of art defined in the US Bankruptcy Code.

priest

References to priests in this book refer to men who have been ordained as priests of the Roman Catholic Church. Ordination is one of the seven sacraments of the Catholic Church, and the importance of the priesthood will be discussed in more detail in chapter four. Priests may be diocesan priests, working under the authority of a bishop, or members of religious orders, and work under the authority of the head of that order.

religious

The word 'religious' has multiple meanings. Members of religious orders, including nuns, monks, and friars, can be referred to as religious. References to 'priests and religious', therefore, are meant to be inclusive of diocesan and religious priests, as well as nuns, monks and friars who are not priests.

religious order

Communities within the Roman Catholic Church, each distinguished by its own liturgical character, history and traditions. Examples of religious orders include Benedictines, Franciscans, Dominicans, Jesuits, Marists, Servants of the Paraclete and Little Sisters of the Poor. Members of religious orders can be referred to as 'religious'.

Royal Commission vs royal commission

For purposes of clarity, Australia's Royal Commission into Institutional Responses to Child Sexual Abuse will be referred to as the Royal Commission, and references to other royal commissions or royal commissions in general will be uncapitalised unless beginning a sentence.

SNAP

Survivors' Network of those Abused by Priests.

Survivors and victims

Many people who have experienced abuse or sexual violence prefer to describe themselves as Survivors, and many people writing about their experience use the term 'Survivor', rather than 'victim', to respect their wishes. I use both terms, generally using 'Survivor' when referring to people who have come forward to demand justice or participate in advocacy groups. I use the term 'victim' when the reference is intended to be broader, and to be inclusive of people who suffered from abuse and did not survive it.

USCCB

United States Conference of Catholic Bishops.

Victorian Inquiry

Parliament of Victoria's 2013 Inquiry into the Handling of Child Abuse by Religious and Other Organisations.

1

Catholic Organisations and Child Sexual Abuse: A Corporate Wrong

I. Dioceses as Case Studies in Corporate Wrongdoing

A. Introduction

From 2008 to 2013, I was a lawyer working on complex, large-scale corporate restructurings in Los Angeles, California. At both of the multinational law firms I worked for, my practice centred on Chapter 11 bankruptcy and corporate reorganization. I decided on that practice area after writing a research paper in law school about three Catholic dioceses that had filed for bankruptcy protection in 2004 and 2005. Having majored in religion as an undergraduate, my law school paper was supervised by an expert in law and religion. I was also taking a class on corporate restructuring, after having taken a class on bankruptcy the previous year. I thought the diocesan bankruptcies would be an interesting subject for a required third-year research paper, and would bring together my existing research interests.

The more I learned about Chapter 11 bankruptcy that semester, the more fascinating I found it. Although bankruptcy has long carried stigma, economies do not function well unless there is a means of dealing with insolvent debtors. Histories of insolvency law point to Biblical passages about jubilee years and other ancient insolvency systems that provide mechanisms for dealing with business failure. Across space and time, insolvency systems change, some of which have been very punitive, like being sold into slavery or sent to a debtors' prison of the sort Dickens described in *Little Dorrit*.[1] The US system of bankruptcy was designed to be more humane, with the possibility of a fresh start one of its central purposes. Chapter 11, the bankruptcy pathway for corporate debtors, is generally seen as more debtor-friendly than other corporate insolvency systems around the world. I will discuss Chapter 11 in more detail in chapter seven, but my initial interest in bankruptcy was sparked by its broad social goals and connections to religious concepts – especially the centrality of forgiveness to both Christian thought and bankruptcy theory.

[1] Charles Dickens, *Little Dorrit* (Ticknor and Fields, 1867).

The diocesan bankruptcy cases drew my attention because they brought to the fore links between debt, harm and sin. Sin, in theological terms, can be conceptualised as the harmful state of being turned away from the Divine. Harm, in secular legal terms, is conceptualised either as crime or tort, depending on whether the party bringing the case is the victim or the state. In tort, the remedy for harm is, typically, a financial award – a debt owed from the tortfeasor to the victim, who is converted to a creditor until the debt is paid. The bankruptcy cases I was writing about involved religious organisations known for a formal ritual of Confession, through which believers access forgiveness of sins. Bankruptcy is a formal, secular process through which people and organisations can access forgiveness of financial debts. In bankruptcy court, these dioceses were seeking secular forgiveness for financial debts that arose from criminal and sinful acts of violence. In the paper I submitted, I meditated on the deep irony of religious organisations known for formal rituals of penance and forgiveness seeking refuge in a secular ritual of forgiveness of economic debts.

Wanting to understand how Chapter 11 functions, I decided to join a corporate law firm and learn about it as a practitioner. As a bankruptcy lawyer, I took part in vibrant, active negotiations between multiple parties, crafting intricate solutions to complex problems. The system in which I was working was designed around the needs of people and organisations like my clients – hedge funds, banks, large businesses and some very wealthy individuals. The system was not perfect, but the structure of Chapter 11 combined with the resources accessible to stakeholders in the kinds of cases I was working on meant that the system works largely as intended for most involved parties.[2] Unsecured creditors and employees of bankrupt firms are not typically thrilled with the outcome of Chapter 11 cases – but resources are allocated from the estate to pay for counsel for committees representing these constituencies, they may have the opportunity to cast a vote on whether or not to adopt a proposed plan, and the bankruptcy court process ensures that they are treated fairly in accordance with the resources available, their legal rights, and the prescribed hierarchies of debt and equity.

As I was becoming well-versed in the practice of Chapter 11 bankruptcy, more Catholic dioceses and religious orders began to file for its protection in courts around the country. I followed the progress of these cases when I could. To a Chapter 11 practitioner, the cases involving Catholic dioceses and religious orders are a type of 'mass tort' bankruptcy. Mass tort proceedings, like the bankruptcy cases of asbestos companies, certain medical device manufacturers and pharmaceutical companies like Purdue Pharma and Johnson & Johnson, are the result of a company facing significant (and difficult to quantify) tort liability. Typically, in mass tort bankruptcies, the cases result in a confirmed plan of reorganization through which the company and its insurers fund a trust. The trust is overseen

[2] See eg Elizabeth Warren and Jay Lawrence Westbrook, 'The Success of Chapter 11: A Challenge to the Critics' (2009) 107 *Michigan Law Review* 603.

by an independent trustee who evaluates the tort claims and pays according to a schedule that was part of the plan the parties voted on.

Following news articles about dioceses and religious orders filing for bankruptcy, I read many quotations from Survivors who had filed tort actions against the dioceses. They were understandably frustrated by the delay and change of venue when a diocese or religious order filed for bankruptcy, and the reporting about the filings were generally critical of the organisations for turning to bankruptcy. I thought, however, that the reporting was missing some potential benefits of the bankruptcy process. For those who had not yet brought claims, the Chapter 11 process could make the ordeal of doing so much less daunting – filing a proof of claim in a Chapter 11 proceeding is much simpler than filing a lawsuit. This might mean that more people would come forward with their claims. It also occurred to me that, with the creative potential of Chapter 11, and the limited funds that would be available for compensation, victims of child sexual abuse might, as a group, feel empowered to seek meaningful non-monetary forms of compensation from dioceses, like personal apologies, public statements of accountability, or disclosure of previously confidential records. As I read through the plans that were being adopted, and spoke with colleagues working on one or more of the cases, I saw that many non-monetary provisions were indeed being included in them. I started to think about revisiting the paper I wrote in law school, and writing about how Chapter 11 bankruptcy might have some surprising benefits for victims of corporate wrongdoing.

I decided to pursue a PhD when a good friend sent me some of John Braithwaite's writing on restorative justice and responsive regulation. I found a lot of similarities between his descriptions of the normative goals of each and principles I knew from Chapter 11 practice. It seemed to me that his descriptions of a flexible approach to regulation had real overlap with the processes of negotiation that I saw every day in my practice. I read about Australia's Royal Commission on Institutional Responses to Child Sexual Abuse and wondered how that process would compare to the Chapter 11 cases of Catholic dioceses in the US. In February 2014, I flew to Canberra to begin my studies at the Australian National University's School of Regulation and Global Governance (RegNet).

I came to RegNet with capacity to make normative arguments, to understand and interpret legal texts, and with a practical understanding of how to navigate legal systems. At RegNet, I learned about social theory, what it means to adopt a research methodology, and about research methods. While social theory tends to embed and draw on normative perspectives and social science research frequently draws conclusions about preferable practices or policies that better conform to normative ideals, its methods of reaching these conclusions are different from the methods typically used by lawyers to argue for or against a normative position. I learned about the history of socio-legal studies (also known as law and society), including the early legal realists who saw factors other than doctrinal argument as central to the outcomes of legal disputes. Over time, legal scholars and social scientists studying legal processes have debated and written volumes about whether legal doctrine or non-law factors such as wealth, access to legal professionals, gender identity, race, religion and political influence are more determinative of legal outcomes. To me, these debates seemed to be missing something. Many were making a case for a dichotomy between law in the books and law in action. To me, the reality is far more complex, and coming to this study after having practised law gave me a different perspective. I felt the debate was overlooking the impact of how legal processes are structured, how they operate in practice. In Chapter 11 practice, for example, I had seen how a multi-stakeholder negotiation works differently from the two-party adversarial nature of most criminal or civil actions. It seemed to me that legal scholars who focus on just doctrine, or just doctrine and procedural law, were sometimes not attending enough to the relevance of social factors, while social scientists were not attending enough to legal processes. But both can miss important factors that relate to the logics, logistics and leverages of practice.

The differences between legal and social science methods became more evident as I read widely about corporate wrongdoing and socio-legal studies in general and the Catholic Church's responsibility for child sexual abuse in particular. Legal scholars tend to write about the proper interpretation of legal text, or to argue for changes to law or policy that would impact how or when legal action might proceed, impose different kinds of penalties for wrongdoing, or otherwise change a specific approach to a particular need or concern. Social scientists writing about these topics tend to use empirical approaches, explaining something about the impact of law, policy or phenomena on people and the communities in which they live. Movements of empirical legal scholars and socio-legal scholars, including New Legal Realists (NLRs), try to bridge the gaps between legal and sociological research. My research is in line with the movement for New Legal Realism (NLR). I use empirical methodologies, but both doctrinal and empirical methods in order to draw conclusions about legal systems. My purpose is to imagine a better system for responding to corporate wrongdoing.

B. Corporate Wrongdoing and Accountability

In 1947, near Jemez Springs, New Mexico, population 198, Father Gerald Fitzgerald founded the Congregation of the Servants of the Paraclete. The *Santa Fe New Mexican* described it as 'a group of priests and religious brothers dedicated to the contemplative life and care of aged and infirm priests'.[3] But, in a 1989 letter produced to the Royal Commission, Liam J Hoare, then Servant General of

[3] 'Byrne Announces Opening of New Jemez Monastery' *Santa Fe New Mexican* (10 January 1947) 1.

the Servants of the Paraclete, wrote to Ronald A Mulkearns, then Bishop of the Diocese of Ballarat, in Victoria, Australia:

> The Servants of the Paraclete have as our mission to provide treatment programs of a therapeutic and spiritual nature for priests and brothers in personal difficulty. This includes the area of sexual misconduct with children and minors.[4]

Jemez Springs is located in the Archdiocese of Santa Fe. Some priests who were sent to the Servants of the Paraclete because they were abusing children in their home dioceses were then sent to work in parishes and schools in nearby dioceses.[5] As discussed in more detail in chapter seven, the Archdiocese of Santa Fe and the nearby Dioceses of Tucson and Gallup have all filed for Chapter 11 bankruptcy protection because of the high numbers of tort claims brought against them related to child sexual abuse. Recruiting priests from the Servants of the Paraclete, which nearby organisations knew was a treatment centre for abusive priests, implicates dioceses as corporate entities. This book is concerned with the way that legal systems address corporate accountability, using diocesan accountability for child sexual abuse as a case study.

In 2015, a lawyer representing victims turned creditors in the Gallup Chapter 11 case told me how important it was to his clients that the truth about the Servants of the Paraclete be made public and widely known. The disclosure of records was one of the most contentious issues in Gallup's case. The bishop's refusal to release those records was highlighted at the confirmation hearing for the plan, at which a Survivor, who had been abused 'on the Navajo Nation by Brother Mark Schornack, a Franciscan friar', spoke of her conflicted feelings about the plan:

> [She] told the bishop he could further her healing process by releasing the files of abusive clergy – something Wall has declined to do.
>
> 'I had been opposed to approving the reorganization plan because the non-monetaries did not include releasing these documents,' [she] said. 'Bishop Wall, the first time we met, I told you I forgave Brother Mark because it was the right thing to do. And I asked you to do the right thing. I'm still waiting.[6]

Many of the professionals who worked on Gallup's case were also involved in the Santa Fe case, and were able to secure a more favourable result for their clients in the bigger, richer Archdiocese's case. The chair of the creditors' committee in the Santa Fe bankruptcy case credited Brad Hall, one of the professionals who represented Survivors in both the Gallup and Santa Fe cases, with suggesting the

[4] Liam J Hoare, 'Letter to The Most Reverent Ronald A. Mulkearns, D.D. from Servant General of the Servants of the Paraclete' Jemez Springs, New Mexico (17 August 1989).

[5] Kathleen Holscher, 'The Trouble of an Indian Diocese: Catholic Priests and Sexual Abuse in Colonized Places' in Tisa Joy Wenger and Sylvester A Johnson (eds), *Religion and US Empire: Critical New Histories* (New York University Press, 2022) 231, 235.

[6] Elizabeth Hardin-Burrola, 'Bishop Apologizes: Bankruptcy Judge Confirms Reorganization Plan' *The Gallup Independent* (22 June 2016).

creation of a document archive of with personnel records from the Archdiocese, the Paracletes and other organisations as a condition of settlement:

> Charles Paez, chairman of the creditors committee, said he suggested an abuse document archive to the archbishop in an initial bankruptcy court hearing called a 341 meeting.
>
> Paez said the idea was first raised by Hall in the committee's early meetings with attorneys for survivors.
>
> 'I think that once he brought it up, I think we all were onboard and thought, "What a great idea this is,"' Paez said in a phone interview.
>
> Paez said he drafted a statement for the 341 meeting that included a request to [Santa Fe Archbishop John] Wester to create a public abuse documents archive. To Paez's surprise, the archbishop agreed.
>
> 'I was surprised that he said yes because I completely expected him to say no,' Paez said. 'I think we all expected him to say no.'
>
> In a phone interview, Wester cited both transparency and healing as the reasons he agreed to establish the archive.
>
> 'I think one way to bring healing is through transparency,' Wester said. 'So, this is an archive, a kind of a public way of people being able to see what happened here. And, of course, for those who have been abused, it helps them to see a certain validation … and they can see some of the facts that might help them in their own healing.'
>
> Wester said it was important to mention the archive is just one of many non-monetary covenants the archdiocese is undertaking. Other non-monetary efforts, he said, include offering restorative justice programs, healing services and meetings with abuse survivors.[7]

The settlement was approved by 99 per cent of the Survivors who submitted a vote. Documents from the Archdiocese, the Servants of the Paraclete and a number of other religious orders will be available online through a public archive hosted by the University of New Mexico.[8]

The Servants of the Paraclete's records are important because they provide documentary evidence of the extent to which dioceses, religious orders and the Church as organisations are culpable in the abuse of children. Priests, monks and brothers were sent to the Servants of the Paraclete by their superiors – bishops and heads of religious orders – and some were then sent to parishes and schools in the Archdiocese of Santa Fe and neighbouring dioceses, like Gallup and Tucson. This would be just one of many examples of Catholic organisations, in control of where known abusers went, sending them to places where they would have access to more children. The records from the Servants of the Paraclete will reveal how many Catholic organisations sent abusers from as far away as Australia to New Mexico, and how many known abusers went to work in local parishes and schools.

[7] Elizabeth Hardin-Burrola, 'New archive of Santa Fe clergy abuse documents hailed as unprecedented' *National Catholic Reporter* (22 February 2023), www.ncronline.org/news/new-archive-santa-fe-clergy-abuse-documents-hailed-unprecedented.

[8] ibid.

The Catholic Church, with its singular position in international, national and sub-national law, occupies a plural and hybrid space. It is not a single entity, but a complex network of separate legal entities. It has its own legal and regulatory systems, organisational culture and relationships with other political and social actors. The Church has deep connections to the development of corporate law and modern understandings of statehood. In some ways, the Church resembles a transnational corporation, and in other ways, it resembles a state. However, dioceses are organised under domestic laws, separate from the Church in Rome. Every diocese and religious order is a separate corporate entity. Each separate entity has its own capacity to engage with the world; their assets belong only to them; they can buy and sell property, enter into and enforce contracts, contribute to society, and engage in wrongdoing separate from any other entity or person.

The complexity and singularity of the Church organisations' responsibility for clerical child sexual abuse make it a good case study for thinking about corporate wrongdoing. As with many other kinds of corporate wrongs, organisational responsibility is triggered by, but is distinct from, the responsibility of human individuals. Like other problems of corporate wrongdoing, the scandal of priests abusing children involves relationships across legal, social and political boundaries: (1) between the Holy See and other nations; (2) between Catholic organisations and states in which they operate; (3) between Catholic organisations and the Holy See; (4) between Catholic organisations (including the Holy See) and faithful Catholics; (5) between Catholic organisations and Survivor advocacy groups; (6) between Catholic organisations and Survivors themselves; and (7) between and among Catholic leaders, parishioners, Survivors, the criminal justice community, families of Survivors, lawyers, journalists and others.

This complexity of relationships reveals something about what it means when one refers to the 'Catholic Church'. The legal existence of the Church's constituent parts are defined, variously, by national, international and canon law. Corporate law is critical to disentangling responsibility in the Church, given its complex multinational structure, just as it is for other multinational organisations. The problem of Church organisations' responsibility for child sexual abuse is an illuminating example of the problem of corporate responsibility for wrongdoing more broadly. As with many types of corporate wrongdoing, it can be difficult to reconcile the degree of harm caused with the degree of culpability attributable to a corporate actor. Dioceses' responsibility for child sexual abuse is difficult to compensate, as are other forms of corporate violence, including environmental destruction or more direct forms of oppression. Not only can there be difficulty in legally linking corporate activity to the harm experienced, but the harms are so extensive that it seems impossible the consequences available for a culpable corporation could be adequate.

Like many other kinds of corporate wrongs, the harms experienced in cases of clerical child sexual abuse are distant from corporate decision-making and the purposes behind corporate policy. The scandal of formula-makers' marketing practices, blamed for the deaths of infants all over the developing world from malnutrition, also caused devastating harm, but the corporate activity at its root was decision-making in offices far removed from the people bearing the consequences of the decisions.[9] It is possible to believe that the bishops moving abusive priests around from parish to parish did not comprehend the gravity of harm they were causing to children, even as their failure to understand is evidence of a serious dearth of empathy or sense of responsibility. As with corporate leadership and governance in business contexts, Church governance is meant to protect and promote the interests of the organisation, and those making decisions to further organisational interests are not always sensitive to the consequences for human beings. In both contexts, the visceral complexity of corporate harms contrasts with seemingly bloodless decision-making in offices far removed from the consequences.

It is not surprising, considering the unique status of the Catholic Church, its patriarchal culture and the severe harms of child sexual abuse in any context, that abuse by Catholic clergy would bring its own unique, and uniquely painful, harms to victims, their families and communities. The harms of child sexual abuse are complex and often life-altering. When committed by priests or others in positions of authority, it has impacts across social, emotional, economic and political dimensions. Legal cases involving claims that Church leaders abused children bring to the fore religious taboos surrounding sexuality, the social implications of blemishes on the Church's reputation, and the Church's unique socio-political positioning, all of which amplify emotional and psychological harms of child sexual abuse. The problem touches on some of society's most meaningful symbols – sex, religion and childhood. Victims, their families and their communities suffer from a wide array of harms arising out of abuse and social reactions to reports of abuse.

The diversity of harms means that even if a legal system designed to address one type of harm is able to meet some stakeholders' interests, there may well be harms that remain unaddressed. A successful legal action may provide plaintiffs with financial recovery, but it does not help one reconnect with a damaged relationship with the Divine, a complicated relationship with community or spiritual disillusionment.

As child sex abuse has been documented or alleged in institutions around the world, the harms arising from pervasive perpetration of child sex abuse and institutional failure to appropriately react are notable in scope and breadth. The severity of abuse in the context of the Catholic Church is not just about rates at which it is perpetrated, but the distinctive harms to individuals and societies when clerics sexually abuse children.[10] There are psychological, spiritual and emotional harms to victims and their communities. Beth Crisp wrote in *Feminist Theology* that in religious contexts with a culture of silence and doctrinal arguments for forgiveness:

> Some perpetrators [of child sexual abuse] even invoke God as a co-conspirator, who will punish those who don't remain silent. While those who have a mature understanding

[9] Colin Boyd, 'The Nestlé Infant Formula Controversy and a Strange Web of Subsequent Business Scandals' (2012) 106 *Journal of Business Ethics* 283.

[10] See eg Amy C Tishelman and Lisa A Fontes, 'Religion in Child Sexual Abuse Forensic Interviews' (2017) 63 *Child Abuse and Neglect* 120.

> of God may be able to reject such notions, those whose understanding of God is less developed (particularly children) may believe what they are told. It is not difficult to make the connection between an all-powerful God who colludes with abuse and the God who smites down his enemies.[11]

She argues that in contexts where 'discussion of even legitimate and non-abusive sexual expression between consenting persons is frequently a taboo subject', an imposed silence is especially painful and damaging.[12]

Survivors frequently report having lost religious faith and becoming disillusioned with the Church. Katherine van Wormer and Lois Berns quote one Survivor, who explained:

> Clergy abuse is so much worse because the priests have more power than anybody and represent … well they are supposed to represent God, and so … they represent not only their position in the Church, but they are supposed to represent Christ [laughs] at Mass. So you know there's a real power play thing going on.[13]

Children who grew up in a Catholic family or were otherwise taught to trust in and respect the authority of Catholic leaders as *alter Christus*, and who were then abused by those very leaders, often report feeling betrayed by the Church or even by God, rather than simply the individual priest.[14] The significance of the priests' role in the Church will be discussed in more detail in chapter four, but it is important to recognise that, even though the purpose of priests' elevated status in the Church is not to facilitate or perpetuate wrongdoing, the status compounds the harms of abuse.

Like other kinds of corporate wrongs, the problem of child sexual abuse is not simply a problem of individual bad actors, but one of social institutions. Religions, schools, corporations and governments around the world have enabled, covered up and feigned ignorance of abuse. The hierarchical and complicated relationships between organisations within the Church, the ways in which the status of religious organisations under state law impacts legal proceedings, and the social power of the Church in communities all contribute complications with holding the Church (and organisations within it) to account. Many see the Church as a whole bearing responsibility for bishops' moving known abusers around and allowing them to continue abusing – and for other kinds of harm. They point to Church dogma related to sexuality and the role of priests as contributors to victim trauma. Others note that the Church's social power and support for patriarchal norms contributes to families and communities not believing victims,

[11] Beth R Crisp, 'Silence and Silenced: Implications for the Spirituality of Survivors of Sexual Abuse' (2010) 18 *Feminist Theology* 277, 283.

[12] ibid, 278–79.

[13] Katherine van Wormer and Lois Berns, 'The Impact of Priest Sexual Abuse: Female Survivors' Narratives' (2004) 19 *Affilia – Journal of Women and Social Work* 53, 60.

[14] See, eg Jennifer M Balboni, *Clergy Sexual Abuse Litigation: Survivors Seeking Justice* (First Forum Press, 2011).

punishing victims for reporting, and enforcing a culture of silence that enables and emboldens abusers.[15]

Although the religious context might make it seem different from other kinds of corporate wrongs, the complexity of the problem actually means that it is more like other kinds of corporate wrongs than it is unlike them, and legal systems' capacity to hold the Church to account is a good indication of their capacity to hold other corporations to account for their wrongs.

II. Corporate Accountability and Legal Systems

The problem of Church responsibility for child sexual abuse is uniquely suited to a comparison of legal systems' treatment of corporate wrongdoing. The Church's unique legal and political positioning, combined with Survivor persistence, means that a wide variety of legal systems have engaged in one way or another with cases arising out of allegations that Catholic priests and religious sexually abused children. Around the world, thousands have joined in a movement of Survivors seeking accountability through creative and dogged action, and their efforts have borne fruit. As literature on the responses to institutional child abuse attests, new laws have been passed, new policies put in place to protect children in the future, and a number of other responses have granted many Survivors forms of redress – notably the hope that fewer children in the future will suffer as they did.[16] This book takes advantage of a rare opportunity created when Survivors' pursuit of justice led to strikingly different legal systems, designed for very different purposes, being tasked with resolving difficult issues arising out of the same corporate wrong. Catholic Church responsibility for child sexual abuse is uniquely suited to a comparative project on legal systems because it is a complex problem that engages with a striking variety of legal systems across and within national and international boundaries, involving what, in another corporate context, would be described as local subsidiaries of the same transnational organisation, and conduct that is remarkably consistent across jurisdictions.

The legal systems employed in assigning responsibility and liability, and sorting out what to do in cases of Catholic priests and religious abusing children have included public inquiries, canon law, civil litigation, criminal law, international law, private law and Chapter 11 bankruptcy law. Some Catholic organisations have implemented quasi-legal systems, like the Australian Catholic Bishops Conference (ACBC)'s Towards Healing programme or the United States Conference of Catholic Bishops (USCCB)'s Dallas Charter. The diversity of legal systems provides a unique opportunity to study how very different systems approach a complex problem.

[15] See eg Crisp (n 11); van Wormer and Berns (n 13).

[16] See, eg Timothy D Lytton, *Holding Bishops Accountable: How Lawsuits Helped the Catholic Church Confront Clergy Sexual Abuse* (Harvard University Press, 2008).

This opportunity allows legal systems to be compared qualitatively as they work in practice. Moving beyond tracing gaps between an ideal of law and lived experience of stakeholders, my intent in this book is to interrogate constituent parts – aspects – of legal systems and describe their character through examining these different aspects as they function. Breaking legal systems into aspects allows for a deeper analysis and comparison of the systems' capacity to hold organisations, like the Church or another corporate actor, responsible for wrongdoing. Studying legal systems requires insight into the internal logic and practical functioning of legal systems. This knowledge was gained through qualitative, doctrinal and archival research, as well as literature reviews drawing on multiple disciplines. Paying attention to legal systems themselves and how they construct and respond to the phenomenon of child sexual abuse provides insight on how legal systems construct ideas of justice, how legal procedures facilitate or hinder the pursuit of stakeholder interests, and how social differences, like location, race, gender and access to resources impact wherewithal to pursue legal rights.

This book focuses on legal processes involving allegations of child sexual abuse and two specific dioceses: The Catholic Diocese of Ballarat, which covers the western third of Victoria, Australia; and the Roman Catholic Church of the Diocese of Gallup, which covers parts of northern Arizona and New Mexico. Both dioceses are located in relatively rural areas, with a similar-sized population of which Catholics are a significant minority. Each has participated in multiple kinds of legal proceedings relating to clerical child sexual abuse. However, they also have some key distinctions that allow for interesting comparisons. Ballarat is located in a relatively wealthy area, home to gold fields and rich agricultural land. The diocese has connections to very powerful people in Australian politics and the global Church. The campaign to hold it accountable has been hard-fought. It has been investigated by state and commonwealth investigative processes, and has been the subject of widely read books and reporting. As a result, Ballarat plays a key role in the Australian public's understanding of the story of abuse in the Catholic Church.

Hundreds of children are also known to have been abused by priests or religious in the Diocese of Gallup, one of the dioceses located close to the Servants of the Paraclete. However, the plight of victims there has not captured the attention of a wider public in the way that the stories from Ballarat have. Gallup is one of the poorest dioceses in the US, containing within it the entirety of the Navajo Nation, as well as a number of other Indigenous and Hispanic communities, many struggling with poverty in the arid, mountainous region home to canyons, coal deposits and a petrified forest. The differences between these two dioceses help isolate and identify the ways in which legal systems may be better, or worse, at enabling full participation for stakeholders regardless of access to resources, and how forms of social difference impact stakeholder participation in legal processes.

In both Ballarat and Gallup, there are overlapping legal orders and semi-autonomous social fields – national and sub-national state law, private law, religious law and community norms. For each diocese, there are two main relevant legal orders: formal state law, and the law of the Catholic Church. Formal state law includes, in Ballarat, Commonwealth (Australian) and Victorian law. In Gallup, it is a bit more complicated. There are federal (US) laws, and then because Gallup spans parts of both Arizona and New Mexico, sometimes the law of one of those states is applicable. The Navajo Nation, like other Native American nations, controls certain legal issues that arise on its sovereign land, to the exclusion of Arizona or New Mexico, but not federal, law. Federal law pre-empts all three, but as discussed in chapter five, undermines Navajo law in cases that involve non-Navajo persons, like the Church.

With both Ballarat and Gallup, then, there is an opportunity to compare systems of law existing and working alongside each other in legally plural environments, including systems that are not generally thought of as relevant for problems like child sexual abuse. In order to compare how these very different systems operate, I consider their theories, purposes, doctrines, procedures and logistics. The diversity of legal responses, actors' positioning, and outcomes in cases arising out of claims of clerical child sexual abuse is testament to the strength of contestation and argument within legal systems.

III. New Legal Realism and Corporate Accountability

This book, as a whole, provides a practical demonstration of how NLR can change the way we think about the structures and theories upon which our legal systems are built, and the roles the systems play in our social worlds. The work of a doctrinal legal scholar is to determine what the 'law in books' says, what it means, and how it might be changed to better correspond to ideals of justice.[17] As recognised by early legal realists, a primarily doctrinal focus risks failing to account for the ways in which social and logistical factors can impact parties' capacity to make effective use of legal process.[18] That being said, classic socio-legal views of 'law on the books' and 'law in action' as a dichotomy between which there is a gap in need of explaining can undervalue the weight of the formal process and substance of law, just as doctrinal scholars can undervalue the weight of social context.[19] A twenty-first-century movement of NLR would collapse this dichotomy and attend to a broader spectrum of factors that impact the functioning of legal systems. This book applies a NLR approach to consider the capacity of legal systems to hold organisations, including multinational corporations, to account.

[17] Roscoe Pound, 'Law in Books and Law in Action' (1940) 44 *American Law Review* 12.

[18] See eg Ann Southworth, Bryant Garth and Catherine Fisk, 'Some Realism about Realism in Teaching about the Legal Profession' in Sally Engle Merry and Heinz Klug (eds), *The New Legal Realism Volume 2: Studying Law Globally* (Cambridge University Press, 2016) 74–94.

[19] Stewart Macaulay, Lawrence M Friedman and Elizabeth Mertz, *Law in Action: A Socio-Legal Reader* (Foundation Press, 2007).

Social science literature on clerical child sexual abuse makes clear that victim desire for, or interest in, accountability, compensation, healing and vindication are often perceived as being thwarted by the very systems meant to meet their interests, often despite changes to law.[20] In classic socio-legal thought, this would be described as a 'gap' between the hoped-for justice and the reality of imperfect legal systems.[21] A classic socio-legal 'gap studies' project on this issue would conduct an empirical test of whether certain changes made to law have narrowed the gap between hoped-for justice and reality of outcomes. Taking a different empirical approach, this book compares legal systems across multiple aspects of their functioning: theory, purpose, doctrine, procedure and logistics. Comparing different systems as they engage with cases involving the same or very similar facts allows for an analysis of how each system functions.

Sex abuse in the Catholic Church involves a complex global organisation causing harm in ways that the existing law cannot fully capture, highlighting the difficulty in holding organisations accountable in this and other contexts. The variety of legal systems tapped to address cases of clerical child sexual abuse mean that the problem makes it possible to compare legal systems responding to corporate wrongdoing across multiple, diverse aspects, shedding new light on the process of holding organisations accountable.

Law is doctrinal and procedural law 'on the books', but law is also socially constructed purposes, theoretical assumptions embraced by legal professionals, and practicalities of access for the various stakeholders, constituencies and individuals who may come into contact with them. Law on the books is not distinct from law in action; they are co-constitutive and together construct legal systems.[22] This book will demonstrate how to evaluate legal systems without reducing their components to a dichotomy. I use both doctrinal and social science methods to open up the black box of how legal systems produce outcomes and break them down into multiple aspects that allow for comparisons while still accounting for real-life complexity.

Child sexual abuse by Catholic priests has been an issue of broad public concern for decades. Critically acclaimed and popular films like *Spotlight*, *Mea Maxima Culpa: Silence in the House of God*, *Calvary*, *Twist of Faith* and *Deliver Us from Evil* evidence intense public interest in stories of abuse by clergy and moral failure by Church leaders. The problem is studied across a number of academic disciplines. There have been evaluations of political and legal responses resulting in suggestions for changes to law or policy produced by criminologists, socio-legal

[20] See, eg Judith Edwina Courtin, 'Sexual Assault and the Catholic Church: Are Victims Finding Justice?' (PhD Thesis, Monash University, 2015); Judith Zatkin, Miranda Sitney and Keith Kaufman, 'The Relationship Between Policy, Media, and Perceptions of Sexual Offenders Between 2007 and 2017: A Review of the Literature' (2022) 23 *Trauma, Violence, and Abuse* 953.

[21] Kitty Calavita, *Invitation to Law and Society*, 2nd edn (University of Chicago Press, 2016).

[22] Stewart Macaulay, 'A New Legal Realism: Elegant Models and the Messy Law in Action' in Elizabeth Mertz, Stewart Macaulay and Thomas W Mitchell (eds), *The New Legal Realism Volume I: Translating Law-and-Society for Today's Legal Practice* (Cambridge University Press, 2016) 29–50.

scholars, psychologists and many others.[23] These related literatures, along with what Michael Andre Guerzoni and Hannah Graham call 'clerical collar crime exposés', and government-led investigations or inquiries, have produced a great deal of knowledge about patterns of abuse, cover-up, institutional failures and the perspectives of victims, perpetrators, institutional leaders and communities.[24] Legal scholars also contribute to the literature. Marci Hamilton has made powerful arguments for further investigations and elimination of statutes of limitations for child sexual abuse allegations.[25] Tim Lytton's *Holding Bishops Accountable* argued that a wave of tort litigation arising out of clerical child sexual abuse led to changes in law and policy, improving the prospects of victims seeking legal redress in the US.[26]

The public concern with child sexual abuse by Catholic priests raises deep questions not just about the phenomena itself, but also about law and law's capacity to respond to wrongdoing by organisations. The academic literature on clerical child sexual abuse reflects the push for justice and accountability. Much of the literature is centred on critiques of the Church and other social and political institutions, advocating for or evaluating the effects of changes to law, contributing to knowledge on abuse and recovery, or researching ways to detect and prevent future abuse. As the Church is condemned for protecting its financial interests and the reputations of those it has declared to be representatives of the Divine on Earth against people abused as children by those representatives, there is also an implicit critique of legal systems' failure hold the Church to account. If only a fraction of victims feels satisfied that justice has been done, cynicism about the capacity of legal systems to meet stakeholder interests reasonably exists alongside critiques of power and corruption in the Church. But cynicism about the capacity of legal systems to address wrongdoing by society's most powerful is hardly limited to the Church's responsibility for abuse: there is a long history of concern with the difficulty of effectively responding to wrongdoing by corporations, entities that have 'no soul to damn, no body to kick'.[27]

While focus on the abuse and culpability of the Church is important, existing work already does that well. If we want to understand how to respond to corporate wrongdoing, we have to carefully consider how legal systems (the whole process,

[23] See eg Michael D White and Karen J Terry, 'Child Sexual Abuse in the Catholic Church: Revisiting the Rotten Apples Explanation' (2008) 35 *Criminal Justice and Behavior* 658; John F Wirenius, '"Command and Coercion": Clerical Immunity, Scandal, and the Sex Abuse Crisis in the Roman Catholic Church' (2012) 27 *The Journal of Law and Religion* 423; Marije Stoltenborgh et al, 'A Global Perspective on Child Sexual Abuse: Meta-Analysis of Prevalence Around the World' (2011) 16 *Child Maltreatment* 79.

[24] Michael Andre Guerzoni and Hannah Graham, 'Catholic Church Responses to Clergy-Child Sexual Abuse and Mandatory Reporting Exemptions in Victoria, Australia: A Discursive Critique.' (2015) 4 *International Journal for Crime, Justice and Social Democracy* 58.

[25] Marci A Hamilton, *God vs. the Gavel* (Cambridge University Press, 2014).

[26] Lytton (n 16).

[27] John C Coffee, '"No Soul to Damn: No Body to Kick": An Unscandalized Inquiry into the Problem of Corporate Punishment' (1981) 79 *Michigan Law Review* 386.

not just the doctrinal law part, but also not forgetting its contribution) actually work. This 'worst case' of corporate wrongdoing creates tough problems across multiple dimensions, revealing weakness in legal systems themselves. Canon law and tort are the established legal systems (in religious and secular jurisdictions) that can be reasonably expected to have rules about what to do in cases of abuse, who/what should be held accountable, and how. If they were working in a way that adequately met the interests of justice, there would never have been a Royal Commission. If tort law was doing a good job of holding corporations accountable for wrongdoing, Chapter 11 bankruptcy would be reserved for financial insolvency, and 'mass tort' would be handled through a system that was designed to assess and respond to wrongdoing – rather than one designed to assess and respond to financial insolvency.

IV. Approach of Book

This book builds on a foundation of scholarship in law, criminology, sociology, psychology and history. Drawing from diverse literatures, archival research, interviews with diverse participants in legal systems and doctrinal research, my purpose is to approach legal systems as social phenomena tasked with a particular problem of corporate wrongdoing. By attending to the underlying logic of each legal system, I compare different ways of understanding social problems in law, different ways of approaching dispute resolution, and different purposes of legal process.

By attending to law as an important mode of pursuing corporate accountability, I show how different aspects of law define what different kinds of claims actors can pursue and the ways they can go about it. Considering multiple formal legal systems at work in two specific places allows for analysis and comparison by isolating their different theoretical, doctrinal and procedural structures, and the ways in which they function within social spaces – purpose and logistics. Among other things, this work shows how different aspects of law operate to promote the goals and interests of some stakeholders while constraining or working against others. The character of a legal system is constructed from elements of law, society and the interaction between the two. A study that looks to the character of legal systems provides a way to compare legal systems empirically and to evaluate their capacity to provide substantive justice for participants.

Chapter two, next, will introduce a framework for assessing responsiveness. Drawing on Nonet and Selznick's classic of socio-legal studies, the chapter makes the case for a critically informed theory of responsive law serving as a normative core for NLR. In doing so, it draws on and adds to a developing literature arguing against using criminal legal processes to respond to corporate wrongdoing more generally. Chapter three will set the scene for the remainder of the book by providing a more fulsome introduction to the two dioceses – Ballarat and Gallup – and discussing what can be learned from considering the similarities and differences between them.

The empirical heart of the book (chapters four to seven) offers an evaluation of different legal systems according to the framework introduced in chapter two – assessing canon law, tort law, Chapter 11 bankruptcy law and the Royal Commission according to three main Selznickian archetypes: repressive, autonomous, or responsive law. Using this framework, the book finds that some of the most important aspects to understand are their underlying purposes – what the systems were designed to do. As discussed in chapter four, canon law's purpose is the internal governance of the Church. It resembles a corporate charter more than it does a code of criminal or civil law. Although behaviour that constitutes clerical child sexual abuse has been prohibited under canon law for centuries, it was not until several years into Francis's papacy that the theory behind the prohibition had relevance to harm imposed on a child. The law's history shows its purpose to be more focused on the Church than the victim. Canon law is, in Selznickian terms, repressive, because it is oriented around protecting the Church as an institution, not establishing truth, resolving disputes or remedying harm.

As discussed in chapter seven, Chapter 11's purpose in reorganizing a corporate entity means it is designed to handle cases involving multiple stakeholders and provides mechanisms through which creditors like employees and tort victims can act collectively. Thus, even though it lacks the investigatory and symbolic power of the Royal Commission or a criminal case, and many in the Survivor movement see bankruptcy filings as an effort to avoid responsibility, more victims in Gallup received compensation through Chapter 11 than likely would have if the diocese had not accessed its protection. Although bankruptcy's purpose tends to obscure the underlying wrongdoing, rendering the court incapable of imposing punishment, the sophisticated understanding of corporate structure embedded within the system has tangible benefits for stakeholders.

Other aspects of legal systems are also important. Doctrine, procedure and the logistics of participating in a legal process are especially relevant for tort law, as discussed in chapter five. The four different jurisdictions where claims in tort have been brought against Ballarat or Gallup have all seen significant reforms to doctrine or procedure specifically intended allow more cases involving child sexual abuse to go forward. Even with changes to law, however, the logistical and practical difficulties of bringing claims still bar many victims, especially those from marginalised communities, from meaningful legal remedies. In tort there is a quasi-mythical promise that those who have been victimised will be compensated, that wrongs will be righted. In practice, however, compensation usually depends on factors unrelated to wrongs or harms. Determining factors can be found in corporate law and procedural law, as well as the socio-economic characteristics of stakeholders. The common law of tort might have been Nonet and Selznick's model for their understanding of autonomous law – it makes promises about equal treatment under law, but in practice, tort's promise of justice is more myth than reality. Despite the best intentions of those changing the law, tort fails to live up to its promises because wealthy, powerful parties, like Catholic dioceses, are advantaged in almost every practical way, with their interests embedded in the structure of tort systems.

The Royal Commission, discussed in chapter six, is determined to be a quasi-responsive system, as is Chapter 11 bankruptcy, but for different reasons. They each demonstrate responsive characteristics, including a purposive approach, procedural flexibility and the deliberate inclusion of multiple stakeholder perspectives. In the case of Chapter 11, this may be somewhat surprising, because it is a process designed to handle the orderly reorganization, sale, or liquidation of an insolvent corporation. The Royal Commission is an inquisitorial, rather than adversarial, fact-finding process, while Chapter 11's process is a structured multi-party negotiation. The Royal Commission produced a credible narration of fact, which contributed to healing and community acceptance, shifting public opinion toward blaming both organisation and individual perpetrators and officials. Chapter 11 has a sophisticated understanding of corporate ontology and a participatory process embedded in its structure, in which victims' leverage plays a significant part within a community of stakeholders making decisions about outcomes. Each seems to address one half of the challenge of responsiveness – if the Royal Commission's narrative power could be somehow combined with a structured multi-stakeholder negotiation like Chapter 11's, we might have an example of a truly responsive system.

Like many cases of serious corporate wrongdoing, child abuse by clerics is a complex problem which pits the interests of vulnerable individuals against the interests of a powerful transnational organisation. Large multinational organisations are uniquely capable of avoiding responsibility in this as in many other examples of mass tort in a globalised economy. Complex corporate and financial structures serve as shields. Harms are concentrated among people with few resources and little social or political power, while corporate leaders are some of the wealthiest and most powerful people in the world. The magnitude of harms to victims is undeniable, but a corporation's legal liability is a more complicated question. The final chapter of this book pulls together the threads of the argument, showing how the framework enables a classification of each of the legal systems as repressive, autonomous or quasi-responsive. Drawing lessons from the Royal Commission and Chapter 11 bankruptcy, chapter eight refines the framework introduced in chapter two, and takes lessons from chapters three to seven to bring responsive law theory into conversation with NLR and identify characteristics of a responsive system for dealing with corporate wrongdoing.

2

Responsiveness and Aspects of Legal Systems: Why *not* Criminal Law?

I. Responsive Law: An Ideal and a Theory

A. Introduction

This chapter explains the framework I use to compare legal systems. As discussed in the previous chapter, a number of very different legal systems have been tasked with resolving legal problems related to sexual abuse of children by Catholic clergy. Although I am using a framework to compare legal systems, I am not doing what is usually called 'comparative law'. Comparative law typically compares legal systems in different places that do similar work – they might compare the operation of child protection law across different countries, for example. I am comparing legal systems which are designed for very different purposes, but which are nonetheless being tasked with resolving problems related to the same set of circumstances. The strategies of comparative law do not work for my purposes. I am interested in the overall character of a legal system, which requires comparisons across more than doctrine, and more than metrics about penalties awarded or avoided.

Selznick's work on responsive law, which is sometimes considered a normative framework for earlier movements of legal realists,[1] is a useful place to begin a normative evaluation of legal systems for a project within the New Legal Realism (NLR) tradition. In line with the responsive law project, I consider the extent to which distinct legal systems can be described in terms of Nonet and Selznick's typologies of repressive, autonomous and responsive law. I also build on responsive law theory in a way that reflects NLR and critical insights, including 'historical, contextual, and sociocultural approaches to understanding how law works'.[2] As Feeley identified, a focus on common law jurisdictions, and especially on American constitutional law, limits Nonet and Selznick's approach as a grand

[1] See Bryant Garth and Joyce Sterling, 'From Legal Realism to Law and Society: Reshaping Law for the Last Stages of the Social Activist State' (1998) 32 *Law & Society Review* 409.

[2] Heinz Klug and Sally Engle Merry, 'Introduction' in Sally Engle Merry and Heinz Klug (eds), *The New Legal Realism Volume 2: Studying Law Globally* (Cambridge University Press, 2016) 1.

theory of law, but their identification of characteristics is nonetheless useful for an analysis of specific legal systems.[3]

My purpose is to use the typologies as descriptors, and though I think responsive law is normatively superior to autonomous law, which in turn is preferable to repressive law, I am not making any claims about these being the only types of law that exist, whether all legal systems could be characterised as one of the three types, or that legal systems necessarily develop from one to another in any particular path. They are, however, useful in helping me explain the differences between legal systems applied to the Catholic dioceses of Ballarat and Gallup, and in providing a base on which to build new insights and developments to responsive law theory. Each of these three types is defined in more detail below.

B. Repressive Law

The prototypical repressive law regime, as Nonet and Selznick describe it, was the dominant form of law in nascent sovereign states where Western law first emerged, and can be found in totalitarian states and other institutions the world over.[4] Repressive legal systems use coercion and domination as primary tools to secure compliance, reinforce class boundaries, and dictate social mores. The fundamental purpose of a repressive law regime is order – keeping the peace. It does so largely through coercion in support of a social order that emphasises the moral legitimacy of its political leaders. Nonet and Selznick identify five characteristics of repressive law, which they discuss in detail in *Law and Society in Transition*. These characteristics are:

(1) Legal institutions are directly accessible to political power; law is identified with the state and subordinated to *raison d'état*.
(2) The conservation of authority is an overriding preoccupation of legal officialdom. In the 'official perspective' that ensues, the benefit of the doubt goes to the system, and administrative convenience weighs heavily.
(3) Specialized agencies of control, such as the police, become independent centres of power; they are isolated from moderating social contexts and capable of resisting political authority.
(4) A regime of 'dual law' institutionalizes class justice by consolidating and legitimating patterns of social subordination.
(5) The criminal code mirrors the dominant mores; legal moralism prevails.[5]

Nonet and Selznick cite Charles Merriam's 'poverty of power' to explain the source of repressive law.[6] If the first goal of law is 'to keep the peace at all events and at any

[3] Malcolm M Feeley, 'Law, Legitimacy, and Symbols: An Expanded View of Law and Society in Transition' (1979) 77 *Michigan Law Review* 899, 902.

[4] Philippe Nonet and Philip Selznick, *Law and Society in Transition: Toward Responsive Law* (Routledge, 2001).

[5] ibid, 33.

[6] ibid, 33, citing Charles Edward Merriam, *Political Power: Its Composition and Incidence* (Mc Graw-Hill, 1934).

price',[7] then repressive law may be the product of a regime with few options available to it to meet that goal other than coercion. This Hobbesian approach to social order has been a primary form of law throughout recorded human history, as few states or governing powers have had the strength to implement any other kind of governance. Other times, repressive law results from government overreach – introducing mechanisms intended to benefit the population, but without the capacity or inclination to do so in a way that meets the needs of the (nominally or honestly) intended beneficiaries. Nonet and Selznick explain that repression can also be a result of limited resources and benign neglect. Repressive systems of government or law resist demands for justice or avoid committing to policies that would provide a public benefit for many reasons, including a lack of resources and tempering public expectations, but always to serve the interests of the state, as understood through the 'official perspective', or to maintain social cohesion through legal moralism.[8] 'The hallmark of the law becomes its association with, and subordination to, the requirements of government.'[9]

C. Autonomous Law

According to Nonet and Selznick, an autonomous legal system is one that functions as, 'a resource for *taming* repression', and autonomous systems form the bases for 'what is celebrated as the "Rule of Law"'.[10] Autonomous legal systems are characterised by 'specialized, relatively autonomous legal institutions that claim a qualified supremacy within defined spheres of competence'.[11] Using this phrase, they explain, 'points to the weaknesses as well as the achievements of the rule of law'.[12] Nonet and Selznick describe the 'chief attributes of autonomous law' as:

1. Law is separated from politics. Characteristically, the system proclaims the independence of the judiciary and draws a sharp line between legislative and judicial functions.
2. The legal order espouses the 'model of rules.' A focus on rules helps enforce a measure of official accountability; at the same time, it limits both the creativity of legal institutions and the risk of their intrusion into the political domain.
3. 'Procedure is the heart of law.' Regularity and fairness, not substantive justice, are the first ends and the main competence of the legal order.
4. '"Fidelity to law" is understood as strict obedience to the rules of positive law. Criticism of existing laws must be channelled through the political process.'[13]

[7] ibid, 34, citing Roscoe Pound, *An Introduction to the Philosophy of Law* (Yale University Press, 1922).

[8] ibid, 37–51.

[9] ibid, 39.

[10] ibid, 53.

[11] ibid, 53 referencing Max Rheinstein (ed), *Max Weber on Law in Economy and Society* (Harvard University Press, 1954) 224 and Roberto M Unger, *Law in Modern Society* (Free Press, 1976) 58.

[12] ibid, 54.

[13] ibid, 54.

Autonomous law is the result of what Nonet and Selznick identify as an historic bargain: procedural autonomy for legal institutions in exchange for substantive subordination of those institutions to political will. It facilitates a professional monopoly on legal proceedings and legitimated forms of justice. Courts remove themselves from the substantive formation of public policy in exchange for their capacity to hold political leaders and institutions to account to the law formed thereby.

Nonet and Selznick's critique of autonomous law lies in its commitment to law as 'an instrument of social control' based on rules rather than values, arguing that its focus on procedural rather than substantive justice limits its value as a normative order.[14] As autonomous legal systems remove themselves from politics and policy-making, they imagine jurists to be 'objective spokesmen for historically established principles, passive dispensers of a received, impersonal justice'.[15] Political leaders establish the content of law, and autonomous legal institutions' procedural independence is purchased at the cost of their refraining from substantive changes to that content.[16] Autonomous legal systems are bound to the rules of positive law, even where that law fails to provide substantive justice, with legal formalism, the model of rules and claims to obedience key attributes, as Nonet and Selznick describe it.[17] 'Legality, understood as close accountability to rules, is the promise of autonomous law; legalism is its affliction.'[18] The formalism and insistence on rule-following can render legal institutions ill-equipped to respond to complexity of real-life problems.

D. Responsive Law

Nonet and Selznick describe responsive law as an ideal, rather than by reference to an established order, acknowledging that 'making law more responsive to social needs', has long been a concern of legal theorists.[19] Quoting Roscoe Pound, they explain that the ideal is for legal systems 'to take more complete and intelligent account of the social facts upon which law must proceed and to which it is to be applied'.[20] As with repressive and autonomous law, they set out a list of characteristics of a responsive legal order. These are:

1. The dynamics of legal development increase the authority of purpose in legal reasoning.

[14] ibid, 63.
[15] ibid, 57.
[16] ibid, 57–60.
[17] ibid, 53–72.
[18] ibid, 64.
[19] ibid, 73 (quoting Jerome Frank, 'Mr. Justice Holmes and Non-Euclidian Legal Thinking' (1932) 17 *Cornell Law Quarterly* 568, 586).
[20] ibid, 73 (quoting Roscoe Pound, *Jurisprudence* (West Publishing, 1959) 350.

2. Purpose makes legal obligation more problematic, thereby relaxing law's claim to obedience and opening the possibility of a less rigid and more civil conception of public order.
3. As law gains openness and flexibility, legal advocacy takes on a political dimension, generating forces that help correct and change legal institutions but threaten to undermine institutional integrity.'
4. Responsive law, which puts pressure on legal institutions' authority and capacity to compel action, depends on the competence of those legal institutions – and so responsive law is possible when legal institutions are capable of securing compliance without resort to coercion.[21]

They describe responsive law as a way of resolving the tension between the 'passive opportunistic adaptation of legal institutions to the social and political environment' embodied by repressive law and the 'overriding preoccupation [with] the preservation of institutional integrity' that is characteristic of autonomous law.[22] While admitting it is a 'risky venture', they argue that a sense of purpose and defined values can allow for critique of established practice while controlling administrative discretion.[23] Although an 'instrumentalist' approach might 'los[e] the ability to moderate the role of power in society [and regress] to repression',[24] 'responsive law presumes that purpose can be made objective enough and authoritative enough to control adaptive rule making'.[25] They hypothesised that a responsive system would qualify the legal profession's monopoly on legitimated justice by enabling a model in which stakeholders do not need to be lawyers to participate effectively.

Selznick continued his work on responsive law in the book *The Moral Commonwealth: Social Theory and the Promise of Community*.[26] He describes responsive law as an approach that involves community participation and flexibility, and combines the 'avoidance of evil [with the] pursuit of the good'.[27] Selznick defines justice as something that 'affirms the moral worth of individuals; sustains autonomy and self-respect; domesticates authority; and establishes a framework for moral discourse on public matters'.[28] Responsive law is defined by a call for a sophisticated understanding of the complexity of social orders combined with a normative perspective opposed to domination of all sorts.

The Moral Commonwealth reflects this sophistication through its theory of organisations. Selznick declares they have moral agency, despite lacking the moral and ontological primacy of human beings. He argues that they can and should be held accountable for wrongdoing, and ultimately 'be judged by the contributions

[21] ibid, 78.
[22] ibid, 76.
[23] ibid, 77.
[24] ibid, 76.
[25] ibid, 77.
[26] Philip Selznick, *The Moral Commonwealth: Social Theory and the Promise of Community* (University of California Press, 1992).
[27] Martin Krygier, 'Walls and Bridges: A Comment on Philip Selznick's "The Moral Commonwealth"' (1994) 82 *California Law Review* 4 73.
[28] Selznick (n 26) 431.

they make to social well-being'.[29] The moral agency of organisations, Selznick argues, exists separately from the moral agency of the individual actors operating within the organisation, although organisations can act only through individuals or technologies that ultimately depend on human action.[30] Selznick's insight about the moral agency of organisations is more significant than simply recognising that organisations are capable of acting and being held responsible for such actions. Few would argue that organisations should not be held accountable for harm, and the literature demonstrating moral failures of entities including governments, corporations and religious institutions is broad. Selznick calls for a more complex view of the nature of organisation, a more sophisticated understanding of their moral capacity and status. He criticises Marx and Foucault for an 'indifference to variation' and failing to distinguish 'discipline that gives coherence to life and sustains autonomous projects from techniques of control that regiment, denude, and degrade'.[31] In other words, context matters, and 'we should ask: what *kinds* of purposive organisation are justified by the nature of the institution? what *kinds* of authority? what *kinds* of subordination?'.[32]

Selznick accounts for critiques of authority and bureaucracy in arguing that responsive mechanisms would empower individuals and communities to respond to repressive power, by whomever wielded. He presents a vision of participatory democracy and shared decision-making that relies on 'sociologically grounded insights into how institutions actually operate' as well as a deep 'understanding of how difficult it is for principles of moral philosophy to penetrate [institutions] and to satisfy human needs'.[33] 'What matters most is effective belonging, which means, among other things, being taken seriously as a person and as a member.'[34] Ensuring that all those with interests in the outcome of a legal issue have the means to effectively and meaningfully participate in legal processes is a cornerstone of responsive law. 'The objective is not harmony based on powerlessness, it is the creation of a civic order, guided by ideals of community, within which the terms of cooperation can be negotiated and decisions can be monitored, criticized, and changed.'[35]

The concept of responsive law is largely aligned with republican theory. Although Selznick himself may have identified as a Trotskyist when young, and later was branded by some a conservative, his concern with freedom and non-domination resembles that of self-proclaimed republicans like Philip Pettit and John Braithwaite. Republican ideals declaring 'freedom as non-domination' as a normative goal call for systems of law and regulation that reduce the amount of

[29] ibid, 243.
[30] ibid, 242.
[31] ibid, 257.
[32] ibid, 263.
[33] JH Skolnick, 'Legacies of Legal Realism: The Sociology of Criminal Law and Criminal Justice' (2012) 8 *Annual Review of Law and Social Science* 1, 1.
[34] Selznick (n 26) 316.
[35] ibid, 318.

domination and increases the quantum of freedom afforded people in the world.[36] The essence of the republican ideal is: (1) good policy is that which advances freedom as non-domination; and (2) checks and balances against arbitrary power are keys to freedom from domination.[37]

Republicans call for flexible, responsive strategies in response to misbehaviour – whether individual, corporate or organisational.[38] This is largely echoed in Selznick's description of responsive law. As Martin Krygier explains, Selznick's theory is grounded in enduring and common features of the natures, circumstances, problems and aspirations of individuals and communities, yet equally in the irreducible variety, particularity and idiosyncrasy that persons exhibit in living their lives.[39] Responsive law imagines a redistribution of power for the benefit of victims of domination through a mechanism steeped in empirical understanding of how that domination is expressed in the lived experience of stakeholders.

NLR builds on previous theories by, among other things, moving away from its American roots to investigate other domestic settings as well as transnational and international contexts. It also adopts what Dagan and Kreitner call 'situated empiricism', combining social science methods with legal craft.[40] A normative framework for NLR that builds on Selznick's ideal of responsive law should incorporate lessons from critical, intersectional and socio-legal scholarship. This means research should attend to how domination and oppression relate to domains of race, class, gender, sexuality and other social markers. Its normative framing requires an acknowledgement of how domination and oppression are often expressed through systemic inequity and call for empirical approaches that are constructed in ways that will help make local, national and global forms of domination and oppression visible.

Just as NLR builds on earlier movements of legal empiricists, a normative framework for NLR is likely to resemble but refine Selznick's view of responsive law. Krygier highlights Selznick's observations that organisational character can reinforce and adopt social hierarchies disadvantaging already disfavoured social groups, even when an organisation holds itself out as a democratising force.[41] It is not sufficient to note the existence of domination; rather, its manifestations and mechanisms should be considered in context and from multiple perspectives. A normative framework for NLR, then, is likely to build on Selznickian ideals and to further develop the theory of responsive law with a normative perspective of intersectionality that seeks to understand domination from the multiple perspectives of those involved – victims, bystanders, perpetrators and wider communities.

[36] Philip Pettit, *Republicanism: A Theory of Freedom and Government* (Clarendon Press, 1997).

[37] John Braithwaite, 'Relational Republican Regulation' (2013) 7 *Regulation & Governance* 124.

[38] See eg John Braithwaite and Philip Pettit, *Not Just Deserts: A Republican Theory of Criminal Justice* (Oxford University Press, 1990).

[39] Martin Krygier, *Philip Selznick Ideals in the World* (Stanford Law Books, 2012).

[40] Hanoch Dagan and Roy Kreitner, 'The New Legal Realism and The Realist View of Law' (2018) 43 *Law & Social Inquiry* 528, 529.

[41] Krygier (n 39) ch 3.

My purpose is to produce a broad and nuanced account of how legal systems operate in real-life settings, paying attention to how social and normative orders existing alongside operative legal systems impact law, and how legal systems construct legal problems. Qualitative methods, including archival research, interviews and observation yielded rich data about professional and community perspectives on legal systems, the problem of child sexual abuse by Catholic priests and religious, and the contexts in which claims are brought. In the next chapter, I describe the historical and social background of Ballarat and Gallup, drawing from archival research, observation, interviews and multiple academic literatures. The purpose is to help the reader put the problem of clerical sexual abuse and the involvement of legal systems into context. The significant social and cultural differences between the two dioceses serve as a way of deepening an understanding of the complexity of the problem and the ways in which legal systems operate. Just as legal problems are constructed by legal systems, they are also socially constructed through the filter of the people and places impacted. Understanding legal systems requires empirical and legal methods.

Law is not just statutes and rules promulgated by the state. It is also a range of social understandings about the role of legal systems, the methods by which legal decisions are made, and much more. Legal systems cannot be separated from their historical development or from their social context, including cultural, political and economic systems.[42] Access to and experience with legal systems is a function of political and material circumstances as much as the specifics of legal doctrine. Successful navigation of legal systems requires resources – financial, social and practical.

In all legal systems, good legal analysis requires an understanding of more than just the text of a specific code or statute. In order for a lawyer to represent a client, they need to know more than just the text of the law – they must understand and be able to navigate multiple aspects of the legal system in order to provide useful advice and representation. This book sets out the following aspects as a way to break down some component parts of legal systems:

(1) Purpose: The general purpose of the legal system – the kinds of problems it is designed to address and the system's role in the larger social order.
(2) Theory: Legal theories express the internal concepts that inform the ideals of justice that a legal system has adopted, the ideas of right and wrong that give shape to decisions within it.
(3) Doctrine: Doctrinal law includes both statutory and, in common law contexts, precedential law.
(4) Procedure: Procedural law governs how cases are brought, who may participate in legal processes, and set out the rules of how cases progress.
(5) Logistics: Practical, localised and material factors that impact stakeholder participation. This includes matters such as courthouse location, judges'

[42] Nicola Lacey, '"Philosophical Foundations of the Common Law": Social not Metaphysical' in Jeremy Horder (ed), *Oxford Essays in Jurisprudence: Fourth Series* (Oxford, 2000) 17, 18–19.

> preferences, local rules of access for court systems, stakeholders' material and social resources, and a range of idiosyncratic circumstances that have real impact on whether or not a legal case is brought, as well as its outcome.

In order to classify legal systems as repressive, autonomous or responsive, I evaluate them by breaking them down into these aspects as variables. This framework allows me to compare legal systems across multiple dimensions, accounting for their purposes within broad social orders, their theories of justice, their express doctrine, the procedural law setting out how the system is meant to work, and the practical factors that fill in the gaps of the procedural law. All of these aspects are important, and together they give shape to the framework of responsive law theory that I use to assess the character of legal systems as repressive, autonomous, or responsive.

II. Aspects of Legal Systems and a Framework for Responsive Law

A. Introduction

This section will introduce and define aspects of legal systems that serve as variables in the framework for evaluating a legal system as repressive, autonomous or responsive. Every legal system is different, and in each system analysed in this book, these aspects play different roles, are more or less developed, and contribute in different ways to how cases are resolved. For some of them, like criminal legal systems, it can be difficult to separate their purposes and theories, while others, like the Royal Commission and Chapter 11 bankruptcy, have very little doctrine. The clear, defined purposes and theories of the Royal Commission and Chapter 11 bankruptcy contribute to their (quasi-) responsiveness, while the focus on doctrine in tort helps identify it as autonomous. This book finds both (corporate) criminal law and canon law to have repressive tendencies because of the way they treat corporations or members of the priesthood as privileged subjects. None of these systems discussed are wholly repressive, autonomous or responsive, but by comparing them across purpose, theory, doctrine, procedure and logistics, it is possible to gain a holistic view of their characters. The subsections that follow will define each aspect and use criminal legal systems' capacity to hold dioceses responsible for child sexual abuse as an example, both to help define the aspect and to explain why criminal legal systems have not, by and large, been used to address diocesan responsibility for abuse. I have written elsewhere of why criminal legal systems are poorly suited to hold corporate wrongdoers to account,[43] and

[43] Meredith Edelman, 'Responsive Law and the Problem of Corporate Crime' (2022) 38 *Australian Journal of Corporate Law* 46; Meredith Edelman, 'Corporate Moral Insolvency: Lessons from Purdue Pharma' (2024) *Griffith Law Review* 1.

I will draw on those arguments to help explain why criminal legal systems have not played a large role in holding dioceses accountable for child sexual abuse.

B. Purpose

Legal philosophers have spilled a lot of ink on abstract questions of the purpose of law as a form of social ordering. I will not add to that. My concern is about the purpose of specific legal systems, not law in general. Each of the legal systems considered here has a unique social purpose separate from larger purpose of law. As Sally Engle Merry wrote, 'Defining the essence of law or custom is less valuable than situating these concepts in particular sets of relations between particular legal orders in particular historical contexts.'[44] Purpose, in my framework of analysis, is a function of legal systems' foundational concerns and their own internal concepts of their purpose. This is along the lines of what Nonet and Selznick called the ends of law – the role each system plays in society. Each system within a plural space constructs its place in part by what kind of problems it seeks to solve.

Purposes and theories (discussed below) are related but not identical concepts in my framework. By purpose, I mean the role the legal system is defined as having in a given polity.

A legal system's purpose affects the kinds of cases it considers, what kinds of relief might be available, the kinds of actors who participate in it, and the ways and places in which the system has authority or can expect its decisions to be enforced. The purpose of a legal system relates to the kinds of problems that come before it, whereas theory relates to the ideals of justice that inform the system's decision-making apparatus. In other words, purpose is what a system claims to do within a community largely recognising the legal system as legitimate, and theories are ideals that those legal systems are structured to recognise and advance. I will discuss theories in more detail in the next section.

In order to understand a legal system's purpose, I find instructive Brian Tamanaha's definition of 'function', ie '"what a thing does" or "what it is used for"'.[45] Each legal system has social purposes – roles proponents assert that a system plays within larger legal and social orders. This helps to define the kind of interests and goals it is designed to recognise as legitimate. Katie Wright uses 'purpose' in a similar way when she calls for understanding the Royal Commission in terms of the forms, history, processes and purposes of public inquiries in polities where they are used.[46] Tamanaha explains that, if law is to be 'understood naturalistically, historically, and holistically',[47] then the roles that legal systems play in social orders are critically important. In his usage,

[44] Sally Engle Merry, 'Legal Pluralism' (1988) 22 *Law & Society Review* 869, 889.

[45] Brian Z Tamanaha, 'Functions of the Rule of Law' in Jens Meierhenrich and Martin Loughlin (eds), *The Cambridge Companion to the Rule of Law* (Cambridge University Press, 2021) 221.

[46] Katie Wright, 'Remaking Collective Knowledge: An Analysis of the Complex and Multiple Effects of Inquiries into Historical Institutional Child Abuse' (2017) 74 *Child Abuse & Neglect* 10, 11.

[47] Brian Tamanaha, 'Law's Evolving Emergent Phenomena: From Rules of Social Intercourse to Rule of Law Society' (2018) 95 *Washington University Law Review* 1149, 1149.

'naturalism views humans as social animals with natural traits and requirements, historicism presents law as historical manifestations that change over time, and holism sees law within social surroundings'.[48]

Realists caution against accepting the claims that legal systems make about effecting justice and warn us not to discount the machinations of power in a legal system's design and effects. Describing system purpose is not meant to suggest that the system entirely or even mostly achieves its purposes, or that purposes are entirely just. Purpose does, however, help explain why systems are constructed as they are and the kinds of problems that they aim to solve. A naturalistic perspective on humanity and our social nature points to the emergence of rules governing social behaviour, indicating that the rules, and by extension legal systems, serve social purposes. While complex legal structures and formal law systems are, historically speaking, relatively new creations, they mediate disputes, adjudicate legitimacy of actions or rules, and institute consequences in response to breaches of rights and rules just as other systems, of varying formality and forms, have taken and continue to take in societies with and without complex systems of formal law.

In common law jurisdictions like Australia and the US, corporations have been subject to criminal legal processes since the mid-nineteenth century, which coincides with the emergence of private business corporations as the drivers of industrialising economies.[49] Before that, and even now in many civil law jurisdictions, it had been understood that corporations were, ontologically speaking, not capable of committing a crime. In order for non-corporeal organisations to be found guilty of crimes with an element of *mens rea* – or guilty state of mind – judges and lawmakers have created, over time, various different means by which corporations can be connected to the *actus reus* of a crime. Corporations can be held criminally liable for the conduct of their employees and agents through vicarious liability,[50] through the identification of a director or manager with a 'directing mind and will',[51] through strict liability offences,[52] or through legislation providing that fault can be attributed to a corporate actor through a permissive or negligent corporate culture.[53] Despite a long history of legislated or judicially developed theories of fault attribution, corporate criminal liability remains a contested issue.

Vincent Chiao began his article, 'What is the Criminal Law For?', by asserting that 'it goes without saying that the criminal law and its associated institutions'

[48] ibid, 1149.

[49] See eg Philip J Stern, 'The Corporation in History' in Grietje Baars and Andre Spicer (eds), *The Corporation: A Critical, Multi-Disciplinary Handbook* (Cambridge University Press, 2017) 21–46.

[50] *New York Central and Hudson River Railroad Company v United States*, 212 US 481 (1909); see also James Edelman, 'Direct and Vicarious Liability of Corporations' in Edwin Peel and Rebecca Probert (eds), *Shaping the Law of Obligations: Essays in Honour of Professor Ewan McKendrick KC* (Oxford University Press, 2023) 211–26.

[51] *Meridian Global Funds Management Asia Limited v Securities Commission* [1995] UKPC 5; see also Samuel Walpole, 'Criminal Responsibility as a Distinctive Form of Corporate Regulation' (2020) 35 *Australian Journal of Corporate Law* 235.

[52] See eg, Corporations Act 2001 (Cth), ss 200B, 791A, 820A, 952J.

[53] See eg, Commonwealth Criminal Code Act 1995, Pt 2.5.

are 'set up to punish people'.[54] Punishment is 'not just hard treatment, but hard treatment motivated by, and expressive of, resentment directed at … morally wrongful conduct'.[55] This helps explain one of the ways that purpose and theory of criminal legal systems are linked: a purpose of criminal legal systems is punishment, and the theory behind that purpose is that morally wrongful conduct should be: a) defined by the state; and b) punished. Doctrinal criminal law, of course, defines wrongful conduct. Criminal laws set out a normative code, one that the state will use its monopoly on legal violence to enforce. Theory connects purpose and doctrine by making normative claims about state power to make judgments, impose penalties, and use violence to enforce these judgments and penalties.

Douglas Husak's list of 10 functions of criminal law outlined many core purposes of criminal legal systems, including: punishing wrongdoers; vindicating rights and condemning wrongs; punishing those guilty of moral transgressions; deterring wrongdoing; and suppressing non-legal violence.[56] Criminal legal systems help legitimate state monopolies on legal violence while expressing social condemnation and meeting a public demand for justice.[57] Chiao's article, despite starting with a reference to punishment, is actually about another purpose: making the rule of law possible.[58]

> Since reasonably stable public institutions are plausibly required to facilitate the realization of whatever other goals it may have, the criminal law's role in stabilizing those institutions enjoys a function priority relative to those other functions. If you think the point of the criminal law is to vindicate a person's natural rights, then you will likely expect a conception of moral wrongdoing to figure prominently in its justification. If, on the other hand, you think the primary job of the criminal law is stabilizing cooperation under shared public institutions, then you will likely expect instead an account of the value of shared life under such institutions to take center stage in justifying the criminal law.[59]

Chiao's point, in Selznick's terms, is that one of the purposes of criminal legal systems is to create sufficiently stable social conditions for autonomous legal systems to exist.[60] Recall that state weakness and social instability are key characteristics of repressive law.

Chiao and Husak are good examples of Nicola Lacey's observation about criminal law jurisprudence, that 'the subject of modern systems of criminal law in and beyond the common law world is generally assumed to be a human individual'.[61]

[54] Vincent Chiao, 'What is the Criminal Law For?' (2016) 35 *Law and Philosophy* 137, 137.
[55] ibid, 137.
[56] Douglas Husak, 'The Price of Criminal Law Skepticism: Ten Functions of the Criminal Law' (2020) 23 *New Criminal Law Review* 27.
[57] ibid.
[58] Chiao (n 54) 138.
[59] ibid, 138.
[60] See eg, ibid, 144.
[61] Nicola Lacey, '"Philosophical Foundations of the Common Law": Social not Metaphysical' in Jeremy Horder (ed), *Oxford Essays in Jurisprudence: Fourth Series* (Oxford, 2000) 17, 25.

More than 80 years after Edwin Sutherland chastised criminology for ignoring the crimes of the powerful, articles on the purpose of criminal legal systems do not even mention corporations as a potential class of offender.[62] Furthermore, as Lacey points out, even the framing of 'white-collar crime' 'implicitly sets up the individual offender as the primary analytic focus'.[63] She observed that discourse on corporate criminal liability, whether from doctrinal scholars of criminal law, legal philosophers, or sociologists of law, is marked by metaphors, contrasts and analogies by which corporations are argued to be either proper or improper subjects of criminal legal systems.[64] Using corporate manslaughter as a case study, she considers various approaches to corporate liability, including the identification doctrine, aggregation doctrine and the corporate culture approach outlined in the Australian Commonwealth Model code, as individualistic or organisational approaches to attributing blame to organisations.[65] She concludes that corporations can be made subjects of criminal legal systems regardless of their metaphysical reality, but that whether or not they should be subjects of criminal legal systems is a question that should be answered only with an understanding of criminal legal systems as a social practice, and not just a legal or normative system.[66] The metaphors and analogies are insufficient – whether or not corporations should be subjects of criminal legal systems deserves more empirical understanding – of both corporations and the social orders in which they operate.

In both Australia and the US, a small number of prosecutors have brought charges against dioceses, religious organisations, or bishops for failing to protect children or criminally endangering them, but very few of these prosecutions have resulted in a conviction. No criminal charges have ever been brought against the Diocese of Ballarat or any of its officials for failing to prevent abuse. No charges have ever been brought against the diocese or a bishop of Gallup either. One man who I interviewed, a victim of abuse in the Diocese of Gallup, went to law school and became a prosecutor in one of the two Arizona counties inside the diocese. I asked him why he never brought a case against the diocese, and he talked with pride about how many individual abusers he had prosecuted, but did not really answer my question about the diocese itself. It may be that, as a devout Catholic, he felt it would be wrong to charge a diocese with a crime. Or, that, as a prosecutor, he did not believe pursuing the diocese would have been a worthwhile use of his time – that diocesan liability was better addressed through civil, rather than criminal

[62] Edwin H Sutherland, 'White-Collar Criminality' (1939) 5 *American Sociological Review* 1.

[63] Lacey (n 61) 25.

[64] ibid, 25.

[65] ibid, 36–37; Australian authorities have been particularly innovative in responding to corporate wrongdoing. Among other things, they have created a system of civil penalty proceedings – a fault-based penalty for corporations that does not require the same high standards of proof as criminal processes, US prosecutors have developed a different approach, using deferred prosecution agreements in order to avoid a long and unpredictable trial.

[66] ibid, 39.

action. Perhaps he did not believe that prosecuting a diocese was congruent with the purpose of the criminal legal system he served.

Kate Gleeson has argued that more leaders and organisations should be prosecuted for systemic failures, lamenting that 'Church representatives continue to describe the organised criminal activity as "an accident of history" and a "disastrous coincidence" of unrelated events and personalities.'[67] Citing US legal scholar Timothy D Lytton, she explained that civil litigation has 'perform[ed] the function of truth recovery by exposing the organisational processes implicated in abuse.'[68] Changing social norms and a movement of Survivors advocating for justice prompted revisions to tort law beginning in the late twentieth century which have allowed for many victims of child sexual abuse to bring claims against corporations, including Catholic dioceses like Ballarat and Gallup. While criminal laws against child sexual abuse have been revised and statutes of limitation expanded, the Survivors movement has, like the former victim turned prosecutor in Arizona, focused on criminal liability for direct perpetrators and civil liability for dioceses. In tort, victims are directly compensated, the burden of proof is significantly lower, and defendants do not benefit from protections of criminal procedure. In sum, there are many different factors that contribute to dioceses, as corporations, only very rarely being prosecuted.

In articles I wrote in 2022 and 2024, I sought to answer questions like those Lacey posed. I argued that some, but not all, functions of criminal legal systems are applicable to corporations. Even if corporations can be subjects of criminal legal systems, the unspoken assumption that civil and regulatory systems are the only alternatives to criminal law is without foundation. As this book demonstrates, there are many different kinds of legal systems. Corporations are capable of blameworthy conduct and, with their immense power to impact life on Earth, it is imperative that there exist a system which effectively incentivises these actors towards pro-social conduct. There is little dispute that corporate wrongdoing triggers a public demand for justice, but it is not possible to punish a corporation in the ways that criminal legal systems punish human beings. A corporation is capable of causing violence, but not perpetrating it in a bodily sense or experiencing it in any sense. The mismatch in purpose may help explain why publics around the world are concerned with lawlessness and harms emanating from corporate actors. My articles and this book argue in favour of a new legal system, one designed around corporate wrongdoing, serving a social function similar to criminal legal systems – encouraging pro-social conduct and deterring anti-social conduct – but designed around and better suited to corporate ontology.

[67] Kate Gleeson, 'Why the Continuous Failures in Justice for Australian Victims and Survivors of Catholic Clerical Child Sexual Abuse?' (2016) 28 *Current Issues in Criminal Justice* 239, 241.

[68] ibid.

C. Theory

Theory can be a confusing term. A great deal of literature traces the history of legal thought and theories of law from Moses and Aristotle through to Machiavelli, Hobbes and Kant, and more recently to Foucault and Dworkin. I will not repeat this history here because I have a narrower definition in mind. I am interested in the normative theories on which legal systems are based. These theories identify the values the system is designed to advance and sets forth the kind of justice that the system takes as ideal. Theories express the ideas of right and wrong that give shape to the cases that a legal system concerns itself with.

For my responsive law framework, purpose identifies the kind of problem a system is designed to address, and theory sets out the values that inform decision-making. Theory, within the framework I use in this book, implicates normative assumptions and understandings that inform how actors within legal systems understand the goals of the law, while purpose implicates the shared understanding of how, why and when the system originated, and social justifications for its role in society. Theories are not static, but are developed and constructed through argument, practice and contestation of norms, ideas and interests. Theory is the foundation upon which doctrine, whether in statute, code or common law, is built.

As I mentioned above, theory and purpose of criminal legal systems are deeply linked. Purposes like the deterrence of non-legal violence and enforcing the state monopoly on legal violence are connected to theories about the right of states to enforce that monopoly, and the wrongfulness of non-legal violence. Criminal legal systems in the common law world construct non-legal violence as a crime against the state, a breach of the peace. The state's right to use violence to enforce criminal adjudications means that the threat of physical, social and material deprivation in jail, or even corporeal punishment or a death penalty, serve as potent threats in coercing compliance. Because only criminal legal systems can impose these penalties, criminal legal systems occupy a unique position within social orders, and conviction of a criminal offence can have serious tangible and social consequences that no other legal system can bring about, at least for human beings.

The theory behind corporate criminal liability is that criminal legal systems' position as the most coercive system will render all those held subject to it similarly coerced. Corporate criminal liability is defended as a means of asserting corporations' subjectivity to the rule of law and communicating that they, like humans, will be held accountable to the law for their wrongdoing. Corporate immunity to violence challenges that theory. It is impossible to put a corporation in a jail cell, or for a corporation to experience embarrassment, pain, hunger, sadness or shame.[69] However impactful it may be for a corporation to be held criminally liable, it is less impactful than a similar conviction would be for a human being. The result is

[69] Edelman (2022) (n 43).

criminal legal systems having two different types of subjects. Even if criminal legal systems had an equal deterrent effect on human and corporate subjects, so long as those systems also have a retributive purpose that can only be fulfilled in the case of human beings, the systems privilege corporations, creating a two-tiered system of law. One type of subject can experience the full weight of the law's power, even as the other type is uniquely capable of causing mass harm.

Diocesan responsibility for child sexual abuse highlights how corporations can be responsible for extraordinary violence and yet not be held to account through criminal legal systems. The dioceses of Ballarat and Gallup allowed priests and religious they knew had previously abused children to hold positions where they would have access to and authority over children, refused to believe children's reports of abuse, covered up evidence (often with the help of local police), and contributed, in many other ways, to victims' trauma. Perpetrators have been sent to prison for abusing individuals, but criminal legal systems offer no comparable punishment to corporations, so even if the dioceses were to be convicted for their contributions to children's' abuse, the penalties would be, at most, similar to the damages awarded in a civil suit. Despite this, neither diocese is likely to ever be charged, much less convicted, of a crime. Corporations are able to cause violence and suffering at unfathomable scale, but because they are incapable of experiencing violence or suffering, criminal legal systems are limited in their capacity to respond to their wrongdoing.

D. Doctrine

Doctrine is the statutory and common law text of law in a given legal discipline. 'Gap' studies scholars might call it the law on the books. William Twining explained a realist perspective on doctrine as 'principles, concepts, and distinctions in addition to rules'.[70] Doctrine is the substantive law, norms and policies (the meaning and proper application of which are the subject of legal argument). Doctrine provides for actors' rights and obligations and establishes a baseline of permitted and forbidden acts. It provides the justification for decision-making about which legitimate goals and interests prevail when more than one such interest is presented. While early legal realists may have discounted the role of doctrine in legal proceedings, and looked to other factors to explain legal determinations, doctrine is a crucial aspect to many legal systems. An NLR approach sees doctrine as an independent variable in legal systems situated within 'formal dimensions of law'.[71] Doctrine is important, even if understanding doctrine alone is insufficient to consistently predict

[70] William Twining, 'Legal R/Realism and Jurisprudence: Ten Theses' in Elizabeth Mertz, Stewart Macaulay and Thomas W Mitchell (eds), *The New Legal Realism Volume I: Translating Law-and-Society for Today's Legal Practice* (Cambridge University Press, 2016) 121, 126.

[71] Sida Liu, 'Law's Social Forms: A Powerless Approach to the Sociology of Law' (2015) 40 *Law & Social Inquiry* 1.

outcomes of legal matters. Twining cites Julie Dickson and Neil MacCormick to argue that 'understanding law needs to combine conceptual, doctrinal, normative, and empirical perspectives in different ways at different levels'.[72] He goes on to argue there is no conflict between legal realism's roots and NLR's increased interest in doctrine: 'The basic realist objection is against the dominance of or an exclusive emphasis on doctrinal studies, not on doctrinal studies as such.'[73]

Doctrine can be a critical variable in determining whether a legal system can be described as autonomous. Repressive law will be designed to serve the interests of the state, allow for powerful interests to avoid accountability, and will legitimise and reinforce existing forms of social subordination. A repressive legal regime will subordinate doctrine to the interests of the established legal order. Autonomous law systems focus on the text and meaning of doctrinal law for the purpose of regularity in application. An emphasis on doctrine and its being fairly applied is a key feature of autonomous legal systems, as well as a key feature of a society that embraces the rule of law. Responsive law, by contrast, may be more flexibly purposive and more likely to allow for normative argument based on principles, rather than requiring textual support in existing law.

Criminal legal systems in Australia and the US rely heavily on doctrine – no one can be criminally prosecuted for an act which is not specifically defined as a crime. Crimes are defined as wrongs perpetrated against the state. If behaviour giving rise to a criminal prosecution caused harm to someone, that injured party may be able to bring a civil claim, but criminal charges are brought in the name of the sovereign – whether that sovereign is styled as Rex/Regina, the People, the State, or the Commonwealth. Prosecutors then must prove that each element of the crime, as that crime is defined by law, has been met. Although ignorance of the law is generally not a defence, Australia and the US both reject that an action (or inaction) can be made criminal ex post.

As Nonet and Selznick discussed, a focus on doctrine and the equal application of law serves as the foundation for autonomous legal systems, and for the rule of law. This echoes Chiao's point about criminal legal systems laying the foundation for the rule of law. However, despite the apparent equal treatment of all subjects, a prohibition against ex post facto criminal punishment, for example, advantages corporations. Corporations, not being alive, do not have a lifespan or other natural limit to their capacity to engage with the world. They can cause or contribute to massacres, famines, mass poisonings and other kinds of violence in countries far removed from where they are organised and headquartered. They can do harm at a scale unimaginable for an individual human being, but corporate harm does not always fit into the neatly prescribed elements set out in criminal law.

Diocesan responsibility for child sexual abuse is an example of how corporate wrongdoing can avoid the scrutiny of criminal legal systems. As discussed in chapter one, religious duress and emotional or spiritual harm impact victims of clerical

[72] Twining (n 70) 124.
[73] ibid 126.

abuse in ways that are qualitatively different from abuse in non-religious settings. Church teachings about the priesthood, sexuality, gender and authority, in conjunction with abuse by priests, give rise to real harm. This harm would not exist but for dioceses placing these men in positions of religious authority, holding them out as intermediaries between the human and the Divine.

Climate change is another example – entire industries used their collective resources to mislead and misinform publics about the dangers of a warming climate and the contributions of fossil fuels to it. Our shared planet is exhibiting signs of climate distress, but most of the activity contributing to that distress is outside the scope of criminal law. Corporate wrongdoing, like corporations themselves, can be idiosyncratic, and may not fit the same patterns of wrongdoing as human beings. Corporations can exist across space and time in ways that human beings cannot, including the capacity to operate in multiple places at once, and to have impact across centuries and cultures.

Just as corporations' economic and social contributions have had massive impact on contemporary societies, so too can their wrongdoing – and this impact can be unanticipated or novel in ways that would make it difficult for the wrong to have been prohibited *ab initio*. Changing the law to retrospectively hold fossil fuel corporations responsible for climate change, or to create a new penalty for religious organisations' responsibility for abuse would violate fundamental tenets of criminal law. But, to the extent these fundamental tenets are designed to protect human beings from arbitrary state violence, which corporations are immune to, the argument supporting their application to corporations is weak.[74]

E. Procedure

Procedural law defines how, when and by whom, decisions are to be made. It governs who can initiate cases against whom, and under what circumstances. It establishes when different kinds of arguments can be presented and the proper format for presenting them. It defines what is allowable as evidence, how evidence can be introduced to proceedings, the purposes for which decision-makers are to consider different types of evidence, the relative reliability and weight carried by different forms of evidence, and even the range of arguments that can be made regarding its admissibility. Procedural rules can have significant consequences to the potential success of cases or the ability of stakeholders to advocate for their interests.

Procedural law has long been a key concern of American legal realists. Karl Llewellyn's admonishment to 'see it as it works' preceded a rising interest in legal procedure as a factor in legal outcomes in succeeding scholarship.[75]

[74] Edelman (2022) and (2024) (n 43).

[75] Tracey E George, Mitu Gulati and Ann C McGinley, 'The New Old Legal Realism' (2011) 105 *Northwestern University Law Review* 689, 736 (citing Karl N Llewellyn, 'A Realistic Jurisprudence-The Next Step' (1930) 30 *Columbia Law Review* 431).

Paul MacMahon argues that the realist tradition has inspired more Americans to be interested in procedure as compared to Anglo (and Australian) scholars, which in turn has increased the significance of procedure in legal practice in the US.[76] He argues that, between the realists and the American reliance on civil litigation as a regulatory practice, associated with class actions and large punitive damages, and the balancing of authority between separate jurisdictions, procedure is a focal point for American academic and professional lawyers.[77] As Cass Sunstein explains:

> American lawyers are 'brought up on sophisticated talk about the fluidity of the line between substance and procedure.' Yet there is rough agreement on what counts as procedure and what counts as substantive law, however poorly theorized that agreement may be. While it may be difficult to tell whether a particular rule is procedural or substantive, the existence of troublesome borderline cases does not make the distinction meaningless.[78]

Chapters five and seven will provide further insight into how this tendency in American legal systems manifests itself in cases involving child sexual abuse in tort and bankruptcy proceedings.

A legal system's approach to procedure shapes the way cases progress and is especially useful in determining its character as repressive, autonomous or responsive. Both reflecting and arising out of the fluidity of the line between procedure and doctrine, responsive law is defined in part by its flexibility of procedure and autonomous law by its rigidity.[79] Procedures in repressive regimes are designed to reinforce and legitimise the interests of established power even if that means flexibility in pursuit of those interests, but autonomous law stakes claim to procedural fairness and submitting the powerful to the rule of law. Responsive law is characterised by flexible procedures that seek to reduce the impact of existing forms of domination and resolve problems through negotiation and consensus, rather than judicial fiat.

Criminal processes, usually, but not exclusively, brought by states, are serious matters. They are designed to be adversarial, and the burden of proof is on the prosecutor. Criminal procedure is a complex set of defined rules that burden prosecutors and largely benefit defendants. Blackstone's maxim, 'the law holds that it is better that ten guilty persons escape, than that one innocent suffer',[80] is often cited in support of these procedural rules. A process that requires the case against an accused person be proved beyond a reasonable doubt is meant to protect against arbitrary enforcement of state power. Criminal procedure and

[76] Paul MacMahon, 'Proceduralism, Civil Justice, and American Legal Thought' (2013) 34 *University of Pennsylvania Journal of International Law* 545, 610.

[77] ibid (citing John Hart Ely, 'The Irrepressible Myth of Erie' (1974) 87 *Harvard Law Review* 693, 724).

[78] Cass R Sunstein, 'Incompletely Theorized Agreements' (1995) 108 *Harvard Law Review* 1733, 1735–36.

[79] Selznick (n 26) 466–67.

[80] William Blackstone, *Commentaries on the Laws of England*, 21st edn (Sweet, Maxwell, Stevens & Norton, 1844).

rights afforded to defendants are designed to make it more difficult for prosecutors in criminal actions than it is for plaintiffs in civil actions. Criminal procedure in Australia and the US is designed to protect those accused of crimes from arbitrary state punishment, to ensure a fair trial, and sets out rights and obligations of relevant parties, as well as mechanisms for their enforcement.

Legal philosopher John Gardner explained how the purpose of these measures relates to the moral dignity of human being:

> Many familiar features of modern criminal law … are supposed to ensure that the trial and punishment for a criminal offence affirms the moral agency and moral responsibility of the offender, and in the process (since moral agency and moral responsibility represent a significant part of what it is to be a human being) affirms the offender's humanity.[81]

Corporations, as non-human creations of state law, are awkward holders of rights embedded in criminal procedure to protect the dignity of human life, because they are not possessed of human life. This is more than simply observing that that corporations have 'no soul to damn and no body to kick'.[82] As Roger A Shiner writes, characteristics of corporations including 'the opaqueness of the corporate veil, the specialized knowledge of corporations, their ready access to the resources for legal representation – all justify measures to ease the burden of proof on the state'.[83]

The Royal Commission's report on the Diocese of Ballarat takes note of one way that the diocese was able to avoid scrutiny – the destruction of records. In 1990, after sending notorious abuser Gerald Ridsdale to the Servants of the Paraclete near the diocese of Gallup, Bishop Mulkearns of Ballarat 'received at least five reports', on Ridsdale, but Father Lechner, the director of the facility in New Mexico,

> asked that Bishop Mulkearns either destroy the reports or return them when he had finished reading them. Father Lechner noted, 'This procedure has been recommended by our legal counsel and also reflects our concern for the priests who come to us and their dioceses.' Bishop Mulkearns apparently followed that advice, as no reports were produced to [the Royal Commission].[84]

Five years later, according to the Royal Commission, 'Victoria Police commenced Operation Arcadia. A number of people were interviewed during this investigation, and at least one search warrant was executed.' It is unclear whether the reports that the Royal Commission assumed Mulkearns destroyed contained information

[81] John Gardner, *Offences and Defences: Selected Essays in the Philosophy of Criminal Law* (Oxford University Press, 2007).

[82] John C Coffee, '"No Soul to Damn: No Body to Kick": An Unscandalized Inquiry into the Problem of Corporate Punishment' (1981) 79 *Michigan Law Review* 386.

[83] Roger A Shiner, 'Corporations and Presumption of Innocence' (2014) 8 *Criminal Law and Philosophy* 485, 487.

[84] Royal Commission into Institutional Responses to Child Sexual Abuse, *Un-redacted Case Study 28: Catholic Church Authorities in Ballarat* (May 2020 (the 'Ballarat Report') 338.

that would have led to a conviction if found in 1995, but if destroying the reports was a regular, recommended procedure of the facility, as the letter to Mulkearns implies, dioceses around the world were able to hide evidence of what they knew about abusive priests, benefiting from the kind of resources and scale that humans might only rarely have access to.

F. Logistics

The final aspect of legal systems that I include in my framework is logistics. Logistics is something of a catch-all, including a wide range of practical and idiosyncratic factors that can impact a legal process, but which are not necessarily relevant to the substance of any legal assertions. These include stakeholders' capacity to secure competent representation and engage meaningfully with systems, as well as the means by which that engagement happens. Logistics include the kinds of resources, knowledge and/or capacities required to be able to participate meaningfully and advocate with reasonable efficacy in pursuit of legally recognisable interests. Personal and professional preferences and associations of judges, clerks and local practice, the proximity of courts to stakeholders, trust in the legal system and a variety of social variables all factor into logistics.

As a new lawyer in practice, a mentor would constantly remind me to be aware of 'logistics'. This meant being aware of how long various processes take, calculating deadlines, knowing local rules (including what we called 'local-local' rules, which are location-specific, judge-specific or even unwritten), and ensuring that the right documents, evidence and arguments are presented at the right time, in the right place, with the right permissions having been obtained, in the right physical or electronic format, to the right audience. Failure to do so can forfeit legitimate substantive claims. Lawyers in all kinds of practice need to be aware of the logistics of practice.

Lawyers' logistics are part of this aspect of legal systems, but logistics of being a party in a legal process are another crucial part. The logistics of being a party relate to access to legal services, the quality of that service, capacity to assess the quality of legal services, capacity to participate in the legal process, finance a case, withstand any social or financial pressures participation brings with it, and process the emotional toll it all takes. Both kinds of logistics are important to understand if we are to achieve a broad perspective of how legal systems operate.

Logistics can also help distinguish a responsive system from repressive and autonomous law systems. Autonomous systems maintain a formal doctrine of fairness, which the logistics of participating can make unfair. For example, in rural areas, especially poor rural areas like most of the Diocese of Gallup, there tends to be a significantly lower proportion of lawyers than in cities or more prosperous areas. Repressive and autonomous systems require participants to adhere to procedural rules, submit specific written documents outlining their legal cases in a particular way and order, and otherwise navigate a complex system. In order to do this effectively, participants need to hire lawyers. For many people, retaining a competent lawyer can be a significant barrier to exercising legal rights.

Responsive systems, on the other hand, actively seek ways to lower the barriers to participation for those most likely to need that help. Responsive systems may not be able to change social or material circumstances, but they can allow for flexibility in how people participate in a legal system. Chapter six will explain some of the ways in which the Royal Commission was proactive about making participation in a fact-finding process simple for those living in remote areas, those who were incarcerated, or those who might otherwise have found participation difficult. With a flexible approach to participation, the Royal Commission demonstrated responsiveness – by allowing victims to submit written statements or provide testimony without facing a cross-examination, the evidence victims submitted would not have been admissible in a criminal case, but the Commissioners were able to consider these statements for more limited purposes.

Dioceses like Ballarat and Gallup, as leading religious organisations in their local areas, have longstanding relationships with Catholic (and non-Catholic) lawyers and other legal professionals, and there are few barriers to their having access to competent legal representation in whatever legal proceeding they may face. But the dioceses' networks also operate to prevent any such legal proceeding from even being contemplated. Recall when I asked the former prosecutor why he never charged the diocese with a crime. He was probably wondering why I would even ask the question. If a district attorney in any of the counties that form the Diocese of Gallup were to bring a criminal case against the diocese, they would face backlash from some of the most powerful people in their communities, as well as many ordinary people who benefit from work the diocese does in the community. Dioceses and other Catholic organisations provide medical services, aid to those living in poverty, education, and advocate for people who need protection from the state (including immigrants), as well as providing social and community identity, spiritual guidance and fellowship, and a place to express communal and social values. District attorneys in Arizona and New Mexico are elected, and prosecuting the local diocese would not bode well for the next election. Dioceses have political, social and material resources that, from a practical (logistical) perspective, advantages them in legal proceedings in ways that have little or nothing to do with the legal substance of those proceedings.

III. Summary

The framework for responsive law developed in this chapter seeks to provide structure for the analysis in the chapters on canon law (chapter four), tort (chapter five), the Royal Commission (chapter six) and Chapter 11 bankruptcy (chapter seven). In each of those chapters, I will evaluate the purposes, theories, doctrine, procedure and logistics of the legal systems, using the definitions for those concepts that have I outlined in this chapter. These legal systems are all very different, and in some cases, the boundaries between purpose, theory, doctrine, procedure and logistics are not easy to identify, and not all of the aspects have the same level of importance in different legal systems. These differences are important, and the relative importance of each aspect in how cases are resolved can help in characterising the systems as repressive, autonomous or responsive.

In this chapter, I have used corporate criminal liability as an example to help me explain what I meant by each of the aspects, and by revisiting the aspects of corporate criminal liability, I have demonstrated how the framework functions. Nonet and Selznick identified criminal legal systems substantially similar to those found in Australia and the US as prototypical examples of autonomous legal systems, but my analysis of corporate criminal liability above has revealed a more complicated picture.

Although the purpose of criminal law generally is quite well theorised, many of its central purposes are inapplicable to corporations. The theory that, by using the same system to hold corporations and humans accountable for their wrongdoing, the state is demonstrating corporations' subjectivity to law, is weak. When corporations and humans are considered alongside each other as subjects of criminal legal systems, the system appears to have two tiers of subject, with human beings treated much more harshly than corporations, a kind of dual-law regime. There is no stated goal of protecting corporations in order to conserve state authority, but the patterns of subordination of life to the interests of capital that Subhabrata Bobby Banerjee described as 'necrocapitalism',[85] as well as logistical advantages that transnational business organisations hold in litigation contribute to duality of legal regimes. Although doctrine has evolved over time to account for corporate liability, criminal procedure's high standards of proof and protections for defendants have largely been applied to corporations, even though the normative justifications for these standards are (at least arguably) not relevant for corporations. Furthermore, the ontological impossibility of punishing a corporation undermines the premise that the impact of a corporation's criminal conviction and a human being's criminal conviction could carry comparable weight.

Criminal legal systems were designed around human beings – our psychology, our corporeality and our desire for freedom. Calls for accountability for dioceses and other organisations whose operations provoke, allow or obscure violence are widespread, but corporate criminal liability's utility is limited. Criminal prosecutions have not been pursued against dioceses, but prosecutors' decisions not to do so have little to do with whether or not they believe dioceses to be responsible for wrongdoing.

[85] Subhabrata Bobby Banerjee, 'Necrocapitalism' (2008) 29 *Organization Studies* 1541; see also Ray Michalowski, 'The Necropolitics of Regulation' (2020) 1 *Journal of White Collar and Corporate Crime* 83.

3

The Dioceses of Ballarat and Gallup

I. Introduction

Ballarat and Gallup are both Catholic dioceses located in wealthy English-speaking settler-colonial nations with complicated histories of contestation between and among multiple racial and ethnic groups. People lived in both places long before Europeans arrived, but the stories of the dioceses begin with the first European people in the areas. Following in Merry's footsteps by taking 'a magnifying glass to [two] small place[s]',[1] this chapter unveils histories of colonialism and their connection to clerical child sexual abuse as a contemporary social problem and, ultimately, a legal problem in the legal systems discussed in later chapters.

Ballarat and Gallup are similar in many ways. Each of them serves a Catholic community that constitutes a significant minority of the population in its geographical territory. Both of these dioceses have employed relatively large numbers of priests and religious known to have abused children – with some individuals in each place responsible for abusing hundreds of children. Documents made available to the public demonstrate at least some Church officials in both Ballarat and Gallup were aware of perpetrators' histories of abuse, while continuing to assign them to positions where they had access to children. In both places, priests and religious who were abusing children were transferred from parish to parish and school to school, leaving traumatised victims behind.

Child sexual abuse is a crime of opportunity, and social conditions contribute to those opportunities. Remote communities, like those in both Ballarat and Gallup, provide opportunities for abusive priests to take advantage of trust placed in them. For example, a typical Sunday for a rural priest requires travel from parish to parish; for many years, priests would typically be accompanied by an altar server in making that journey, which facilitated abuse.

But abusers were not just protected and enabled by diocesan leadership. In both Ballarat and Gallup, perpetrators were also protected and defended by local officials, including police. Documents made public through state-law legal proceedings and published Survivor accounts evidence that police in both places were aware of some perpetrators' abuse of children, and not only failed to bring

[1] Martha Merrill Umphrey, 'Review' (2004) 38 *Law & Society Review* 833, 833 (quoting Sally Engle Merry, *Colonizing Hawai'i: The Cultural Power of Law* (Princeton University Press, 1999)).

charges against them, did not even intervene to stop them from continuing in positions with authority over children.

Children may even have faced disbelief within their own families. In both places (at least historically), communities have been divided along sectarian lines. In both places, Catholic children through the twentieth century spent the vast majority of their time with their families, at church, or in schools where most of the children shared their own religious and cultural backgrounds. Psychiatrist Carolyn Quadrio told the Royal Commission that in communities and families strongly associated with religion, children's disclosures about abuse by religious authorities are often met with 'a bad reception and [being] told [that] they're lying, it can't be true. The negative response from family and community can really compound the damage enormously.'[2]

Despite the above-listed similarities, the dioceses also have significant differences. Although both can be described as rural, the population of Ballarat is more concentrated in town centres, and more economically secure than the more remote, poorer population of Gallup.[3] The majority of Catholics in Ballarat are members of Australia's dominant ethnic group and the majority of Catholics in Gallup (although not most of those in the priesthood or diocesan leadership) are either Native American or Hispanic – both disfavoured minority groups in the US. Other differences will be discussed in more detail below, allowing for a reflection on the ways that race, class, gender, political power and wealth or poverty can impact the rates, impacts and contexts of child sexual abuse.

Ballarat and Gallup provide the framework for the study of legal systems' responses to diocesan responsibility for abuse, providing insight into how legal systems work in practice. Their similarities and differences highlight how patterns of conduct by abusers and their enablers could repeat themselves around the world even as a wide range of localised factors complicate legal processes. Locating the study in these places allows for a grounded perspective, giving readers a sense for the relationships between individual cases and broader trends. The heterogeneous data available on the social conditions of Ballarat and Gallup tell interesting stories about how culture, economics and temporal change, as well as social, political and economic conditions, shape the impacts that corporate wrongdoing has on its victims and the capacity of legal systems to respond to it.

The next section will introduce the Diocese of Ballarat, with a focus on how its history and social context contributed to the ways in which abuse was perpetrated and enabled. Following that is a section introducing the Diocese of Gallup, and then a discussion comparing the two.

[2] Royal Commission into Institutional Responses to Child Sexual Abuse, *Un-redacted Case Study 28: Catholic Church Authorities in Ballarat* (May 2020) (the 'Ballarat Report') 433, quoting Evidence of Carolyn Quadrio to Royal Commission into Institutional Responses to Child Sexual Abuse, Ballarat, 25 May 2015, 8471:36–47.

[3] Robert Tanton, Dominic Peel and Yogi Vidyattama, 'Every suburb Every town: Poverty in Victoria' National Centre for Social and Economic Modelling (November 2018).

II. The Diocese of Ballarat

The Archdiocese of Melbourne is the head of the ecclesiastical province of Melbourne (co-extensive with the State of Victoria). Sandhurst, Sale and Ballarat are suffragan dioceses within the ecclesiastical territory.[4] The Diocese of Ballarat describes itself as

> a diverse and geographically extensive Diocese of twenty-nine parishes which covers the western third of Victoria, extending from the Murray River in the North to the Southern Ocean. To the west it is bounded by the Archdiocese of Adelaide and the Diocese of Port Pirie, to the north by the Diocese of Wilcannia-Forbes and to the east by the Diocese of Sandhurst and the Archdiocese of Melbourne.[5]

The Diocese of Ballarat is located on land identified as having traditional owners including the Gunditjmara, Eastern Maar, Wotjobaluk, Jaadwa, Jadawadjali, Wergaia, Jupagalk, Dja Dja Wurrung, Wadawurrung, and Millewa-Mallee Peoples and Nations.[6] The Australian Bureau of Statistics estimates that there were about 2,500 Indigenous persons living in all of Victoria in 1854. They further estimate that by 1891, that number dipped below 1,000 persons and did not return to more than 2,000 persons until the 1960s.[7] The 2016 Census reveals Victoria to have the smallest percentage of Indigenous persons in Australia, at 0.9 per cent of the population.[8] The Catholic Church's expansion in Victoria cannot be separated from the settler-colonial project – its growth benefited from and coexisted with the effective genocide of Indigenous people. Genocide has been a feature of colonialism across Australia, as it has in Africa, Asia and the Americas.[9] Lyndall Ryan explains that Indigenous peoples' 'virtual disappearance' in Victoria between 1835 and 1851 is a classic example of genocide facilitating the material gains of setter-colonial enterprises.[10]

The 1841 census counted 203 Catholic people living in Portland, Victoria's first permanent European settlement. The Ballarat Parish was established in 1852, and the Diocese recounts that in 1853 the number of children on the Ballarat 'diggings'

[4] Archdiocese of Melbourne, 'Archidioecesis Melburnensis', www.catholic-hierarchy.org/diocese/dmelb.html.

[5] 'Our Diocese', Catholic Diocese of Ballarat, www.ballarat.catholic.org.au/our-diocese.

[6] Victorian Government, 'Welcome to Country and Acknowledgments Map', Aboriginal Cultural Heritage and Information System, achris.vic.gov.au/weave/wca.html.

[7] Australian Historical Population Statistics, *Aboriginal and Torres Strait Islander Census counts and estimates of the population, states and territories, 1836 onwards* (Table 10.2, 2019).

[8] Australian Bureau of Statistics, *Estimates of Aboriginal and Torres Strait Islander Australians, June 2016*, www.abs.gov.au/ausstats.

[9] See eg, Adhikari Mohamed (ed), *Genocide on Settler Frontiers: When Hunter-Gatherers and Commercial Stock Farmers Clash* (Oxford Press, 2015).

[10] Ryan Lyndall '"No Right to the Land": The Role of the Wool Industry in the Destruction of Aboriginal Societies in Tasmania (1817–1832) and Victoria (1835–1851) Compared' in Mohamed Adhikari (ed), *Genocide on Settler Frontiers: When Hunter-Gatherers and Commercial Stock Farmers Clash* (Oxford Press, 2015); see also Fred Cahir, *Black Gold: Aboriginal People on the Goldfields of Victoria, 1850–1870* (Australian National University E Press, 2012).

increased from 850 to 3,600, demonstrating the remarkably fast growth of European settler population in the area, at the same time the Indigenous population was nearly extinguished.[11] The Diocese of Ballarat was erected in March 1874 by Pope Pius IX, and Bishop Michael O'Connor was installed as the first Bishop. Since that time, there have been seven bishops, including the current Bishop of Ballarat, Paul Bernard Bird, CSSR, appointed 1 August 2012, upon the retirement of Bishop Peter Joseph Connors, who himself was preceded by Bishop Ronald Mulkearns.[12]

The rapid changes in the region in the mid-nineteenth century were due to a series of gold strikes, which brought thousands of Europeans in search of fortune.[13] Many of the new arrivals were Catholic, so the gold mines and the Diocese of Ballarat grew rapidly together, both crucial parts of the settler-colonial project in Victoria; and the city of Ballarat, which houses the cathedral, became a wealthy regional centre.[14]

For people in the Diocese between the mid-nineteenth and mid-late twentieth centuries, whether one was a Catholic or a Protestant determined both identity and community. There was hostility between the groups; they were schooled separately; and intermarriage was rare.[15] This environment of social segregation and closeness of the Catholic community set the scene for the diocese later becoming known as the 'epicentre' of clerical child sexual abuse.[16] The Royal Commission's report on Ballarat highlighted testimony from victims of Ballarat's abusive priests about how the closed nature of the Catholic community in the diocese impacted family and community responses:

> [One victim,] told us Ballarat is a very Catholic town and the Catholic community is very closed. He continued, 'Coming forward and talking publicly about child sex abuse in Catholic institutions not only has repercussions at a family level, but also at the business and social level in Ballarat.'
>
> …
>
> [Another victim] said that, after he and his brother came forward about the sexual abuse, his family lost Catholic friends. He said, 'In my experience, victims and their families often feel ostracised because people don't understand what has happened and are awkward because they don't know what to say.'

[11] Catholic Diocese of Ballarat, 'Diocesan Timeline', www.ballarat.catholic.org.au/our-diocese/history-2.

[12] Catholic Diocese of Ballarat, 'Our Diocese: Bishop Paul Bird', www.ballarat.catholic.org.au/our-diocese/bishop-paul-bird; Opening Address by Senior Counsel Assisting to Royal Commission into Institutional Responses to Child Sexual Abuse, *Case Study No 28*, Ballarat (19 May 2015).

[13] See eg William Bramwell Withers, *History of Ballarat and Some Ballarat Reminiscences* (Ballarat Heritage Services, 1999).

[14] See eg ibid.

[15] Timothy Willem Jones and Clare Wright, 'The Goldfields' Sabbath: A Postsecular Analysis of Social Cohesion and Social Control on the Ballarat Goldfields, 1854' (2019) 43 *Journal of Religious History* 447; see also John McKinnon, *Report on a Survey of the Religious Attitudes of the Diocese of Ballarat* (Diocese of Ballarat, 1973) ii.

[16] Greg Gliddon, 'Ballarat an "Epicentre" of Institutional Child Abuse' *The Ballarat Courier* (27 June 2018) 2.

> Mr BAV told us that, as a result of speaking out about the sexual abuse, he has been excluded from social events and experienced forms of bullying in the community. Mr BAV told the Royal Commission that he believed he had also lost work opportunities, as people refuse to hire him because he has spoken out against the Catholic Church.[17]

The way in which social segregation, including within the police forces, contributed to official protection of abusive priests and religious is also detailed in a memoir of a police officer trying, unsuccessfully, to prosecute an abuser. Denis Ryan's *Unholy Trinity: The Hunt for the Paedophile Priest Monsignor John Day*[18] provides a crucial insider's perspective on how the police forces in the Diocese of Ballarat responded to allegations of child sexual abuse. He writes of 'a group of police officers, known as the Catholic Mafia, [that] actively suppressed investigations into paedophile priests'.[19] His story gives critical insight into how child sexual abuse can be enabled by the kind of closed, patriarchal and hierarchical institutional cultures exhibited by the Diocese of Ballarat and the Victorian police.

The 'Catholic Mafia' Ryan wrote of developed in a Victoria police force that reflected the 'sectarianism in Australian society at the time', between Catholics and Protestants (connected, in his telling, with Freemasonry).[20] 'For a young uniform copper not long out of the academy, the Catholic-Mason divide operated almost invisibly.'[21] However, Ryan writes that, as he moved up the ranks, he was invited to join

> a group of [Victoria police officers] who, at the request of the Cathedral, look into instances where priests have been charged with offences to see if we can have these matters dropped or dismissed so the Church's good name will not be brought into disrepute.[22]

Although Ryan declined to join, he writes that he assumed the crimes being dropped or dismissed were relatively minor affairs, 'misdemeanours, traffic offences, drink driving and so forth, … crimes that were of no profound criminality but would necessarily bring embarrassment to the Church'.[23] However, when Ryan was later transferred to Mildura, in the Diocese of Ballarat, he became aware of serious offending by John Day, one of the diocese's most notorious abusers. He wrote about his struggle to hold Day accountable – his collection of evidence and compassion for victims, his fight against his superiors in the Victoria Police working against his efforts, and his ultimately being fired from the Victoria Police when he refused to back down from his efforts to bring Day to justice. More than a simple story of one man's struggle to bring justice to abused children, Ryan's

[17] Royal Commission into Institutional Responses to Child Sexual Abuse, *Unredacted Ballarat Report* (May 2020) 434 (citations omitted) ('Unredacted Ballarat Report').

[18] Denis Ryan and Peter Hoysted, *Unholy Trinity: The Hunt for the Paedophile Priest Monsignor John Day* (Allen & Unwin, 2013).

[19] ibid, 8.

[20] ibid, 24.

[21] ibid, 24.

[22] ibid, 24.

[23] ibid, 24.

memoir provides insight into how abusers have been protected by both the state and the Church, while linking that protection to broader social forces of sectarianism and community segregation.

Ryan served in the Victoria Police from 1956 to 1972. 'In 1978, Michael Glennon, a Catholic priest, would be the first cleric to go before the courts.'[24] Glennon was convicted of having abused of 10-year-old girl, but was released and allowed to work as a priest in the 1980s 'mainly to immigrant and Aboriginal communities', where he abused more children.[25] He continued to abuse children even while out on bail and facing new charges.[26] The social conditions that facilitated such repeated offending were supported by religious authorities, as well as lay people:

> In one of [Glennon's] trials a woman gave evidence that she saw Glennon in a bed with a boy one night, but thought nothing of it because she trusted him. 'Well, of course I did. I'm a Catholic, aren't I?' she told the jury. 'I mean, you go by the cloth. Who else do you trust in this world?'[27]

The story of *Unholy Trinity* is a story of justice delayed by systems privileging the powerful over the weak, and social conditions that benefit and protect abusers. Church and police officials had been aware of abuse for decades, but child sexual abuse by Catholic priests only became an issue of concern to the broader Australian public in the 1990s, with the Wood Royal Commission in New South Wales.

In response to civil claims and public outcry in the 1990s, the Australian Catholic Bishops Conference (ACBC) determined to implement a change. While the Archdiocese of Melbourne launched the Melbourne Response,[28] other Catholic organisations in Australia, including the Diocese of Ballarat, launched Towards Healing, 'a process offered by the Church to a person who has been abused by a priest, religious or other Catholic Church personnel'.[29] From the late 1990s and through the 2000s, as more people disclosed having been abused, Towards Healing and other Church initiatives were increasingly perceived as being insufficient to meet the needs of victims, their loved ones and communities. Around the same time as *Unholy Trinity*'s publication in 2013, the Victorian Parliament requested its Family and Community Development Committee provide a report on 'the processes by which religious and other non-government organisations

[24] ibid, 200.

[25] Mark Butler, 'Pedophile Priest Michael Charles Glennon Dies in Jail' *Herald Sun* (1 January 2014), www.heraldsun.com.au/news/law-order/pedophile-priest-michael-charles-glennon-dies-in-jail/news-story/d12cc8b85c8f364722c61fd7175de3a3.

[26] ibid.

[27] ibid.

[28] Royal Commission into Institutional Responses to Child Sexual Abuse, *Case Study 16: The Melbourne Response* (August 2014).

[29] Professional Standards Office: Catholic Church Queensland, 'Towards Healing', psoqld.catholic.net.au/documents/towardshealing.html.

respond to the criminal abuse of children by personnel within their organisations'.[30] The report, *Betrayal of Trust: Inquiry into the Handling of Child Abuse by Religious and Other Non-Government Organisations*, made a number of recommendations, many of which were taken up by the Victorian Government (the 'Victorian Inquiry').[31]

The Royal Commission, established in 2013 and discussed in more detail in chapter six, dedicated multiple days for hearings in three different sessions to sexual abuse allegations in the Diocese of Ballarat. Those hearings were closely watched across Australia and around the world.[32] The Diocese of Ballarat was characterised as the 'epicentre' of clerical child sexual abuse in Australia, not just because the number of perpetrators and rate of victimisation in the diocese is relatively high,[33] but also because, even before the Royal Commission, the perpetrators and their crimes had become known to the public, their stories told through news reports, major governmental enquiries and widely read publications. The Royal Commission's public hearings related to the Diocese of Ballarat, especially those involving its famous former leader, Cardinal George Pell, garnered intense public interest. When Ballarat's officials, many of them retired, were cross-examined in public and on video-link, Australians were watching.

> In hearing rooms across the country, church and state came face to face before the commission. Ambushes were sprung and confessions extracted. Men of faith were made to deal in facts. Fragile survivors were led gently through appalling revelations of abuse. Memories failed. Lies were told blind.
>
> All this was streamed to the world. In New York and Israel, members of the Yeshiva sect watched as their leaders faced public interrogation. Unprecedented, too, was the grilling of leaders of another secretive sect, the Jehovah's Witnesses, and 22,000 viewers followed that contest live.
>
> But the ratings winner in all the years of hearings turned out to be Case Study 28: Catholic Church authorities in Ballarat. It's no surprise. In the public imagination, Ballarat was the epicentre of neglect, abuse and the outrageous protection of the notorious paedophile Father Gerald Ridsdale. Fifty-four thousand viewers watched as these horrors were brought to light.[34]

[30] Family and Community Development Committee, Parliament of Victoria, *Betrayal of Trust: Inquiry into the Handling of Child Abuse by Religious and Non-Government Organisations* (November 2013) vol 1, v.

[31] Royal Commission into Institutional Responses to Child Sexual Abuse, *Redress and Civil Litigation Report* (September 2015).

[32] See eg, Hilary Whiteman, Anna Coren and Jo Shelley, 'Pell's Hometown Ballarat at the Center of Australia's Sex Abuse Scandal' CNN (24 March, 2019), edition.cnn.com/2019/03/23/australia/george-pell-ballarat-catholic-abuse-intl/index.html.

[33] See eg, Barney Zwartz, 'Catholic Response "unChristlike"' *The Sunday Age* (30 April 2013) 1; Michael Short, 'Hell on Earth: Judy Courtin Says the Rape of Children by Catholic Priests is Best Dealt with by a Royal Commission', *The Sydney Morning Herald* (25 June 2012), www.smh.com.au/national/hell-on-earth-20120624-20wa8.html.

[34] David Marr, 'Grappling with Rome: David Marr's Lessons from the Royal Commission' *The Guardian* (12 December 2017), www.theguardian.com/australia-news/2017/dec/13/grappling-with-rome-david-marrs-lessons-from-the-royal-commission.

The Royal Commission published reports for each of their case studies. Its report into the Diocese of Ballarat (the 'Ballarat Report')[35] details its investigation into the abuse and findings after considering hours of testimony (in hearings both public and private) and reams of documents handed over by the diocese and other entities.[36] The Ballarat Report details known events of abuse; children's reports to parents; and parents' complaints to school, Church, and police officials – repeated failures by authorities to protect children. It sets out who knew what and when about particular allegations of abuse, responses to allegations, and when and why abusive priests and brothers were transferred from school to school and parish to parish. It details the meetings of officials, conversations with insurance companies, and letters to and from mental health professionals. It lays out the stories of abuse told by the victims themselves and compares those stories with the testimony of officials and documentary evidence to piece together a narrative that spans decades. This tracing of events is a crucial reconstruction, and, as will be discussed in chapter six, furthers a narrative of truth about the problem of child sex abuse in institutional settings that has been truly consequential for victims and their communities across Australia.

There is broad agreement that the abuse perpetrated in Ballarat constitutes a cluster, and that the rate of abuse was unacceptably high, which justified the Royal Commission's significant investment of time and resources in the case study of the Diocese of Ballarat.[37] The quantitative data produced by the Royal Commission into rates of abuse in institutional settings across Australia, however, suggests that, while the rates of abuse in Ballarat are high, there are a number of places where significantly higher percentages of those working in the institutions were abusive.

In February 2017, the Royal Commission, through a public hearing, ran an institutional review of all Catholic Church authorities operating in Australia, considering evidence 'in relation to child protection and child-safe standards, including responding to allegation of child sexual abuse'. This review, with data collected through the Royal Commission process, formed the 'Catholic Report'.[38] On 15 December 2017, the Royal Commission presented its multi-part final report (hereinafter, the 'Final Report'), 'detailing the culmination of a five year inquiry into institutional responses to child sexual abuse and related matters'.[39]

The Catholic Report detailed statistics about reports of child sexual abuse in Catholic institutions. As opposed to the detailed account of instances of abuse and institutional action (or inaction) found in the Ballarat Report, the Catholic Report provides statistics about all of the dioceses and religious communities in Australia,

[35] Unredacted Ballarat Report (n 17).

[36] ibid.

[37] See eg Kate Gleeson, 'Exceptional Sexual Harms: The Catholic Church and Child Sexual Abuse Claims in Australia' (2018) 27 *Social and Legal Studies* 734.

[38] Royal Commission into Institutional Responses to Child Sexual Abuse, *Case Study 50: Institutional Review of Catholic Church Authorities* (February 2017) ('Case Study 50').

[39] Royal Commission into Institutional Responses to Child Sexual Abuse, *Final Report 'Preface and Executive Summary'* (December 2017).

including the Diocese of Ballarat and the religious institutions operating therein.[40] It finds that 139 people made a claim of child sexual abuse against the Diocese of Ballarat, which constitutes three per cent of all claims of child sexual abuse received by Catholic institutions in Australia.[41]

In the Catholic Report, we also find that the Diocese of Ballarat reported that 98 of the claims against it resulted in a payment or payments, whether those payments consisted of compensation, treatment, legal or other costs. The diocese paid a total of AUD4.96 million on account of these claims. Of those 98 claims, 38 were brought in civil courts, of which 87 per cent (33) resulted in monetary compensation, totalling AUD2.31 million. A total of 84 claims went through Towards Healing, of which 47 claims made to Towards Healing claims resulted in monetary compensation through that programme, totalling AUD1.97 million. Although the specific amounts paid to individual claimants is not public information, the AUD2.31 million paid to 33 victims through the civil claims process averaged AUD70,000 per claim, while the AUD1.97 million paid to 47 victims through Towards Healing averaged just under AUD42,000.

The Catholic Report listed 21 alleged perpetrators as being subject to one or more claims of child sexual abuse received by the Diocese of Ballarat, of whom 20 were identified by name. All were male. Of the alleged perpetrators subject to one or more claims of child sexual abuse, 81 per cent (17) were reported to be priests while three were reported to be non-priest religious. Six alleged perpetrators were the subject of 10 or more claims, while one was the subject of 78 claims.[42] With a total of 199 priests serving the Diocese of Ballarat during the relevant time period, the Royal Commission found that 8.7 per cent of the total number of priests in the diocese had been accused of abuse.[43]

This figure is slightly higher than the proportion of abusive priests in Australia as a whole, but several other dioceses had rates that were higher still, and many religious orders had significantly higher rates.[44] The dioceses and orders with the highest rates of abuse are those that regularly operated schools, orphanages or other facilities that put their members in positions with direct authority over children.[45] There was far less variation among dioceses than among religious

[40] Case Study 50 (n 38).

[41] ibid.

[42] ibid.

[43] ibid.

[44] ibid. Listing an average rate of 7.9% for diocesan Church authorities and 7.0% for Australian Church authorities including religious orders). The Archdiocese of Brisbane (9.3%), the Diocese of Lismore (13.9%), the Diocese of Port Pirie (14.1%), the Diocese of Sale (15.1%), the Diocese of Sandhurst (14.7%) and the Diocese of Wollongong (11.7%) have higher rates of abuse. Of religious institutes, the Christian Brothers (22.0%), the De La Salle Brothers (13.8%), the Marist Brothers (20.4%), the Salesians of Don Bosco (non-ordained) (20.9%), the St John of God Brothers (40.4%), the Marist Fathers (13.9%), the Benedictine Community of New Norcia (21.5%), the Pallottines – Society of the Catholic Apostolate (13.7%) and the Salesians of Don Bosco (ordained) (17.2%) also have rates of abuse higher than that of the Diocese of Ballarat.

[45] ibid.

institutes, many of which operated schools or orphanages as their primary activity. In general, religious institutes operated by women and those in which members did not interact with children in any capacity had the lowest rates of all types of institutions, and those run by men and which operated residential facilities for vulnerable young people had the highest rates.[46]

The Christian Brothers, a religious institute with a high rate of abuse (22 per cent of its members were credibly accused), is responsible for much of the abuse discussed in the Ballarat Report.[47] Many known abusers were assigned to work at Christian Brothers schools, as well as other schools throughout Australia. Although the Christian Brothers and the Diocese of Ballarat were treated separately for purposes of data in the Catholic Report, the Ballarat Report considered the local Christian Brothers' community alongside the Diocese of Ballarat in order to gather information on abuse occurring in the geographical area, regardless of the order or diocese to which the priest or religious belonged.[48]

The relationship between the Christian Brothers and the Diocese of Ballarat during the period studied by the Royal Commission was considered during the inquiry, and although the two organisations had separate formal leadership, the Royal Commission's evidence demonstrated that the two organisations worked closely together, and that Cardinal Pell and other leaders were apprised of allegations against both diocesan priests and Christian Brothers, and would have had the authority to take action with respect to those allegations.[49] Officials of both organisations were involved in the schools where abuse was reported to the Royal Commission. The Royal Commission examined how officials in both organisations discussed events and issues arising in the schools. But the Christian Brothers and the Diocese of Ballarat were not the only organisations implicated in the Ballarat Report. The Royal Commission heard, and reported on, evidence that the Victoria Police were aware of claims that priests in the Diocese of Ballarat were abusing children.[50]

The evidence collected and made public by the Royal Commission gives insight into how Church and state authorities responded to reports of abuse. There are letters, reports, records of meetings and days of testimony about transferring offenders to new locations, convincing parents and victims to not report abuse to the police, or otherwise covering up the abuse. The Ballarat Report describes instances of Victoria Police notifying diocesan officials of decisions not to act on reports of abuse against individual priests and religious, and contrasts those with public statements by those same authorities claiming they had not known about those individuals' abuse.[51]

[46] ibid.
[47] Unredacted Ballarat Report (n 17) 21.
[48] ibid.
[49] ibid, 158.
[50] ibid, 225.
[51] ibid, 226.

The abusers who haunted Ballarat and the Church officials who enabled them are notorious, villains in a well-known chapter of the Australian public's understanding of the problem of child sexual abuse. The history of child sexual abuse by priests and religious in Ballarat is serious; the recidivism is particularly disturbing; and the stories that have made Ballarat known for the problem of clerical child sexual abuse in Australia are well worth telling, reading, hearing and studying. They provide insight into the circumstances, patterns and reactions to child sexual abuse in Catholic institutions in Australia, as well as providing critical information into how wider social patterns can impact the capacity and willingness of law enforcement and other authorities to act on reports of abuse.

Yet the rhetoric surrounding Ballarat – that it represents a cluster with higher rates of abuse than other areas in Australia or the world – deserves scrutiny. The stories of abuse, cover-up and institutional bias against the protection of children serve as critical focus points that have advanced the Australian public's understanding of the problem of child sexual abuse in institutional settings, without which the Royal Commission may not have even been launched. The involvement of and lack of action by the Victoria Police, however, demonstrates the importance of considering the wider social context. This will be seen in the next section, which discusses a diocese with many apparent similarities to Ballarat, but which is not nearly as well known.

III. The Diocese of Gallup

The Diocese of Gallup, like the Diocese of Ballarat, was founded on land occupied by Indigenous people who were not, before colonisation, Catholic. Beginning in 1539, with the arrival of Franciscan friar Marcos de Niza, the Catholic Church was centrally involved with cycles of colonisation, domination, conversion and violence in and around the area now forming the Diocese of Gallup.[52] The process of this early colonisation was particularly brutal, even for the sensibilities of a Spanish monk during the time of the Spanish Inquisition. A letter from Franciscan Brother Juan de Escalona in 1601 to the Spanish Viceroy is sharply critical of the violent and oppressive treatment of Pueblo peoples, including the forcible taking of food, blankets and other supplies.[53] As the diocese tells the story on its 'History of the Diocese of Gallup' webpage, the three centuries of Spanish colonisation, during which the region was a part of the Diocese of Durango, was a time of incredible brutality, with revolts, slavery and violence characterising the relationships between different peoples.[54] By the end of the seventeenth century, most

[52] Janet Lecompte, 'Coronado and Conquest' (1989) 64 *New Mexico Historical Review* 279, 282–93.

[53] Edwin S Gaustad (ed), *A Documentary History of Religion in America to the Civil War* (Eerdmans Publishing Company, 1993) 70, citing GP Hammond and Agapito Rey, *Don Juan de Oñate, Colonizer of New Mexico, 1595-1628* (University of New Mexico Press, 1953) Pt II, 692–95.

[54] Diocese of Gallup, 'History of the Diocese of Gallup', dioceseofgallup.org/about/our-history.

Pueblo people had submitted to Spanish colonisation, while Navajo and Apache peoples continued to raid Spanish and Pueblo settlements, missions and towns.[55]

As the diocese explains, Mexico's 1821 independence from Spain saw missions secularised, Franciscans expelled and churches falling into disrepair.[56] 1846 brought a US military occupation and the 1848 Treaty of Guadalupe Hidalgo established the area as a US territory, prompting Pope Pius IX to erect the Vicariate Apostolic of New Mexico in 1850, later establishing it as the Diocese of Santa Fe.[57] As Laura Gómez explains, the US acquisition gave rise to a form of 'double-colonization' where US authorities 'encountered an entrenched set of European-origin political and social institutions' operated mostly by descendants of Spanish and Indigenous people and Pueblo communities.[58] The social hierarchies of double-colonisation saw Anglo-Americans and certain Mexican-Americans become elites while lower-status Mexican-American and Pueblo people occupied an intermediate status above Navajo, Apache and other Indigenous peoples.[59]

The elevation of the Diocese of Santa Fe to an archdiocese in 1875 took place in a time of significant change. In the 1880s, the railroad through what are now New Mexico and Arizona was completed, bringing new peoples and industries to the area.[60] The town of Gallup, New Mexico was founded during this period, located close to rich coal fields adjacent to the railroad.[61] The last decades of the nineteenth century also saw well-publicised conflicts in Arizona and New Mexico territories between the US Government and Indigenous peoples, including the Chiricahua Apache band led by Geronimo.[62] As Indigenous people in the region were, tribe by tribe and band by band, confined to reservations, the US Government and the Catholic Church began establishing schools for Indigenous children, including boarding and day schools.[63] Katherine Drexel, the daughter of a wealthy Philadelphia banker and later Mother Superior of the Sisters of the Blessed Sacrament, a religious order she founded, was a prominent figure in the establishment of mission schools in the region. Drexel brought Franciscans back to the area when the Franciscan Fathers of Cincinnati acceded her request for

[55] ibid.

[56] ibid.

[57] Laura E Gómez, 'Off-White in an Age of White Supremacy: Mexican Elites and the Rights of Indians and Blacks in Nineteenth-Century New Mexico' (2005) 25 *Chicano-Latino Law Review* 9, 14.

[58] ibid, 14.

[59] ibid, 14.

[60] See eg Laura E. Gómez, 'Race, Colonialsim, and Criminal Law: Mexicans and the American Criminal Justice System in Territorial New Mexico' (2000) 34 *Law & Society Review* 1129, 1137.

[61] Diocese of Gallup, 'About the Diocese of Gallup', dioceseofgallup.org/about.

[62] See eg John R Welch and Robert C Brauchli, '"Subject to the Right of the Secretary of the Interior": the White Mountain Apache Reclamation of the Fort Apache and Theodore Roosevelt School Historic District' (2010) 25 *Wicazo Sa Review* 47.

[63] See eg Debra K Barker, 'Kill the Indian, Save the Child: Cultural Genocide and the Boarding School' in Dane Anthony Morrison (ed), *American Indian Studies: An Interdisciplinary Approach to Contemporary Issues* (Peter Lang, 1997) 47; David Wallace Adams, *Education for Extinction* (University of Oklahoma Press, 1995).

missionaries to work with Navajo people.[64] Schools she established include the St Michael Indian School, still operated by the diocese in St Michaels, Arizona.[65] The Franciscans, organised as a separate entity from the Diocese of Gallup, much as the Christian Brothers are separate from the Diocese of Ballarat, also operated the St John's Indian School where many children from Colorado River Indian Tribes, Gila River Indian Community, Pascua Yaqui Tribe, San Carlos Apache Tribe, Tohono O'odham Nation and White Mountain Apache Tribe in Arizona, and the Mescalero Apache Tribe in New Mexico, were sent, until it closed in 1981.[66]

Whatever benevolent intentions Drexel, who was canonised in 2000, may have had, they did not prevent her schools from causing serious harm to Indigenous children and communities. Activist Mary Crow Dog, who attended a school founded by Drexel, called it a 'curse for our family for generations'.[67] Debra KS Barker characterised the schools as 'an instrument that emotionally scarred generations of Indian children, leaving them and their children, as well, victims of institutionalised cultural genocide'.[68] The cultural genocide experienced by Indigenous children in what is now called the Diocese of Gallup reflected express US policy 'to culturally assimilate Indigenous children by forcibly relocating them from their families and communities to distant residential facilities where their … identities, languages, and beliefs were to be forcibly suppressed'.[69] The purpose of 'civilising' Indigenous people has come to be defined as cultural genocide, and a characteristic of the settler-colonial project in Australia, Canada and the US, among other places. Residential schools around the world designed for the purpose of educating Indigenous children were hotbeds of cultural, spiritual, physical, emotional and sexual abuse.

In 1939, Pope Pius XII issued a Papal Decree establishing the Diocese of Gallup out of the northern part of Arizona and the north-western part of New Mexico, crossing state borders to include all of the Navajo Nation.[70] The city of Gallup had, in 1922, begun hosting an Inter-Tribal Indian Ceremonial celebrating Indigenous people that, by the late 1930s, was attended by Navajo, Hopi, Zuni, Pueblo,

[64] 'Declaration of Bishop James S. Wall in Support of Chapter 11 Petition and First Day Motions' *In re Roman Catholic Church of the Diocese of Gallup*, No 13-13676 (Bankr DNM 12 November 2013) ('Wall Declaration').

[65] St Michael Indian School, 'Home', www.stmichaelindianschool.org.

[66] Elizabeth Hardin-Burrola, 'Franciscan Friars of California ask to extend abuse claim deadline' *National Catholic Reporter* (3 July 2024), www.ncronline.org/news/franciscan-friars-california-ask-extend-abuse-claim-deadline.

[67] Mary Crow Dog and Richard Erodes, *Lakota Woman* (Harper Perennial, 1991) 31.

[68] Barker (n 63) 47.

[69] Memorandum on Federal Indian Boarding School Initiative from Secretary of the Interior Deb Haaland to Assistant Secretaries, Principal Deputy Assistant Secretaries, and Heads of Bureaus and Offices of the Department of the Interior (22 June 2021), www.doi.gov/sites/doi.gov/files/secint-memo-esb46-01914-federal-indian-boarding-school-truth-initiative-2021-06-22-final508-1.pdf.

[70] Diocese of Gallup, 'Pope Pius XII Forms Gallup Diocese', www.dioceseofgallup.org/history.html; see also Kathleen Holscher, 'The Trouble of an Indian Diocese: Catholic Priests and Sexual Abuse in Colonized Places' in Tisa Joy Wenger and Sylvester A Johnson (eds), *Religion and US Empire: Critical New Histories* (New York University Press, 2022), 231, 236.

Kiowa, Apache and Mission peoples from as far away as Southern California.[71] Then-Archbishop of Santa Fe, Rudolph Gerken, declared the diocese of Gallup to 'represent[] a foreign mission field in our country [and that it] was primarily established … that a bishop might live in the midst of the largest and most populous Indian territory in the United States'.[72] In 1940, Bishop Bernard T Espelage, a Franciscan born in Ohio, was appointed the first bishop of Gallup.

Espelage served as bishop of Gallup until his retirement in 1969. Bishop Jerome J Hastrich was appointed in 1969, but to a smaller diocese, with all but Navajo and Apache counties in Arizona being ceded to the newly established Diocese of Phoenix.[73] In 1990, Hastrich retired and Bishop Donald Pelotte, the first Indigenous American to be appointed a Catholic bishop in the US, became the third bishop of Gallup.[74] Bishop James Wall was appointed in 2009 and described it in 2015 as 'the poorest diocese in the United States':[75]

> There are no large metropolitan areas within the Diocese, and the geographic area of the Diocese includes significantly poor and underdeveloped areas where there is high unemployment and low income. In many of the counties within the Diocese, approximately forty-three percent (43%) of the people live below the poverty level, and the unemployment rate is approximately forty percent (40%) on the Native American reservations which comprise a large part of the Diocese.[76]

As with the Diocese of Ballarat, many priests and religious serving the diocese in the twentieth century are now known to have been serial abusers.[77] While the story of Ballarat was thoroughly investigated through the Royal Commission, no such comprehensive investigation or report has been conducted with respect to Gallup. However, child sexual abuse in the Diocese of Gallup took place in the schools set up for Indigenous children, and has been widespread across parishes serving primarily poor Hispanic and Indigenous communities.

As a part of the bankruptcy settlement (discussed in chapter seven), the diocese has released and continues to update a list of priests and religious who have lived or worked in the diocese, and who the diocese admits have been credibly accused of child sexual abuse (the 'Credibly Accused List'.[78] At the time of writing, there

[71] Martin Link, '1920s' and '1930s' *102nd Gallup Inter-Tribal Indian Ceremonial Magazine*, 24–25, gallupceremonial.com/ceremonial-magazine.

[72] Holscher (n 70), 231, 237 (quoting 'Indian Capital Becomes a Bishopric' *Indian Sentinel 20.9* (November 1940) 141–42).

[73] Diocese of Gallup (n 54).

[74] Catholic Hierarchy, 'Bishop Donald Edmond Pelotte, S.S.S.', www.catholic-hierarchy.org/bishop/bpelotte.html; Catholic News Agency, 'Bishop Emeritus of Gallup Donald E. Pelotte Dies at 64' (8 January 2010), www.catholicnewsagency.com/news/bishop_emeritus_of_gallup_donald_e._pelotte_dies_at_64. Pelotte's father was a member of the Abenaki First Nation, a people from an area far to the east of New Mexico, and he grew up in Maine.

[75] Wall Declaration (n 64).

[76] ibid, [II.E].

[77] Diocese of Gallup, 'Credibly Accused List', dioceseofgallup.org/youth-protection/credibly-accused-list ('Credibly Accused List').

[78] ibid.

are 61 names on the list. The list includes locations where these individuals were assigned by the diocese and the years of those assignments. Some individuals have multiple assignments, and others only a few. There is at least one diocesan priest named in a claim alleging child sexual abuse who does not appear on the Credibly Accused List.[79] The list includes 34 individuals who served as priests or religious in the diocese during Bishop Espelage's tenure, 24 individuals during Bishop Hastrich's tenure, 10 during Bishop Pelotte's tenure, and one during Bishop Wall's tenure. Of the 221 assignments of credibly accused priests or religious reported, 48 of these were on Navajo Nation land, eight in the Fort Apache reservation, where the White Mountain Apache Tribe is, two at a location serving the Laguna Pueblo, and one each in the Acoma and Zuni Pueblos. Of the remaining assignments, most were to small towns with relatively high proportions of people living in poverty, Indigenous people or Hispanic people.

Whereas in Ballarat, the community has historically split between Catholic and Protestant, in Gallup there are three main population groups: white people (mostly in the Arizona counties), typically called 'Anglos', the vast majority of whom are either members of the Church of Latter-Day Saints (often referred to as 'LDS' or 'Mormon' people) or are Evangelical Protestants; Hispanic people (some recent immigrants, but mostly descendants of people who have lived in the area for generations, often called 'Hispanos'), most of whom are Catholic; and Native American (Indigenous, but sometimes called 'Indian') people. There are seven Indigenous nations within the boundaries of the diocese: Acoma Pueblo, Laguna Pueblo, Zuni Pueblo, Jicarilla Apache Nation, White Mountain Apache Tribe, Hopi Tribe, and the Navajo Nation, the largest of the seven. 'On Navajo land, participation in traditional Navajo practices exists side by side with activity in the Native American Church, Catholic parishes, and all kinds of mainstream, Pentecostal, and Evangelical Protestant churches.'[80]

People in rural Arizona and New Mexico are more religious than the US average.[81] Even those who rarely attend services are affiliated with one of the main religious traditions, and have family or close friends who attend services regularly. Much of daily life in the area is centred around religious and family life. Growing up in Pinetop-Lakeside, Arizona, a small town in the Diocese of Gallup, in an 'Anglo' family of mixed religious traditions, none of them Catholic, Evangelical or Latter-Day Saint, I was keenly aware of the importance of religion in my community. The Credibly Accused List shows two assignments to St Mary of the Angels, the parish in Pinetop-Lakeside, which was across a small country lane from the Presbyterian church where I was a member and, as a teenager, a deacon.

[79] Hannah Grover, 'Former Farmington Pries Allegedly Sexually Abused Children, Covered Up Abuse for Other Priests,' *Daily Times* (5 September 2013).

[80] Jay Youngdahl, *Working on the Railroad, Walking in Beauty: Navajos, Hózhǫ́, and Track Work* (Utah State University Press, 2011) 45.

[81] Clifford Grammich et al, 'U.S. Religion Census: Religious Congregations & Membership Study' (Census, Association of Statisticians of American Religious Bodies, 2010).

Pinetop-Lakeside is one of the more prosperous towns in the area – its high elevation makes it heavily wooded and relatively cool in the summer, and thus a tourist destination for outdoor recreation or escaping the desert heat. Looking at the places on the Credibly Accused List, it is notable to me that the parishes listed most often are those in the towns and villages where the majority of people are Indigenous or Hispanic, and where most of the people live in poverty.

Local newspaper reporter Elizabeth Hardin-Burrola has covered the Diocese of Gallup and reports of abuse by its priests for decades. Speaking on a local radio programme, she commented:

> [T]he abusers were mostly sent to small, rural communities with a lot of Hispanic parishes full of very devout Hispanic Catholic families and also to remote Native American communities where people would be struggling with language differences, poverty, probably not inclined to report.[82]

Plaintiffs' attorneys I interviewed made similar observations, pointing to segregation between social groups before noting that most of the serial abusers working in the Diocese of Gallup tended to be stationed in the poorest and most rural areas of the diocese. One of these lawyers told me that the bishop knew:

> 'Don't shit in your own bed.' They didn't put them at the cathedral or St Francis [in Gallup]. Some rural place – Holbrook, Winslow, Camp Verde. Largely Hispanic, places look like shanty towns. Do you think the mother who's trying to get money together to make a pot of beans is going to say 'hey Father, you touched my kid!'? No, they're trying to do more basic stuff like food. And she would see the priest as someone that would take care of her kid and not hurt him. Little did she know.[83]

From 1965 to 1975, Clement Hageman was assigned to the Madre de Dios Parish in Winslow, Arizona. Madre de Dios is one of two Catholic parishes in the town of just under 10,000 people, 'a tiny church on the edge of town … ringed by ramshackle homes and a vacant field'.[84] The Diocese lists 22 assignments in Winslow.[85] In 2024, the per capita income of Winslow was USD19,946 – less than 50 per cent of the US average of USD43,289. Winslow is 27.4 per cent white, 35.4 per cent Hispanic or Latino, 39.9 per cent Native American, and 3.9 per cent Black.[86] Hageman, now known as a prolific abuser, is one of the 16 individuals who appears on the diocese's Credibly Accused List with assignments between 1954 and 1989 to one of Winslow's two parishes.[87] In 1940, Bishop Emmanuel Ledvina, then the bishop of Corpus Christi in Texas, wrote to Bishop Espelage, who was

[82] 'Dark Canyon Part Nine: The Diocese of Gallup' KSFR (14 December 2017), www.ksfr.org/dark-canyon.

[83] Interview with anonymous plaintiffs' lawyer in 2015.

[84] Dan Frosch, 'Accusations of Abuse by Priest Dating to Early 1940s' *The New York Times* (10 July 2011), www.nytimes.com/2011/07/11/us/11priest.html.

[85] United States Census Bureau, 'Quick Facts: Winslow City, Arizona; United States', www.census.gov/quickfacts/table/POP010210/0483930,00.

[86] ibid.

[87] Credibly Accused List (n 71).

considering appointing Hageman to work in the newly created diocese, and told him that Hageman had been 'guilty of playing with boys'.[88] Yet Espelage assigned him to Holbrook, Humbolt, Kingman and Winslow, Arizona, where he worked until he retired in 1975.[89]

Joseph M Baca's *Constant Reminder: A Memoir of Priest Abuse and Recovery* is a self-published, unedited memoir of life in Winslow that Hardin-Burrola described as an 'unvarnished story stand[ing] as a frank testament to the hellish abuse one child endured and then managed to survive'.[90] Baca describes encounters with Hageman and Monsignor James Lindenmeyer, who was vicar general under Bishop Espelage in the 1960s.[91] Baca and his adult brother Leonard told Lindenmeyer that Hageman was abusing him,[92] which only resulted in more abuse for Baca. As he recounted, Hageman 'cursed me with hell and damnation', and raped him again.[93] When, as a teenager, Baca was convicted of a stealing a car for a joyride and sentenced to probation, Lindenmeyer was the Navajo County probation officer assigned to his case:

> Lindenmeyer confined me to a small cell and started his interrogation. He demanded to know how many people were aware of Father Clement Hageman's pedophile activities. I told him the truth – my mother, father, brother and family doctor … [He] threatened to incarcerate me for a long time if I told anybody else. Before he left, [Lindenmeyer], who called himself a man of God, directed me to pray for forgiveness.[94]

Baca may have been unaware, but Lindenmeyer was known to be a close friend of Hageman.[95] Hageman has been named by at least 16 victims in Winslow,[96] as well as victims in Holbrook[97] and Thoreau New Mexico.[98]

Plaintiffs' lawyers told me that they were aware of lawyers who, during Pelotte's time as bishop, represented a number of victims who brought claims against the

[88] 'Rev. Clement A. Hageman of the Corpus Christi Diocese: His File from the Diocese of Gallup' Bishop Accountability.org, www.bishop-accountability.org/docs/corpus_christi/hageman; see also Dan Frosch, 'Accusations of Abuse by Priest Dating to Early 1940s' *The New York Times* (10 July 2011), www.nytimes.com/2011/07/11/us/11priest.html.

[89] ibid.

[90] Elizabeth Hardin-Burrola, 'Local Clergy-abuse Survivor Writes Memoir' *Gallup Independent* (8 November 2011).

[91] Joseph M Baca, *Constant Reminder: A Memoir of Priest Abuse and Recovery* (CreateSpace Independent Publishing Platform, 2013) 45.

[92] ibid, 45–46.

[93] ibid, 47.

[94] ibid, 48.

[95] 'Rev. Clement Hageman: 1927–1975', Bishop Accountability.org (Letter to Madre de Dios Parish, 15 July 1975), www.bishop-accountability.org/docs/corpus_christi/hageman/Hageman_Rev_Clement_A.pdf.

[96] 'Database of Publicly Accused Priests in the United States', Bishop Accountability.org, bishop-accountability.org/priestdb/PriestDBbylastName-H.html.

[97] *Moya v Roman Catholic Church of the Diocese of Gallup, et al*, CV-2010-00713 (Superior Court Arizona, Coconino County, 12 August 2010).

[98] Olivier Uyttebrouck, 'Gallup Diocese Bankruptcy Raises Question of How Many More Victims There Are' *The Albuquerque Journal* (14 December 2013).

diocese 'settling cases for cheap'.[99] Baca is one of these victims. Baca's description of the process reveals that the money he would receive in compensation was, to him, less important than the apologies he received from diocesan representatives including Bishop Pelotte. 'Although my lawyer emphasized that some sort of financial award is expected, I delegated all activity and concern in that regard to him.'[100] The plaintiffs' lawyers I spoke with were more cynical. They told me that these lawyers had a pattern: rather than file a formal complaint, they would call the diocese, secure a payment – 'usually enough for the Survivor to buy a truck' – the parties would sign a non-disclosure agreement, and no records would be made public.[101] The lawyers I spoke with believed they would have, at a minimum, secured more compensation.

In 2005, Bishop Pelotte publicly apologised to survivors at a Mass he gave in St Joseph's Church in Winslow. Hardin-Burrola's article describing the Mass and reactions to it was positive. She quoted an attendee referring to the bishop's homily as 'the best thing in the world'.[102] She also wrote about how that man and the bishop later met in person, along with three others. The bishop apologised to them personally and promised to investigate a list of priests the group gave him.[103] As Hardin-Burrola explained to me, her opinion of Pelotte changed over time. She later contrasted Pelotte's warmth in dealing directly with people and the diocese's cold treatment of people under his leadership – including a lack of action to remove priests accused of abuse.

In July 2007, Bishop Pelotte was seriously injured under somewhat mysterious circumstances, and never recovered.[104] On 5 February 2009, Bishop James S Wall was appointed.[105] A number of interview participants told me that as a priest in the diocese of Phoenix, Bishop Wall had been close with Bishop Thomas J Olmsted of the Diocese of Phoenix, who administered the diocese from Bishop Pelotte's injury until Bishop Wall's appointment.[106] Bishop Olmsted is regarded as a conservative bishop.[107] He once made news when he excommunicated a nun who authorised an abortion at a Catholic hospital in order to save the life of the mother.[108] Interviews with diocesan officials confirmed that Bishop Wall is a conservative Catholic whose

[99] Interview with anonymous plaintiffs' lawyer in 2015.

[100] Baca (n 92) 112.

[101] Interviews with anonymous plaintiffs' lawyers in 2015; see also Uyttebrouck (n 99).

[102] Elizabeth Hardin-Burrola, 'Bishop Apologizes for Abuse: Pelotte Speaks to Winslow Parishioners' *Gallup Independent* (20 September 2005).

[103] Elizabeth Hardin-Burrola, 'Bishop Talks with Victims of Abuse: Outreach to Native Victims is Discussed', *Gallup Independent* (9 May 2005).

[104] Elizabeth Hardin-Burrola, 'What Caused Pelotte's Injury? Catholic Bishop Insists He Wasn't "Beat Up"' *Gallup Independent* (30 July 2007).

[105] Diocese of Gallup, 'About Our Bishop', dioceseofgallup.org/about/our-bishop.

[106] Elizabeth Hardin-Burrola, 'Pope Steps in, Phoenix Bishop Appointed as Temporary Head of Gallup Diocese' *Gallup Independent* (4 January 2008).

[107] Michael Clancy, 'Olmsted Bringing Changes to Diocese, Liberals Concerned, Conservatives Cheer' *The Arizona Republic* (3 May 2004).

[108] Bill Tammeus, 'Thomas J. Olmsted: Portrait of a '"Policy-Driven" Bishop' *National Catholic Reporter* (3 June 2010), www.ncronline.org/news/people/thomas-j-olmsted-portrait-policy-driven-bishop.

views are more in line with those of Pope Benedict XVI than Pope Francis.[109] Bishop Pelotte was understood to be more of a moderate.[110] Chapter five on canon law will explain more about the theological implications of political positioning within the Church, but Wall's conservative views align him with positions strongly in favour of preserving patriarchal traditions like all-male leadership and celibacy for priests, and sceptical of the reforms called for by the Second Vatican Council, Vatican II.

Around the same time as the disruption in leadership in Gallup precipitated by Bishop Pelotte's injury, lawsuits alleging abuse by priests and religious began to be filed against the diocese. In November of 2007, one suit was filed in a Navajo Nation District Court alleging that Charles 'Chuck' Cichanowicz, a Franciscan priest who had served at Catholic parishes in St Michaels Arizona and Shiprock New Mexico had abused a child on the reservation. By May 2009, two more lawsuits were filed in Navajo District Court.[111] These were litigated and ultimately settled for undisclosed amounts. Later, more lawsuits were filed in state courts, and some of these led to significant settlements. Ultimately, settlements and anticipated further liability related to litigation in Arizona superior courts, New Mexico district courts and Navajo tribal courts led the diocese to file for bankruptcy protection in 2013.

Interviews with influential members of the Gallup Catholic community in 2015 showed a continued reluctance to engage with the problem of abuse generally, including with the role or responsibility borne by the diocese. Every person affiliated with the diocese that I spoke with sought to convince me that most abuse was history, that most happened in the 1960s and 1970s, that most leaders in the diocese did not know the abuse was taking place at the time, that most priests in the diocese were unaware that anyone, much less a priest, would abuse children. I got the sense that these officials were of the belief that the diocese should not be legally liable for the behaviour of individual priests. People told me that the Credibly Accused List was complete, and that there were no people currently abusing children in the diocese.[112] Since that time, several names have been added to it.[113]

Interviews with victims and local journalists suggested that many, perhaps even most, victims of abuse in the diocese have not come forward, and implied that many of them believed there might be abusers even among the contemporaneously active priests and religious in the diocese. One Survivor said those who had not come forward were concerned about their families – they had children and didn't want to explain to them what had happened; or they were concerned that their families would not believe or support them.[114]

[109] Interviews with anonymous officials in 2015; see also 'Do Good and Avoid Evil' Bishop James Wall (blog, 3–4 November 2014), dioceseofgallup.org/bishopwallblog/117.
[110] Interviews with anonymous officials in 2015.
[111] Elizabeth Hardin-Burrola, 'Third Priest Sex Abuse Lawsuit Filed' *Gallup Independent* (13 May 2009).
[112] Interviews with anonymous officials in 2015.
[113] Credibly Accused List (n 71).
[114] Interviews with anonymous Survivor advocates in 2015.

IV. Comparing the Dioceses

Child sexual abuse is widely underreported.[115] 'It is estimated that between 55% and 70% of victims [of child sexual abuse] do not tell anyone that they have been abused before adulthood.'[116] Sociodemographic characteristics, socio-economic status, exposure to stress and adversity, and other experiences that contribute to harsh and inconsistent parenting are risk factors for abuse and also 'make it more difficult for children to talk about the abusive experience'.[117] Underreporting is even more prevalent in marginalised communities, whether from limited access to legal services, limited time or resources to access help, shame or fear of social stigma.[118] Victims' advocates with whom I spoke told me that they were aware of many victims, especially those from marginalised communities, who had not come forward with their stories because of shame and fear of not being believed.[119]

The reasons victims may not seek justice through legal systems are multiple and complex. Lawyers and Church officials told me how bringing claims against the Church is especially complicated for those whose families and communities benefit from the Church's financial, legal and political support.[120] One plaintiff's lawyer explained how systematic criminalisation of alcoholism and drug use in marginalised communities (as opposed to medicalisation) meant many, if not most, of his clients have criminal records, making recoveries through legal systems far less likely, because a criminal conviction makes a litigant less credible in evidentiary law, blunting the impact of testimony by those who have previously been convicted of a crime.[121]

Major studies of historical institutional child abuse have consistently found high rates of abuse in institutions serving Indigenous people, and those with other kinds of disfavoured statuses.[122] The Catholic Report shows that 75 per cent of the claims of child sexual abuse against a Catholic entity in Australia arose in schools, orphanages and residential facilities: places which housed Indigenous or disabled children taken from their parents, or children sent to these facilities from Great Britain – some orphans and others taken from their families.[123] Of the 28 institutions with 20 or more claims against them, 17 housed poor, disabled, orphaned or

[115] See eg Patrick Parkinson, 'Child Sexual Abuse and the Churches: A Story of Moral Failure?' (2014) 26 *Current Issues in Criminal Justice* 119.

[116] AM Reitsema and H Grietens, 'Is Anybody Listening? The Literature on the Dialogical Process of Child Sexual Abuse Disclosure Reviewed' (2016) 17 *Trauma, Violence & Abuse* 330, 330.

[117] ibid, 332.

[118] See eg Paul D Steele, 'Child Sexual Abuse among Socially Marginalized Groups: Cultural and Governmental Influences Perpetuating Maltreatment in American Indian Country' (2009) 1 *Forum on Public Policy*.

[119] Interview with anonymous plaintiffs' lawyer in 2015.

[120] ibid.

[121] ibid.

[122] See eg Kathleen Daly, *Redressing Institutional Abuse of Children* (Palgrave Macmillan Limited, 2014).

[123] Case Study 50 (n 38).

Indigenous children.[124] Of the 10 institutions with the most claims against them, all but one housed poor, disabled, orphaned or Indigenous children.[125] 40 per cent of the total number of St John of God Brothers, who operated schools for boys with learning difficulties between 1950 and 2010, were alleged perpetrators.[126] 22 per cent of the Christian Brothers, a religious order that once operated numerous schools, residential institutions for poor, orphaned and Indigenous children in Australia,[127] were alleged perpetrators. Between those years, the comparable figure for the Church as a whole was seven per cent.[128]

Similar patterns are apparent across the US, even as the kind of comprehensive data produced by the Royal Commission is lacking.[129] In interviews across Australia and the US, plaintiffs' lawyers, community members, advocates and journalists told me that after complaints were made about abusive priests in wealthier areas, they were likely to be assigned to work in communities where the populations predominately consisted of members of disfavoured social groups, including Indigenous people, Black people, immigrants, people living in poverty or in rural areas, people living with disabilities, as well as people inhabiting other disfavoured identities.[130] As one lawyer told me, the Archdiocese of Los Angeles sending abusive priests to marginalised communities in Arizona or New Mexico, 'was not an accident, not a coincidence'.[131]

The diocese of Great Falls-Billings in Montana filed for bankruptcy in March 2017, citing debt arising out of claims of child sexual abuse. Although Montana is nearly 90 per cent white, and less than seven per cent Native American,[132] of the cases brought against the diocese, 'a majority of those who have come forward with names and locations were allegedly abused on the remote Indian reservations', and the remainder mostly from an orphanage or very rural areas of the diocese.[133] The Jesuits in the Northwest, which operated missions and boarding schools in Washington, Oregon and Alaska, settled the claims of over 500 people, almost all of them Indigenous, who had been abused at missions

[124] ibid, table 50, 71.

[125] ibid.

[126] Stephanie Anderson, 'Royal Commission into Sexual Abuse: Who are the Brothers of St John of God?' ABC News (6 February 2017), www.abc.net.au/news/2017-02-06/who-are-the-brothers-of-st-john-of-god/8245306.

[127] Christian Brothers Oceania Province, 'Our History', Edmund Rice (2019), www.edmundrice.org/our-history.html; Case Study 50 (n 38).

[128] Case Study 50 (n 38) 16.

[129] See eg Holscher (n 70) 231.

[130] Interviews with anonymous participants in 2015.

[131] Interview with anonymous plaintiffs' lawyer in 2015; see also Stephanie Innes, 'Tucson a "dumping ground" for abusive priests' *The Arizona Daily Star* (24 February, 2013, updated 20 November 2017), tucson.com/news/local/tucson-a-dumping-ground-for-abusive-priests/article_99076313-f4df-5602-8a11-f50efd923736.html.

[132] United States Census Bureau, 'Quick Facts: Montana', www.census.gov/quickfacts/fact/table/MT/PST045216.

[133] Seaborn Larson, 'Montana Reservations Reportedly "Dumping Grounds" for Predatory Priests' *Great Falls Tribune* (16 August 2017), www.greatfallstribune.com/story/news/2017/08/16/montanas-reservations-were-dumping-grounds-predatory-priests-suit-alleges/504576001.

and schools across the Pacific Northwest and Alaska.[134] The Diocese of Fairbanks, in its bankruptcy case, identified that most of the victims of child sexual abuse in that diocese were, 'native Athabaskan, Yup'ik Eskimo, or Inupiat Eskimo'.[135] In a single Indigenous village in Alaska, 80 per cent of the children were found to have been sexually abused by Catholic officials.[136]

Victims in Ballarat were likely from the most vulnerable families in the area, and many have disclosed significant personal struggles, but their visibility as worldwide leaders in the Survivor movement is a result of their having, collectively, the wherewithal to organise themselves as advocates and bring attention to the harms that were allowed to be perpetrated against them. They brought the world's attention to those who had protected abusers at their expense. As adults they found power they did not have as children. This has proven more difficult for victims from Gallup. Kathleen Holscher described Gallup as a 'dumping ground' for 'clerical refuse' because the 'racial, economic, and political structures that sustain settler colonialism' place little value on the lives and welfare of Indigenous and Hispanic children.[137]

Victims in Gallup are likely to have grown up in poverty, to have limited access to legal, medical and mental health services. Catholic communities in the diocese of Gallup tend to be highly religious and embrace traditional ideas of gender, childhood and sexuality – conditions that literature suggests are correlated with high rates of abuse and low rates of disclosure.[138] As will be discussed in chapter five, bringing claims in Gallup is especially difficult because people tend to live in remote locations, have little access to legal services and the legal process is full of difficulties. Although stories from places like Ballarat have dominated public perceptions of Church responsibility for abuse, we cannot assume that all victims will have the same capacity to navigate legal systems, and we should consider how well those legal systems facilitate participation by those who have little capacity to advocate for themselves.

Table 3.1 below compares some of the data on populations and numbers of clerics accused of abuse, the number of claims, and data on money paid on account of abuse claims in Ballarat and Gallup. Ballarat has a smaller overall population and half the landmass, while Gallup has nearly twice the number of parishes. Ballarat has significantly more schools, programmes, social welfare and pastoral services

[134] 'Oregon Jesuits to Pay $166 Million to Abuse Victims' *National Catholic Reporter* (15 April 2011) 3.

[135] 'Third Amended and Restated Disclosure Statement in Support of Debtor's and the Official Committee of Unsecured Creditors' Third Amended and Restated Joint Plan of Reorganization for Catholic Bishop of Northern Alaska Dated December 16, 2009' *Catholic Bishop of Northern Alaska*, No 08-00110-DMD (Bankr CD Alaska).

[136] 'Frontline: The Silence' PBS (19 April 2011), www.pbs.org/video/frontline-the-silence-1.

[137] Holscher (n 70) 233.

[138] See eg Mary E Becker, 'The Abuse Excuse and Patriarchal Narratives' (1998) 92 *Northwestern University Law Review* 1459; Aileen Moreton-Robinson, 'Imagining the Good Indigenous Citizen: Race War and the Pathology of Patriarchal White Sovereignty' (2009) 15 *Cultural Studies Review* 61; Katherine Beckett, 'Culture and the Politics of Signification: The Case of Child Sexual Abuse' (1996) 43 *Social Problems* 57.

than does Gallup. The Royal Commission reported that 21 of Ballarat's diocesan personnel were accused of abuse during the time of its study, while the Diocese of Gallup acknowledges 61.

A consistent refrain I heard from Survivors brave enough to become advocates was that they represent the tip of the iceberg – that far more people have been victims than are able to speak publicly about their experiences. The purpose of comparing Ballarat with Gallup is to highlight why we should listen to those Survivors. The challenge, for a responsive system of law, is to ensure that justice is accessible to everyone, especially for the majority for whom it has historically been inaccessible. People who face multiple kinds of disadvantage or vulnerability can be expected to face additional difficulties in bringing their claims forward. A responsive system would actively gather information to learn about the kinds of barriers different constituencies face, and work to remove or lower those barriers to ensure equitable access to justice.

Table 3.1 Comparing the Dioceses of Ballarat and Gallup

	Ballarat[139]	**Gallup**[140]
Total population in diocese area	407,400	490,000
Total land mass	58,000 km^2 22,000 mi^2	143,660 km^2 55,468 mi^2
Population of largest city in diocese	~116,000 (Ballarat)	~20,500 (Gallup)
Number of parishes	29	56
Catholic schools	63	13
Number of priests, religious, or other diocesan personnel listed by the Royal Commission or Diocese of Gallup as accused of abuse	21	61

[139] Catholic Diocese of Ballarat, 'Our Diocese', www.ballarat.catholic.org.au/our-diocese/dsp-default.cfm?loadref=103; Australian Bureau of Statistics, *Ballarat* (12 July 2019), www.abs.gov.au/methodologies/data-region-methodology/2011-24#data-downloads.

[140] Diocese of Gallup, 'About Us', dioceseofgallup.org/about.

4

Canon Law

I. Canon Law and its Critics

Canonist Sister Moya Hanlen described Divine law to the Royal Commission as 'the law as it comes from God, which we will find in the scriptures and in documents like the Ten Commandments'.[1] Canon law, by contrast, is drafted and interpreted by humans and given force by human effort.[2] Canon law's approach to clerical sexual abuse is discussed by canonists, those in the Survivor advocacy movement, reporters, lawyers, scholars of secular law, judges, commissioners and politicians. Some of these authors are insiders, canonists with degrees in canon law, bishops or other officials whose work is guided by canon law. Among these there are two main groups: conservative Catholics and the Catholic left. Outsiders who write about canon law and clerical sexual abuse tend to be in the Survivor movement or are advocates for victims. These include lawyers or academics whose expertise is in a different area of law or a different discipline altogether.

Discussions of the Church's application of canon law to the problem of clerical child sexual abuse, whether by insiders or outsiders, tend to engage with one or more of the following issues:

(1) the extent to which canon law encourages, prevents or discourages bishops and other Church leaders from reporting knowledge or suspicions of abuse to civil law authorities, or has done so in the past;[3]
(2) the prohibition of child sexual abuse and prescribed punishments available under canon law, whether or not they have been imposed on abusive priests, and why this is the case;[4]

[1] Royal Commission into Institutional Responses to Child Sexual Abuse, Transcript (9 February 2017, Day C245) C25038 [18-25], testimony of Moya Hanlen, www.childabuseroyalcommission.gov.au/case-studies/case-study-50-institutional-review-catholic-church-authorities.

[2] ibid.

[3] See eg Patrick Parkinson, 'Child Sexual Abuse and the Churches: A Story of Moral Failure?' (2014) 26 *Current Issues in Criminal Justice* 119; Doyle, Sipe and Wall, *Sex, Priests, and Secret Codes: The Catholic Church's 2,000-Year Paper Trail of Sexual Abuse* (Volt Press, 2006).

[4] Charles G Renati, 'Prescription and Derogation from Prescription in Sexual Abuse of Minor Cases' (2007) 67 *The Jurist: Studies in Church Law and Ministry* 503; John P Beal, 'Doing What One Can: Canon Law and Clerical Sexual Misconduct' (1992) 52 *The Jurist* 642; Thomas J Green, 'Clerical Sexual Abuse of Minors: Some Canonical Reflections' (2003) 63 *The Jurist* 366.

(3) the legal and political environments in which canon law operates and whether they privilege the Church, its reputation, or the interests of the clerical caste above those of victims and the faithful;[5]
(4) the question of whether canon law is capable of meeting the justice interests of victims;[6] or
(5) the governance structures established by canon law and how these structures impact rates and/or likelihood of an abuser being caught, reported to authorities and/or punished.[7]

Disapproving discussions of canon law in this context include those of the United Nations Committee on the Rights of the Child (CRC). In its report and observations pursuant to a periodic review of the Holy See's compliance with the Charter on the Rights of the Child, the committee wrote of its concerns about the use of canon law.[8] In its view, state authorities should have primary competency for crimes against children. It was particularly critical of canon law in that it 'contain[s] no provision for the protection, support, rehabilitation and compensation of child victims'.[9] Law professor Patrick Parkinson was similarly critical, writing that 'it is no part of canonical thinking that child sexual abuse is a crime that ought routinely to be reported to the police and dealt with by the criminal courts'.[10] The purpose of this chapter is not to add to this criticism, but rather to dig in to the ways that canon law shows how a legal system's purpose and theory influence its construction of the issues it is tasked with resolving – how changes in doctrine alone can fail to make the changes that reformers seek.

The chapter is organised into sections that reflect the different aspects of law set out in chapter two. In section II on purpose I will explain some of the history of canon law and its contemporary concern with internal affairs, most notably the priesthood. Section III on theory will discuss how the role of the priesthood and relationships between actors within the Church has shaped the way Church leaders understand the problem of child sexual abuse by clerics. Section IV on doctrine will discuss what discourse on interpretation of a papal instruction about secrecy reveals about how insiders construct the problem of clerical child sexual abuse. Section V on procedure will explain how a system of rights established in

[5] Royal Commission into Institutional Responses to Child Sexual Abuse (n 1) C25031 [41-7], testimony of Thomas Doyle; see also Dublin Archdiocese: Commission of Investigation, *Report into the Catholic Archdiocese of Dublin* (Report, 2009) ch 4 ('Murphy Report'); Kieran Tapsell, *Potiphar's Wife: The Vatican's Secret and Child Sexual Abuse* (ATF Press, 2014) 207.

[6] Elizabeth M Delaney, 'Canonical Implications of the Response of the Catholic Church in Australia to Child Sexual Abuse' (PhD Thesis, University of Ottawa, 2004) ch 3.

[7] Green (n 4); Renati (n 4); Abby Ohlheiser, 'The Vatican Defrocked 848 Priests for Child Abuse in the Past 10 Years' *The Atlantic* (6 May 2014), theatlantic.com/international/archive/2014/05/the-vatican-defrocked-848-priests-for-child-abuse-in-the-past-10-years/361821; Thomas P Doyle, 'Clericalism: Enabler of Clergy Sexual Abuse' (2006) 54 *Pastoral Psychology* 189.

[8] United Nations Committee on the Rights of the Child, *Concluding Observations on the Second Periodic Report of the Holy See*, CRC/C/VAT/CO/2 (31 January 2014).

[9] ibid.

[10] Parkinson (n 3) 129.

canon law contributes to a dual law regime where members of the priesthood are privileged over others. Section VI on logistics will discuss how criticism of canon law is deflected, highlighting the priority of administrative convenience in constructing the 'official perspective' for canon law. Finally, the chapter will conclude with a discussion of whether the characteristics discussed in sections II–VI render canon law fundamentally repressive.

II. Purpose: Canon Law and the Nature of Priesthood

As discussed in chapter two, a legal system's purpose is the role it plays in the broader social order, the kinds of problems it seeks to solve. Today, canon law's role within the large and complicated organisation broadly referred to as the Catholic Church can be aptly compared to the bye-laws of a multinational corporation or a national constitution. It establishes the roles, rights and responsibilities of various stakeholders. It sets out how and by whom decisions will be made. It defines the types of issues that various decision-making and adjudicatory processes can handle, and the powers of various stakeholders to enforce or interpret the meaning of canonical text or tradition. However, canon law's purpose has changed a great deal over the millennia of its existence. This history sheds light on how the priesthood became central to canon law's contemporary purpose.

Harold Berman's *Law and Revolution* explained how the Gregorian Revolution (1075–1122) changed the Church's relationship with other political powers, as the Church became an independent political agent with the Vatican as a seat of power (mostly) independent of royal authority.[11] In much of Western Europe, before the Gregorian Revolution, ecclesiastical courts handled many types of legal disputes, including ordinary contract disputes and trials of both laypersons and clerics accused of crime. The Gregorian Revolution produced the first collection of canon law, the *Decretum Gratiani*, which reconciled the law of the Church of Rome from councils and synods dating to the earliest days of Christianity. With this, 'The clergy became the first translocal, transtribal, transfeudal, transnational class in Europe to achieve political and legal unity.'[12]

The centralisation of power in the Vatican ultimately enabled the rise of the modern state in Europe and precipitated the first collections and systematisations of what became law in secular states. Between the eleventh and nineteenth centuries, relationships between the Church and states were dynamic, responding to and shaped by social and political movements as well as global forces.[13] As time went on, states' authority grew in relation to that of the Church – with secular

[11] Harold J Berman, *Law and Revolution: The Formation of the Western Legal Tradition* (Harvard University Press, 1983).

[12] ibid, 108.

[13] Charles Donahue Jr, 'A Crisis of Law? Reflections on the Church and the Law over the Centuries' (2005) 65 *The Jurist* 1.

states asserting jurisdiction over trials and punishments for accused criminals, even as the Church continued to claim parallel jurisdiction in other areas of law – notably the right to discipline priests and religious.[14]

Canon law confronted a legitimacy crisis after the excesses of the Spanish Inquisition in the fifteenth and sixteenth centuries, and entered a stage of decline, eventually being relegated almost exclusively to Church governance and adjudications related to marriage. State legal systems became the primary location for the resolution of most legal matters, including prosecutions of priests accused of crimes.[15] By 1885, Pope Leo XIII wrote that 'the state and the Church should be understood as two independent and sovereign societies concerned with different matters: the spiritual and the worldly'.[16]

In 1904, Pope Pius X initiated a process of reform and codification of canon law.[17] In 1917, Pope Benedict XV promulgated the resulting '1917 Code' (also known as the 'Pio-Benedictine Code'), which brought together and organised existing doctrine and canon law. The 1917 Code was compiled from the accumulated law of the Church spanning more than 1,500 years, some of which had been seen as outdated even before codification. It was not long before reform was again determined to be necessary. The revision and modernisation of canon law was one of the goals when, in 1959, Pope John XXIII called for a Second Vatican Council ('Vatican II') with the overall aim of modernising the Church. Vatican II, 'the most important event in the history of modern Catholicism after the Council of Trent',[18] convened in 1962 and officially concluded in 1965.[19] During that time, Pope Paul VI, who became pope in 1963, commissioned a revision and update to canon law which ultimately took two decades to complete (the '1983 Code').[20]

Since Vatican II, internal discourse about Church governance has been centred on the role of the priesthood and the relationship between priests and laity. Different factions within the Church use this discourse as a frame for their discussion of the crisis of sexual abuse, agreeing that issues central to Church governance should also be understood as central to the Church's response to clerical child sexual abuse, even as they endorse different approaches to both governance and the scandal. The priesthood and the theology surrounding it was a central issue of Vatican II and remains

[14] See eg R Genestal, 'Les Origines du Privilege Clerical' (1908) 32 *Nouvelle Revue Historique de Droit Francais et Etranger* 161.

[15] See eg Robert I Burns (ed), *Las Siete Partidas*, vol 1, tr Samuel Parsons Scott (University of Pennsylvania Press, 2000) Alfonso X, Partida I, Title VI, L-LXII; *Benefit of the Clergy Act 1575* (UK) 18 Elizabeth I c 7.

[16] Rodger Austin, 'Canon Law', Submission prepared by the Truth Justice and Healing Council, *Royal Commission into Institutional Responses to Child Sexual Abuse*, (28 November 2016) [3] quoting Leo XIII, *On the Christian Constitution of States* [*Immortale Dei*] (Encyclical Letter, 1 November 1885) 35.

[17] ibid, 8 (citing Albert Gauthier, *Roman Law and its Contribution to the Development of Canon Law* (St Paul University, 1996) 3–15).

[18] Massimo Faggioli, *A Council for the Global Church: Receiving Vatican II in History* (Augsburg Fortress Publishers, 2015) 1–10.

[19] ibid, 9, citing Pope John XXIII (Address, 25 January 1959).

[20] Dublin Archdiocese: Commission of Investigation, *Report into the Catholic Archdiocese of Dublin* (Report, 2009) ch 4.

one of the most significant points of theological disagreement within the Church. This discourse is often framed through contested concepts of 'collegiality' and 'clericalism', each of which feature in discourse about the priesthood, clerical child sexual abuse, and the governance and future of the Church. Only priests can be bishops, and bishops have essentially monarchical power in their dioceses, just as the Pope does over certain aspects of the Church organisation. Thus, the priests' role is important not only because of its symbolic and ritual importance, but because priests have a unique capacity to hold positions of authority. This role is of critical importance to people of faith while also the subject of intense disagreement and concern.[21]

Mary McAleese argues that this contestation in the twenty-first century takes place largely through discussions about the meaning of the term collegiality, and the relationship between collegiality and the Vatican II reform effort.[22] McAleese was the president of Ireland during the 2000s, during which time the Irish Government convened several inquiries into child sexual abuse in institutional settings (the vast majority of which were Church institutions). She left office in 2011 and began a PhD in canon law, explaining her interest by referring to reports that 'in not one single incidence of sexual abuse had canon law been able to do anything on the victim's side, nothing useful or helpful'.[23] Her book, *Quo Vadis? Collegiality in the Code of Canon Law*, explains how definitions of collegiality reflect the worldviews and theological perspectives of different factions within the Church.[24] She explains that there are two primary definitions of the term: collegiality as a relatively broad democratic approach (where priests and laity together are responsible for Church governance) and a narrower definition that describes a healthy relationship between bishops as leaders in the Church.

The contest between these two different visions of the Church and the appropriate relationship between the laity and ordained priests is at the heart of post-Vatican II relationships and politics in the Church.[25] Popes John Paul II and Benedict XVI were both conservatives who resisted the changes of Vatican II, while Pope Francis was a moderate who wanted to see the whole Church embrace these changes, albeit at a slower pace than many to his left would prefer.[26] Pope Leo XIV is also understood to be a moderate, and in his first formal audience, 'told the cardinals who elected him that he was fully committed' to Vatican II's reforms.[27]

[21] See eg Brendan Daly, 'Priestly Celibacy: The Obligations of Continence and Celibacy for Priests' (2009) 4 *Compass* 20, 25 (discussing Paul VI, *Sacerdotalis caelibatus* (Encyclical, 24 June,1967) 14–15).

[22] Mary McAleese, *Quo Vadis? Collegiality in the Code of Canon Law* (Columba Press, 2012).

[23] Mary McAleese, 'Politics are About Getting Through the Things You Need to Get Through' *Boston College News* (2013), www.bc.edu/content/bc-web/bcnews/news-archive-2011-to-2015/chronicle/2013/topstories/q-a--mary-mcaleese.html#.

[24] McAleese (n 22) 12.

[25] ibid, ch 4.

[26] See, eg Royal Commission into Institutional Responses to Child Sexual Abuse, Transcript (21 February 2017, Day C252) C25779, testimony of Bishop Vincent Long, www.childabuseroyalcommission.gov.au/case-studies/case-study-50-institutional-review-catholic-church-authorities.

[27] Nicole Winfield, 'Pope Leo XIV pledges to pursue the reforms of Pope Francis' *National Catholic Reporter* (10 May, 2025), www.ncronline.org/vatican/pope-leo-xiv-pledges-pursue-reforms-pope-francis.

Sociologist Bill McSweeney, writing in the aftermath of Vatican II, explained that the Church had 'take[n] dramatic steps towards a more democratic "Protestant" conception of the priesthood', but that the change was limited to theology, and not the everyday lived experience of the faithful.[28] McSweeney described the priesthood as a 'power system in which the three components of religion – ritual, myth and discipline – are interrelated'.[29] He described how priests were, despite the Vatican II theological change, generally still understood as ontologically different from other people, quoting: 'The mediatorial priest, standing between God and man, personally endowed with the supernatural power of offering sacrifice, and capable of using that power on behalf of any he wished to benefit.'[30] Canonist Brendan Daly's 2009 discussion of priests' ontological identification with Christ, in which he cited a General Audience of Pope John Paul II, suggests that the conception of a mediatorial priest remains prominent.:

> A Priest acts 'in the person of Christ the Head.' By virtue of his ordination, a priest is sacramentally configured and ontologically identified with Christ. The priest is not simply another Christ, like every baptised Christian. Rather a priest represents Christ precisely in his leadership role as head of the body the Church. Just as Jesus does not marry and is totally committed to His mission, the Church requires that those to be ordained as priests have discerned a vocation to celibacy, before they are ordained and act in His name. Their celibacy expresses their complete and total identification with Christ and their commitment to continuing His mission.[31]

Discussion of the Church's response to clerical child sexual abuse from the Catholic left often points to how the social and theological positions of the priesthood contribute to the issue, labelling problematic positioning as 'clericalism'.[32] 'Clericalism', as defined by canonist and Dominican priest Thomas P Doyle, is:

> The radical misunderstanding of the place of clerics (deacons, priests, bishops) in the Catholic Church and in secular society. This pejorative 'ism' is grounded in the erroneous belief that clerics constitute an elite group and, because of their powers as sacramental ministers, they are superior to the laity.[33]

Archbishop of Brisbane, Mark Coleridge, testifying before the Royal Commission, identified clericalism as a destructive perversion of the power granted priests in Catholic teaching, describing clericalism as 'power used destructively'.[34] Doyle and psychiatrist Marianne Benkert linked clericalism with a concept they call 'religious

[28] Bill McSweeny, 'The Priesthood in Sociological Theory' (1974) 21 *Social Compass* 5, 8.

[29] ibid, 17.

[30] ibid, 17 (quoting AH Couratin, 'Liturgy' in Jean Daniélou, AH Couratin and John Kent (eds), *Historical Theology* (Penguin, 1969) 225).

[31] Daly 9 (n 21) 30, citing '*in persona Christi capitis*', LG 10.

[32] See eg Amanda M Pike, 'Discovering Records Beneath the Robes: Canonical Protection and Civil Resurrection of the Boston Archdiocese Secret Archives' (2010) 19 *Journal of Information Ethics* 86.

[33] Doyle (n 7) 190.

[34] Royal Commission into Institutional Responses to Child Sexual Abuse, Transcript (23 February 2017, Day C254) C26038 [17-20], testimony of Archbishop Mark Coleridge, www.childabuseroyalcommission.gov.au/case-studies/case-study-50-institutional-review-catholic-church-authorities.

duress', which they define as 'the internal pressure experienced by a person as a result of fear-based beliefs'.[35] They link religious duress with 'the notion of *reverential fear*, a well-established category in Catholic Canon Law. This is a fear that is induced not from an unjust force from without but from the reverence one has for an authority figure'.[36] They identify religious duress as a frequent symptom of having been sexually abused by a Catholic priest because of the reverential fear that the faithful, and especially children, have for the person of a Catholic priest.[37]

Doyle notes: 'The self-identification of clerics with the favour of the Almighty led to a variety of social and legal privileges, expected deference, vast power, and an aura of fear':[38]

> Although there is ample historical evidence to clearly demonstrate that priests, bishops, cardinals, and popes remain human in spite of the sacred ceremonies that elevate them to their lofty positions, there persists a belief that erring clerics are somehow above the law and beyond most forms of accountability. In spite of ample evidence of individual and institutionalized corruption, the deep roots of clericalism have enabled the ecclesiastical world to slip into deep denial when faced with the possibility that clerics really are no different and no better than mere mortals.[39]

The importance of these issues to the Church was highlighted by the Vatican's 2022 theological symposium, 'Toward a Fundamental Theology of the Priesthood', which was described as being concerned with 'the clerical sexual abuse crisis and the problem of clericalism, which Pope Francis has often condemned, and many have faulted as a contributing factor to clerical abuses of power, authority, and sexuality'.[40]

Canon law has, over time, come to focus on Church governance. Only priests are able to serve as bishops, a position with monarchical authority in dioceses, and the priesthood is a central concern of canon law. While the Catholic right and left may disagree about how the priesthood should be understood and the appropriate relationship between priest and laity, they agree that these questions are of central importance to Church governance and canon law.

III. Theory of Canon Law on Child Sexual Abuse

Chapter two defined theory in my framework as aspects of law that set out the normative ideals that the system embraces. Despite the separate social and spiritual

[35] Marianne Benkert and Thomas Doyle, 'Clericalism, Religious Duress and Its Psychological Impact on Victims of Clergy Sexual Abuse' (2009) 58 *Pastoral Psychology* 223.
[36] ibid, 224.
[37] ibid, 236.
[38] Doyle (n 7) 194.
[39] ibid, 195.
[40] Elise Ann Allen, 'Vatican event on priesthood to explore topic of celibacy' Crux (13 April 2021), cruxnow.com/vatican/2021/04/vatican-event-on-priesthood-to-explore-topic-of-celibacy.

realms for Church and secular state law, and canon law's purpose of internal Church governance, sexuality, sexual behaviour and marriage have continued to be spaces where both states and the Church claim the right to enforce their own law. Importantly, canon law has never relinquished its claim to special jurisdiction over the sexual conduct of priests and religious. Texts from across centuries evidence deep concern with regulating the sexual behaviour of clerics, extending beyond the well-known prohibition on priests or religious marrying.[41] Canon law continues to impose strict rules on priests and religious that prohibit behaviour that is entirely legal under secular law in contemporary Australia or the US.

There is a long history of canon law prohibiting sexual contact between priests and (at least) some classes of children. However, the theory behind the law – the normative idea that these laws were written to protect – is different from that of contemporary laws against child sexual abuse. Cultural and social understandings of childhood, sexuality and gender have shifted dramatically over time, and some conduct now condemned as child sexual abuse was not always understood as criminal or deviant – or the theory of the wrong was centred on the gender of parties involved rather than age or consent. Texts reflect the issues of the day in which they are written, and later generations do not always interpret those texts within the historical context. For example, some critics of the Church's response to abuse have pointed to the *Book of Gomorrah*, by St Peter Damian, as evidence that the Church has long been aware of child sexual abuse within the priesthood.[42] However, when canonists refer to this text it is usually in the context of the Church's teaching on homosexuality – it has been understood as primarily about sexual activity between men.[43]

One of the earliest Christian condemnations of adults engaging in sexual behaviour with children dates to 153 CE. The *Didache* lists 'corrupting boys' alongside committing murder, adultery, fornication, stealing, practising magic, using enchantments, abortion, infanticide, speaking evil of others, bearing false witness, being double-minded or double-tongued, and coveting.[44] Behaviour now described as sexual abuse of children continued to be outlawed by various Church documents, including the *Canons of the Council of Elvira*;[45] the *Penitentials*, attributed to, among others, the Venerable Bede;[46] as well as the *Book of Gomorrah*,

[41] Doyle, Sipe and Wall (n 3) 4.

[42] See eg Kieran Tapsell, *Potiphar's Wife: The Vatican's Secret and Child Sexual Abuse* (ATF Press, 2014).

[43] Conrad Leyser, 'Cities of the Plain: The Rhetoric of Sodomy in Peter Damian's "Book of Gomorrah"' (1995) 86 *Romanic Review* 191, 199 (citing John Boswell, *Christianity, Social Tolerance, and Homosexuality: Gay People in Western Europe from the Beginning of the Christian Era to the Fourteenth Century* (University of Chicago Press, 1980)).

[44] See eg Aaron Milavec, *The Didache: Text, Translation, Analysis, and Commentary* (Liturgical Press, 2003).

[45] See eg Karl Joseph von Hefele, Joseph Hergenröther and Alois Knöpfler, *Histoire Des Conciles d'Après Les Documents Originaux* (Ulan Press, 2012); Samuel Laeuchli, *Power and Sexuality: The Emergency of Canon Law at the Synod of Elvira* (Temple University Press, 1972) 134.

[46] Allen J Frantzen, 'The Penitentials Attributed to Bede' (1983) 58 *Speculum* 573.

dated 1051.[47] This complicated history impacts how texts condemning behaviour we would today call child sexual abuse should be understood. When considered in context, much of this early teaching suggests that child sexual abuse has been prohibited because it is a breach of a vow of celibacy or because it involves sexual activity between two people of the same gender.

Translations of this early canon law suggest that the theory behind the law relates to sexual deviancy, not with protection of children as a vulnerable class of person. Presbyterian theologian Samuel Laeuchli translated the Council of Elvira's work as 'men who sexually abuse boys shall not be given communion even at the end'.[48] Being denied communion was among the harshest penalties these canons meted out – understood in the context of belief that not receiving communion may damn a soul for eternity. This denial carried a great deal of weight. The English translations of these works, including Laeuchli's, do not include explanations of why only boys, and not all children, were to be protected. Scholars of religion, history and theology debate how to understand teachings about gender and sexuality in religious texts and leading interpretations of texts have changed over time.[49] Doyle, Sipe and Wall write of centuries of Christian taboos and sex-negative teachings, tracing how 'Church authorities from the second century onward have repeatedly disparaged sex in all its human forms as dirty, sinful, unclean, and even unnatural.'[50] They explain how, over time, this disparagement came to focus on condemnations and prosecution of sexual contact between adult men, or between men and boys.[51]

Catholic historian C Colt Anderson explains that laws which have historically prohibited child sexual abuse have been primarily concerned with clerical celibacy.[52] He explains how the term 'sexual abuse' has been and continues to be used to describe: clerics cohabitating with adult women;[53] 'coerced and consensual sexual acts between clergy and adult men'; and 'seducing or compelling boys and adolescents to submit to sodomy'.[54] He noted that these relationships involved significant discrepancies of power that led to serious abuses, especially as unmarried cohabitants had few rights in eleventh-century Europe, but that Church authorities were concerned with ritual purity and inheritance rights, not the well-being of vulnerable people.[55] Rashid and Barron describe:

> A case study from the late 16th century in Italy, where a priest was tried by a Church court for sodomising a 13-year-old boy, defrocked, and then handed over to secular

[47] Peter Damian, *Book of Gomorrah*, tr Pierre J Payer (Wilfrid Laurier University Press, 1982).

[48] Laeuchli (n 45) 134.

[49] See eg. Rosemary Radford Ruether, *Women and Redemption: A Theological History* (Fortress Press, 1998); Kilian McDonnell 'Feminist Mariologies: Heteronomy/ Subordination and the Scandal of Christology' (2005) 66(3) *Theological Studies* 527; Julie Faith Parker 'Blaming Eve Alone: Translation, Omission, and Implications of עמה in Genesis 3:6' (2013) 132 *Journal of Biblical Literature* 729.

[50] Doyle, Sipe and Wall (n 3) 5.

[51] ibid, 360–67.

[52] C Colt Anderson, 'When Magisterium Becomes Imperium: Peter Damian on the Accountability of Bishops for Scandal' (2004) 65 *Theological Studies* 741.

[53] ibid, 748.

[54] ibid, 749.

[55] ibid, 748.

> authorities who carried out the death sentence through decapitation. The death penalties awarded for indulgence into sexual crimes in Italian and Spanish territories could therefore be categorized to fall in line with the 1568 'Apostolic Constitution' by Pope Pius V calling for the death penalty for pedophilia, child sexual abuse, and sodomy.[56]

However, Richard Sherr, after reviewing the contemporaneous records of the case used by Rashid and Barron for their gruesome description, finds that 'it becomes clear that the major object of concern was the possible involvement of the canon, Luigi Fontino, in homosexual acts'.[57] The concern was not for the victim, who himself was whipped after 'confessing' to sexual activity with the priest, after which he 'was banned from the Papal States'.[58] Furthermore, far from the standard response to reports of deviant sexual behaviour, the harsh punishments meted out in this case were a confluence of timing, politics and relationships with powerful people. Sherr describes another case of students at a seminary in a nearby city complaining 'in explicit terms' about their rector. While the rector was sent to prison, 'special measures were taken to see that he had some degree of comfort'.[59]

The 1917 Code listed adultery, debauchery, sodomy, bestiality and the sexual abuse of persons under 16 years of age as canonical 'delicts' or crimes, which could be committed by clerics and laity alike.[60] Canonist John P Beal, commenting on the delicts in the 1917 Code, explained that the code reflected longstanding prejudices connecting disfavoured sexual behaviour with heresy.[61] Beal cautions contemporary readers not to assume that the 1917 Code was designed to protect children from predation, even when its provisions could be read as criminalising child sexual abuse, explaining that scholars discussing the reasons for reserving the delict to the Congregation for the Doctrine of the Faith (CDF) suggest the following as motivating factors: (1) 'protecting the integrity of the sacraments by ensuring the worthiness of their ministers'; (2) the crimes are subject to the jurisdiction of the both the state and the Church, so 'it would be a source of scandal if a perpetrator were hauled before a secular court for such a scandalous offense while still a cleric'; and (3) 'the longstanding conviction … that those who engaged in deviant sexual behaviour were heretics or at least suspect of heresy'.[62]

The 1983 Code made significant changes to canon law in this area, providing that priests and religious laity could be prosecuted under canon law for sexual abuse, but did not address, within the text, any change to the theory behind the

[56] Faisal Rashid and Ian Barron, 'The Roman Catholic Church: A Centuries Old History of Awareness of Clerical Child Sexual Abuse (from the First to the 19th Century' (2018) 27 *Journal of Child Sexual Abuse* 778, 785.

[57] Richard Sherr, 'A Canon, A Choirboy, and Homosexuality in Late Sixteenth-Century Italy' (1991) 21 *Journal of Homosexuality* 1, 4.

[58] ibid, 9.

[59] ibid, 10.

[60] Codex Iuris Canonici 1917 (the '1917 Code').

[61] John P Beal, 'The 1962 Instruction *Crimen sollicitationis*: Caught Red-Handed or Handed a Red Herring?' (2007) 41 *Studia Canonica* 199, 202.

[62] ibid, 206–07.

law. Canon 1395 §2, previously located in a section entitled 'Delicts Against Special Obligations,' provided:

> A cleric who in another way has committed an offense against the sixth commandment of the Decalogue, if the delict was committed by force or threats or publicly or with a minor below the age of sixteen years, is to be punished with just penalties, not excluding dismissal from the clerical state if the case so warrants.[63]

Delaney explains how the theory of the harm being an offence against the Church rather than the victim was enshrined in Canon law by the placement of canon 1395 under the title 'Offences against Special Obligations'.[64] It communicated that the Church's concern was with the harm suffered by the office of the priesthood rather than children.[65] Delicts against special obligations, defined by canons 1392 to 1396, are crimes that, by definition, only priests, deacons and religious laity who owe special duties under canon law can commit. Other delicts against special obligation include priests and religious marrying, living with a partner, or engaging in certain kinds of business or trade.

Delaney argued that including laity in this delict would 'be more consistent with the present reality in which the number of lay persons who are engaged in the Church's pastoral care, including health and education, far outweighs the number of clerics or religious'.[66] As long as the delict was based in the special obligations of priests and religious, however, the theory of wrong was harm to the Church, not harm to victims.[67] Like traditional criminal law theory, which sees offending as crimes against the state, canon law framed child sexual abuse as a crime against the Church. This centring of clerics and other consecrated persons may arise from an organisational culture centring on the Church's concerns – or as the Catholic left might identify it, from clericalism. The Church and the accused perpetrator are the key parties, and the victim's role is limited to that of witness. A canon law that theorises clerical child sexual abuse as an abuse of the office, rather than abuse of a child, meets Nonet and Seznick's definition of repressive: an overriding concern with conservation of power and control.

In 2021, Pope Francis issued an Apostolic Constitution *Pascite Gregem Dei*, reforming Book VI of the 1983 Code to include moving the previous prohibition to Title VI, 'Offences Against Human Life, Dignity, and Liberty'.[68] Effective on 8 December 2021, this reform includes the laity, and prohibits the grooming or abuse of minors or vulnerable persons.[69] Effective 11 February, 2022, Pope Francis

[63] 1983 Code. Note that the Decalogue, or Ten Commandments, in the Catholic tradition, lists 'You shall not commit adultery' as the sixth Commandment. *Catechism of the Catholic Church*, Section 3:2.

[64] Delaney (n 6) 268.

[65] ibid, 268.

[66] ibid, 268.

[67] ibid, ch 3.

[68] Francis, *Pascite Gregem Dei* (Apostolic Constitution, 23 May 2021).

[69] John Lavenburg, 'U.S. Church Leaders Welcome Changes to Canon Law on Sexual Abuse' Crux (3 June 2021).

issued Apostolic Letter *Fidem servare*, which changed the internal structure of the CDF, separating the functions related to doctrine and marriage from the functions related to disciplinary issues, such as sexual abuse.[70] Time will tell whether these changes result in less abuse or more abusers being caught and stopped, but the intent seems to be to change the theory of wrong from one of wrong against the Church to wrong against a vulnerable person, which is a real step toward more holistic justice.

IV. Canonical Doctrine

In 1922, Pope Pius XI issued a *pagella*, an instruction, which provided that proceedings of canonical trials convened to address claims against clerics be subject to a 'pontifical secret', preventing disclosure of the subject matter of the trial.[71] This instruction, *Crimen sollicitationis*, was reissued with minor changes in 1962. John Paul II's 2001 *motu proprio*, *Sacramentorum Sanctitatis Tutela*, which referenced *Crimen sollicitationis*, made certain changes to canon law applicable to the whole world that had previously only applied to the US. These changes clarified the CDF's jurisdiction over cases of clerical child sexual abuse, extended the prescription period to allow suits to begin within 10 years after the victim turns 18, and clarified the kinds of acts that constitute child sexual abuse under canon law.[72] The United States Conference of Catholic Bishops (USCCB) and the Australian Catholic Bishops Conference (ACBC) were leaders among regional bishops' conferences in pushing for the substance of these changes, and the USCCB's Dallas Charter and the ACBC's Towards Healing were seen within the Church as model responses.[73] As discussed above in section III, the canonical provisions remained in the section on 'delicts against special obligations', with a theory of wrong having been done to the Church, rather than the victim, for another two decades.

Plaintiffs' lawyers and media saw *Crimen sollicitationis* as evidence of cover-up. Similarly critical of the instruction, legal counsel assisting the Australian Royal Commission described *Crimen sollicitationis* as binding bishops, administrators, victims and witnesses to keep secret the information discovered in an inquiry into allegations about a priest abusing children. This statement was made before questioning Bishop Geoffrey Robinson, an Australian bishop and canonist who was deeply involved in the creation of Towards Healing. Counsel assisting noted that canon law requires secrecy of those involved with canonical trials and observed that Bishop Robinson and the ACBC had acted contrary to those laws when developing the Towards Healing programme.[74] The Irish Murphy Report identified the

[70] Francis, *Fidem Servare* (Apostolic Letter issued 'Motu Proprio', 11 February 2022).
[71] Beal (n 61) 201–02.
[72] ibid, 201–02.
[73] Interview with anon Vatican official in 2015.
[74] Royal Commission into Institutional Responses to Child Sexual Abuse, Transcript (24 August 2015, Day 156) C16007-8.

same documents and instructions, and what it called a 'culture of secrecy' that bishops felt bound by, even though they knew secrecy was incompatible with protecting children.[75]

For canonists, interpretation of the instruction appears more complicated than it might seem from this discourse.[76] Beal notes that the instruction for secrecy has been misunderstood because, although by its terms it applies to all involved with a proceeding, accusers and witnesses are not to be censured if they breach those terms. Delaney, similarly, explains the instruction requires secrecy to 'prevent harm to the accused or to witnesses'. She links the instruction to deep concern in canon law for a person's right to a reputation: 'Because a person's good name is held to be sacred, anyone who violates someone's reputation is bound, both morally and in law, to make amends and may be subject to punishment.'[77] Beal also explains that the instruction reserves two delicts to the jurisdiction of the CDF: 'The delict committed by a confessor who solicited a penitent for a sexual sin and the delict referred to somewhat euphemistically as 'the worst crime (*crimen pessimum*)':[78]

> Although the 1962 Instruction included the sexual abuse of minors by clerics among the species of the *crimen pessimum*, the sexual abuse of minors was not its primary meaning. The primary meaning of the term *crimen pessimum* in the 1962 Instruction and its principal focus was what the canonists who wrote it would call homosexual sodomy. To the extent that the drafters of the 1962 Instruction (as well as its 1922 predecessor) might have been prompted to append a section on the *crimen pessimum* by concern about contemporary problems of which the Holy Office had become aware, the tenor of the document suggests that these problems would have been priests engaged in homosexual activities with other adults.[79]

Secular legal authorities, in multiple jurisdictions, including Ireland, the United States, Canada, the Dominican Republic, Australia and many other places, have repeatedly concluded that a culture of secrecy protected the institution at the expense of children. Canonist literature, as just explained, focuses on the intent of the secrecy provision and how the language should be interpreted. They critique the use of the secrecy doctrine because it led Church leaders to believe that they should not report abuse to civil authorities, and because it had the effect of protecting the Church at the expense of victims and communities. Beal's suggestion that bishops might have conflated child sexual abuse and consensual sexual conduct that breaches Church doctrine provides unfortunate support for my conclusions in section III above, ie that the theory of the prohibition against child sexual abuse was, until 2021, about controlling the sexual behaviour of priests, rather than the protection of children.

[75] Murphy Report (n 5) ch 4.
[76] ibid.
[77] Delaney (n 6) 152.
[78] ibid, 152.
[79] Beal (n 61) 225.

V. Procedure

In 2014, the Vatican announced that 848 priests had been defrocked using canonical processes, apparently in order to demonstrate its seriousness in addressing the problem of sexual abuse.[80] In 2017, the Royal Commission's Final Report identified 1,880 alleged perpetrators in Catholic organisations in Australia, of whom 572 were priests.[81] The worldwide number of abusive priests would likely be orders of magnitude higher than the number for Australia, suggesting canon law was being applied in only a fraction of cases of abusive priests.

This chapter has suggested some reasons for canonical processes being little used. As canon law has over time ceded ground to civil law in the realm of interpersonal harms, the legal theory underlying the canonical prohibition of child sexual abuse has been, for most of the Church's history, more concerned with the relationship between priest and Church than the harm imposed on children. The doctrinal history and placement of the law in the Code of Canon Law conflated consensual adult behaviour that violated commitments to celibacy or norms against sexual conduct between persons of the same gender with criminal sexual abuse of children. The increase in canonical proceedings and laicisation can be traced to relatively recent changes to the 1983 Code that have, among other things: (1) broadened and clarified the scope of prohibited behaviour to include sexual abuse of people under the age of 18 and vulnerable people of any age; (2) made compulsory reporting to civil authorities where required by civil law; (3) extended the number of years in the prescription periods (that is, the time in which a case must be brought);[82] and (4) clarified the procedures that must be followed in cases in which clerical child sexual abuse is alleged.[83]

The proceedings, even with the recent changes, are quite different from the proceedings typical of common law countries. First, resembling the civil law of continental Europe, canon law is based on a code which does not include the concept of binding precedent. Canonical interpretation is derived from opinions and recommendations from papal, conciliar and curial documents. Different kinds of documents from those three sources have different degrees of authority, and their legal significance is a matter of debate.[84] Second, legal procedure is not set out in a single body of text or made clear through a collected statement of rules as in both civil and common law jurisdictions.[85] Third, the bishop of a diocese is

[80] 'Vatican Defrocked 848 Priests for Abuse', SBS News (7 May 2014), www.sbs.com.au/news/vatican-defrocked-848-priests-for-abuse.

[81] Royal Commission into Institutional Responses to Child Sexual Abuse, *Final Report 'Preface and Executive Summary'* (December 2017).

[82] See eg Renati (n 4).

[83] Thomas J Green, 'CDF Circular Letter on Episcopal Conference Guidelines for Cases of Clerical Sexual Abuse of Minors: Some Initial Observations' (2013) 73 *The Jurist* 151.

[84] See eg Green (n 4).

[85] James T O'Reilly and Margaret SP Chalmers, *The Clergy Sex Abuse Crisis and the Legal Responses* (Oxford University Press, 2014) 314.

deeply involved in the process in many ways: he is required to act as mentor to all priests in the diocese, while also being the person who has final say on whether a report progresses to a trial, the representative of the interests of the diocese as a whole, and the person who often has final say over what will happen to a priest once a determination has been made. The opacity and inaccessibility of procedural law and conflation between the judicial and political function of the bishop are classic characteristics of repressive law regimes.

Conservative canonist Thomas Green argued in 2003 that bishops should have been using canon law processes throughout the twentieth century, but that a post-Vatican II 'antinomianism' (ie belief in faith to the exclusion of law as basis for salvation) led bishops to rely on psychology, rather than canon law, to deal with abusive priests.[86] Other canonists point to the ways in which the structure of the law itself made cases difficult. John Beal, writing in 1992, highlighted procedural and logistical difficulties even as he opined that more canonical prosecutions would have helped 'dispel the widespread perception that church authorities are more prone to cover-up than to address complaints of clerical misconduct, demonstrate that they have exercised a reasonable standard of care, and honour the obligations assumed toward clerics at ordination'.[87]

Bishops have unique power over and responsibility to the priests in their dioceses.[88] 'It is the bishop's responsibility, through his delegates, to initiate, pursue and bring closure to the process for dealing with an allegation against a priest of his diocese.'[89] This responsibility to hold the priest to account is paired with a personal responsibility for the priest and his well-being:

> [T]he bishop has special responsibilities toward clerics, those genuinely accused (and in a special way, those falsely accused) of sexual misconduct. The bishop is not in an adversarial role toward his clergy, but must 'attend' to his presbyters with special concern. He is to 'protect their rights and see to it that they correctly fulfil the obligations proper to their state,' and is to make sure that they have the spiritual, intellectual, and material means they need (c. 384). There may be a need to distance the diocese as much as possible from the sexual misconduct of a cleric, but the bishop cannot distance himself from the person of the cleric himself without violating a grave responsibility of his office.[90]

Green explains that canon law provides for a special relationship between diocesan bishops and the priests they supervise, which has significant impacts on prosecutions or other disciplinary measures related to clerical wrongdoing.[91] Bishops are required to 'cultivate a special personal and professional relationship with [their]

[86] Green (n 4).
[87] Beal (n 4).
[88] O'Reilly and Chalmers (n 85) 254.
[89] John J Coughlin, 'The Clergy Sexual Abuse Crisis and the Spirit of Canon Law' (2003) 44 *Boston College Law Review* 977, 978.
[90] James H Provost, 'Some Canonical Considerations Relative to Clerical Sexual Misconduct' (1992) 52 *Jurist* 615, 616.
[91] Green (n 4) 368.

priests'.[92] Canon law discourages formal trials in favour of informal resolutions of conflict; and before initiating a formal process, a bishop must ask himself whether 'scandal [can] be repaired, justice restored, and the offender reformed without a penal process'.[93]

The bishop, notwithstanding the personal and professional relationship he is required to cultivate with all the priests in his diocese, is uniquely powerful in the canonical process, giving rise to the kind of conflicts of interest that legal systems embracing the rule of law ideal have long criticised. Once a complaint is received by a diocese, the bishop must ensure that there is a preliminary investigation that 'is meant to give the [bishop] a sense of probability that a delict [crime] did or did not occur'.[94] After the preliminary investigation, bishops are required to undertake a more formal investigation. While the law considers that bishops may themselves conduct investigations, it is seen as better practice to appoint someone else.[95] Once the investigation is over, the results are given to the bishop, who is to consult with his diocesan review board to make a determination as to whether the allegations 'at least seem true'.[96] If the bishop makes a positive determination, then he must write his canonical opinions as to how the case should be handled, and he then submits the case to the CDF, which will either take the matter under consideration itself or direct the bishop on what should be done next. From this point, there is a range of procedural options, depending on the decisions made by the CDF and the bishop. Throughout, a bishop's central role and authority is a constant.

The bishop is separately obligated to protect the people of his diocese and the priests in his diocese, and to further the interests of justice. If a priest begins harming the people in the diocese, the bishop's position becomes incredibly difficult. The separation of powers between judicial and political roles is one of the most important characteristics of autonomous law and a key feature of the rule of law. Canon law requires that bishops play both judicial and political roles. The critique of bishops' failure to use canon law comes from those who feel canon law could have helped the Church avoid the scandal of child sexual abuse, yet it is canon law that sets up bishops to fail by requiring that they play contradictory roles in these proceedings. That contradiction ultimately benefits the interests of the most powerful, those who are authority figures in the hierarchical and monarchical political orders in which repressive law systems typically exist.

Legal historians Charles J Reid Jr and John Witte Jr explain that modern constitutional law the world over owes much to theories of representation, consent and rights first developed by canonists.[97] Protecting defendants' rights is meant to increase the difficulty of conviction and can restrain over-zealous prosecutors.

[92] ibid, 368.
[93] ibid, 369.
[94] O'Reilly and Chalmers (n 85) 320 (citations omitted).
[95] ibid, 326.
[96] ibid, 335.
[97] Charles J Reid Jr and John Witte Jr, 'In the Steps of Gratian: Writing the History of Canon Law in the 1990s' (1999) 48 *Emory Law Journal* 647.

But not all rights schemes are the same or protect the same interests. In canon law, a defendant's rights include:

(1) a right to a good reputation (c 220);
(2) a right to privacy (c 220);
(3) a right to choose one's state of life (c 219);
(4) a right to defend one's right (c 221);
(5) a right not to incriminate oneself (c 1728);
(6) a right not to be punished with canonical penalties except according to law (c 221); and for those who are priests,
(7) a right to a relationship with the diocesan bishop, to the support of brother priests, to tangible support, and (in some cases) to ones' ministry.[98]

Some of these, like a right to not incriminate oneself, and a right not to be punished except according to law, are similar to the rights that defendants have today in criminal trials Australia and the US. Others, like a priest's right to a relationship with a bishop, are not.

Delaney argues that the robust rights regime afforded priests reflects the seriousness with which canon law and the Church understand what it means to be a priest.[99] In the common law tradition, few ideals are as cherished as protection of liberty, which is a fundamental interest that justifies weighing the scales in favour of the defendant. Atticus Finch from the novel *To Kill a Mockingbird*[100] and John Adams are heroes of the American criminal defence bar in part because they represented unpopular defendants. There is a strong normative current in this perspective: liberty is so important that we cannot allow anyone to be deprived of it unless it is proven beyond a reasonable doubt that they are guilty of a crime meriting such punishment. Delaney shows how being a priest is, within the framework of canon law, so important that being stripped of that office requires the kind of prophylactic rights that the loss of freedom has to criminal defence lawyers.[101]

It is not the protection of rights in general but the specific rights granted to priests that grant additional privilege to the already powerful. The right to a good reputation, a right to ministry, a right to a relationship with the bishop, and particular ways of interpreting apparently familiar rights (such as a right to privacy, a right to choose one's state in life, and a right to defend one's rights) are likely to benefit priests accused of abuse, binding people to secrecy, hampering investigations and creating unavoidable conflicts for the bishop in executing his required duties. It provides rights to priests that others do not have, a classic characteristic of a dual-law system – two classes of people, with one privileged over the other.

[98] Delaney (n 6).
[99] ibid.
[100] Harper Lee, *To Kill a Mockingbird* (Lippincott, 1960).
[101] Delaney (n 6).

VI. Logistics

Logistics, as set out in chapter two, consists of a wide range of practical factors that might impact a party's experience with a legal case or legal system. As discussed in section V, there have been relatively few canonical proceedings related to clerical child sexual abuse, and these are prosecutions of individual abusers, not the leaders or organisation that enabled the abuse. The Church has made significant changes to canon law in recent years, following decades of Survivor advocacy and programmes like Towards Healing and the Dallas Charter.

In 2011, the CDF issued guidance requiring bishops and leaders to comply with civil laws concerning mandatory reporting of child sexual abuse.[102] The Royal Commission questioned Church leaders about whether bishops and others interpreted this guidance to require reporting only in those jurisdictions where it was required under secular law. The Commission received only relatively vague and inconclusive answers from the canonists they questioned.[103] The line of questioning by the Royal Commission may have been influenced by reporting about a training manual for new bishops, made available to the public in 2015. This manual triggered criticism because it included a passage arguing that deciding to report sexual abuse to secular authorities should be a decision left to individual bishops.[104] The manual also provided that whether a bishop voluntarily reports or is required to report depends on the law of the country in which the bishop works.[105] The author of the controversial chapter of the manual, who was known for homophobic comments, was later removed from ministry after allegations of abuse were raised against him.[106]

Some argue that bishops might not always be serving the best interests of victims in reporting allegations of abuse to civil authorities. John J Allen Jr, editor of *Crux*, a leading source for news and observations about the Vatican, had a pithy explanation: 'It's the universality, stupid.'[107] Allen notes that 'two-thirds of the Church's 1.2 billion people live outside the West', and that the Church operates in

[102] William Levada and Luis F Ladaria, 'Circular Letter to Assist Episcopal Conferences in Developing Guidelines for Dealing with Cases of Sexual Abuses of Minors Perpetrated by Clerics' The Holy See (Circular, 3 May 2011).

[103] See generally, Royal Commission into Institutional Responses to Child Sexual Abuse, Transcript (30 June 2015, Day C143).

[104] Christine Kearney, 'Vatican advises bishops it's "not necessarily" their duty to always report abuse to authorities' *ABC News* (12 February 2016), www.abc.net.au/news/2016-02-12/anger-over-vatican-bishop-training/7164636.

[105] Tony Anatrella, 'La relation pastorale, l'équilibre de la vie affective des prêtres et problems de déviances' in *Testimoni Del Risorto: Atti del Corso Annuale di Formazione Per I Nuovo Vescovi* (Libreria Editrice Vaticana, 2015).

[106] 'Priest Who Denied a Duty to Report Abuse Faces Abuse Charges' Crux (20 February 2017), cruxnow.com/global-church/2017/02/priest-denied-duty-report-abuse-faces-abuse-charges; Robert Shine, 'Prominent Anti-Gay Priest Removed from Ministry for Sexually Abusing Patients' New Ways Ministry (6 August 2018), www.newwaysministry.org/2018/08/06/prominent-anti-gay-priest-removed-from-ministry-for-sexually-abusing-patients.

[107] John J Allen Jr, 'Politics of Baby Bishops' School: "It's the Universality, Stupid!" The Crux (7 October 2016), cruxnow.com/analysis/2016/10/politics-baby-bishops-school-universality-stupid.

societies with significant legal and cultural differences.[108] Similarly, writing about the CRC report criticising the Vatican's position, Grant Gallicho, another journalist covering the Vatican, wrote that the committee failed to take context into consideration that rules developed to respond to a problem in one place might have unintended consequences in other places.[109] An official with the Pontifical Commission remarked in an interview that there may be good reasons to keep information from local authorities in countries where a bishop has reason not to trust local authorities to take a claim of sexual abuse seriously, or where local taboos and laws against people of the same gender engaging in sexual behaviour give rise to concerns for the safety of victims.[110]

This argument rests on flawed premises. Drawing on stereotypes of non-Western or developing countries as backwards, it ignores that policy can be adopted which accommodates for circumstances where reporting sexual abuse might create risks for victims. Officials could be advised that they should report abuse to civil officials except when reporting would cause or risk further harm to victims. Special processes and guidance for how to respond to priests or religious abusing children in jurisdictions where officials do not trust local authorities to adequately protect victims can be designed. The Church, with its moral authority, could use canon law to demonstrate to the world how to protect children from predation, and arguments that defend the Church's failure to do so by allusion to stereotypes about less developed countries are unpersuasive at best. The weakness of these arguments suggests an adoption of what Nonet and Selznick described as an 'official perspective', resolving doubts in favour of the system and prioritising administrative convenience over substantive justice or the interests of parties who have been wronged.

VII. Conclusion

The state law systems that developed alongside of and in relationship with canon law in Western Europe are the systems Nonet and Selznick identify as prototypical repressive law regimes. Foucault called the corresponding approach to monarchical government a 'self-referring circularity of sovereignty or principality' that seeks to protect at all costs the power and control of the sovereign over the subject territory or people.[111] The fundamental purpose of a repressive law regime is keeping the peace, maintaining order and buttressing the moral legitimacy of its political leaders.

Although the mission of the Church may be to spread the light of the Divine and bring hope to the world, the mission of canon law is to govern and protect the Church. As a legal system that is primarily focused on Church governance, the

[108] ibid.

[109] Grant Gallicho, 'Vatican Responds to UN Report on Sexual Abuse' Commonweal (7 February 2014), www.commonwealmagazine.org/blog/vatican-responds-un-report-sexual-abuse.

[110] Interview with anonymous Vatican official in 2015.

[111] Michel Foucault, *Power*, tr James D Faubion (Allen Lane, 2001) 210.

debate between clericalism and collegiality reveals the centrality of the priesthood to that governance. Nonet and Selznick described dual law systems as those in which people are subject to different laws based on their status. This is clearly the case for canon law, and while there are factions within the Church that denounce clericalism and push for the democratising aims of Vatican II, whether or not someone is a priest is incredibly important to their treatment in canonical proceedings. A vision of the priesthood as an ontologically different state of existence subject to a different form of law is a powerful idea that has shaped perceptions of clerical abuse and responses to it. Doyle's critique of clericalism, McAleese's examination of collegiality and Coughlin's discussion of antinomianism all centre on the role of the priesthood, including its theological and legal status and what that means for Church governance. These discussions link the scandal of clerical sexual abuse with Vatican II and the future of the Church.

The theological and canonical theories of the priesthood are deeply connected to clerical child sexual abuse, intensifying and shaping the harm inflicted on victims, defining the kind of harm cognisable through canon law, and shielding accused priests with special rights not afforded to others. The patterns of social and political subordination lay members of the Church to priests is made clear in Kathleen Holscher's description of how priests sent to the Servants of the Paraclete from places around the world ended up abusing children living in poverty in New Mexico and Arizona:

> Via Coeli offered monastic seclusion; Fitzgerald created it to be a place where priests could devote their lives to prayer, along with physical healing, to achieve their souls' sanctification. 'Returning a priest to grace, not necessarily returning him to the active ministry, was the essence of rehabilitation to Father Gerald,' one former Servant explained. 'A priest out of favor with the Church could not obtain salvation.'
>
> By the midsixties, however, the Servants' strategy – or what the order offered as the path to 'fixing broken priesthoods' – shifted in a devastating way. Relying upon new psychological therapies, the Servants began to partner with bishops to reintroduce 'guests' to ministry in nearby parishes, as part of a program of 'graduated rehabilitation.' 'The men must be prudently tried on various social levels if their rehabilitation was to be complete,' a staff psychologist for the Servants now explained. 'The dignity and integrity of the human person demanded this.' Of course, when the Servants reintroduced abusive priests to ministry, they did so at the expense of people in parishes where those men relocated. At least a half-dozen priests, and likely more, later accused of abuse within the Diocese of Gallup made their way into its churches via the Jemez Springs monastery. Within the Archdiocese of Santa Fe, which actually encompasses the Jemez region and Via Coeli itself, the number of former residents accused of abuse is higher still. 'New Mexico is in the middle of nowhere,' explained one attorney representing abuse victims. 'If you want to store nuclear waste, you do it here. If you want to set off nuclear bombs, you do it here. If you need a place to send pedophiles, well, there's always New Mexico.'[112]

[112] Kathleen Holscher, 'The Trouble of an Indian Diocese: Catholic Priests and Sexual Abuse in Colonized Places' in Tisa Joy Wenger and Sylvester A Johnson (eds), *Religion and US Empire: Critical New Histories* (New York University Press, 2022) 231, 245–46.

5

Tort Law in Victoria, Arizona, New Mexico and the Navajo Nation

I. Introduction

This chapter on tort, or the law of civil wrongs, discusses the primary means in common law systems by which private parties seek redress from those who have harmed them. Unlike canon law, tort law is at least relatively familiar to most people living in Ballarat and Gallup, and records and other information about cases proceeding in both those sites arising from cases of clerical child sexual abuse are publicly available. But whereas canon law is largely the same throughout the entire Church, there are significant differences between the law of tort as it is understood, applied and experienced, depending on where claims are brought.

The common law of tort is a judicially created doctrine with theories of liability that draw directly from its purpose of resolving disputes about accidental and intentional harms and wrongs. The common law of tort forms the basis for tort law in Victoria, Arizona and New Mexico, and influences the law in the Navajo Nation. Tort cases against the Diocese of Ballarat are subject to Commonwealth law on tort and insurance, and those brought in the civil circuit court for Ballarat are subject to the authority of the Supreme Court of Victoria, where Victorian civil procedure applies. Cases proceeding against the Diocese of Gallup have been filed in three different jurisdictions. Two of these, New Mexico and Arizona, are US states. The other is the Navajo Nation, considered a 'dependent sovereign' under US law.[1] Arizona, New Mexico and the Navajo Nation all have their own laws of tort, insurance and procedure.

The point of this chapter is not to compare tort law in the two common-law countries. This has been competently done by others.[2] Many of the relevant 'structural and systemic differences' between the two are explained in Peter Cane's discussion of the legal systems in the US, Australia and New Zealand, including the relative isolation of the US vis-à-vis Commonwealth countries.[3] Importantly

[1] *Cherokee Nation v Georgia*, 30 US 1 (1831).

[2] See eg RH Graveson, 'The Task of Comparative Law in Common Law Systems' (1959) 34 *Indiana Law Journal* 571; Frank Bates, 'Comparative Common Law: A Justification' (1981) 14 *The Comparative and International Law Journal of Southern Africa* 259.

[3] Peter Cane, 'Searching for United States Tort Law in the Antipodes' (2011) 38 *Pepperdine Law Review* 257, 274–79.

for this analysis, the US does not have a national common law of tort. Each state's common law is independent, with the highest court in the state being the final arbiter of state law. In Australia, there is one High Court, which serves as the final arbiter of tort law for the whole nation.[4]

As was discussed in chapter one, literature on law and the problem of clerical child sexual abuse tends to focus on tort cases, as tort is the primary means of seeking redress through formal state law. Many critics focus on the people whose claims are barred through operation of a procedural device and legal positions taken by Church organisations. Critics are particularly concerned with the applicability of statutes of limitation, the shifting of responsibility from a diocese to a religious order, the difficulty in compelling dioceses to disclose records kept on individual priests and religious, corporate law allowing Church organisations to evade liability, and strategies through which dioceses delay and resist claims.

A common thread of these critiques is the way in which the law does not work indiscriminately, but for the benefit of powerful interests. This chapter, building from the critiques, demonstrates how the interests of powerful stakeholders are embedded within tort as a legal system, at least in three of the four jurisdictions. Furthermore, it explains how, despite reforms intended to address critics' concerns, the embeddedness of the interests on the powerful in the system itself continues to impact its potential for substantive justice.

II. Purpose, or Theory of Tort

Sir William Blackstone, an early commenter on common law, coined the maxim 'that every right when withheld must have a remedy, and every injury its proper redress', which tort law scholars often cite as a foundational precept, at least in common law settings.[5] A major purpose of tort, according to tort law theorists, is the provision of a forum for private parties to bring claims against those whose action or failure to act (where legally required) has caused harm.[6] Unlike canon law, with its focus on governance and the Church, tort law is a form of private law – plaintiffs and defendants in tort actions are usually private parties (such as individuals, businesses, non-profit or charitable organisations), and the range of harms that are cognisable in tort is broad.[7] Tort's purpose of resolving private disputes through a formal process is one of the basic functions that legal systems have long claimed to provide. While critics might say it creates an appearance of

[4] ibid, 274–79.

[5] William Blackstone, *Commentaries on the Laws of England*, 21st edn (Sweet, Maxwell, Stevens & Norton, 1844) vol 3, 109.

[6] See eg John CP Goldberg, 'The Constitutional Status of Tort Law: Due Process and the Right to a Law for the Redress of Wrongs' (2005) 115 *Yale Law Journal* 524; Peter Cane, 'Distributive Justice and Tort Law' (2001) 4 *New Zealand Law Review* 401, 403.

[7] See eg John CP Goldberg and Benjamin C Zipursky, 'Civil Recourse Defended: A Reply to Posner, Calabresi, Rustad, Chamallas, and Robinette' (2013) 88 *Indiana Law Journal* 569, 610; Richard Posner, 'Instrumental and Noninstrumental Theories of Tort Law' (2013) 88 *Indiana Law Journal* 469, 470.

remedy to private disputes that are in practice almost always sorted informally, a more nuanced perspective might point to the law's existence as a frame for informal resolution, by serving as a backstop when informal dispute resolution breaks down, even if threats of legal action are largely empty. I have combined the discussion of purpose and theory for tort law because these aspects are so closely linked for tort; there is little daylight between the purpose of a forum to resolve private disputes and the theory of injuries requiring redress.

Philosopher RA Duff explained tort law by reference to criminal law. Criminal law, like delicts in canon law, conceives of a wrong having been committed against the sovereign – the state in the case of the criminal law and the Church in the case of delicts.[8] By contrast, Duff describes torts as being

> focused on harms: typically, harms that have occurred and can (to at least some extent) be repaired. The law enables one who suffers harm at another's hands to shift the cost of that harm onto the other person, by proving that he was legally responsible for it.[9]

Once legal responsibility and harm have been established, remedies are awarded or determined for purposes including compensation, deterrence and loss-spreading.[10]

Although in other common law jurisdictions, corrective justice is the most accepted theory of tort, in the US, the law and economics movement has focused on tort as a mechanism of cost allocation and deterrence.[11] They describe tort as a cost-shifting mechanism, for which the purpose is to deter or minimise the costs of harms.[12] Guido Calabresi wrote that it is 'axiomatic that the principal function of accident law is to reduce the sum of the costs of accidents and the costs of avoiding accidents'.[13] This movement has been dominant among tort law scholars in the US for some time, taught in law schools and built into the way many lawyers there understand the role of tort. Civil recourse theorists in the US, with a different perspective that has growing support in the twenty-first century, reject a view of tort as means of social control and public benefit for one centred on tort as a private right.[14] They argue that the law and economics focus on tort as a means of allocating costs of accidents fails to account for personal wrongs.[15] These scholars focus on tort as a relational and private concept, looking to early commenters like

[8] RA Duff, 'Repairing Harms and Answering for Wrongs' in John Oberdiek (ed), *Philosophical Foundations of the Law of Torts* (Oxford University Press, 2014) 212.

[9] ibid, 216.

[10] See eg, Pam Stewart and Anita Stuhmcke, *Australian Principles of Tort Law*, 3rd edn (The Federation Press, 2012) 6, citing *Pyrenees Shire Council v Day* (1998) 192 CLR 330 [123] (Gummow J).

[11] See eg Guido Calabresi, *The Cost of Accidents: A Legal and Economic Analysis* (Yale University Press, 1970).

[12] Posner (n 7) 470.

[13] Calabresi (n 11) 26.

[14] Michael L Rustad, 'Twenty-First-Century Tort Theories: The Internalist/Externalist Debate' (2013) 88 *Indiana Law Journal* 419.

[15] ibid.

Blackstone to argue that tort law should be seen as a 'basic category of law', that is concerned primarily with private wrongs and not a means of social control.[16]

In 2003, Peter Cane explained some of the ways that Australian tort law theory differed from the US:

> United States tort scholarship is generally much more oriented towards viewing tort law as a tool for regulating individual and, especially, corporate behaviour, than Commonwealth tort scholarship, most of which is more inclined to treat tort law as primarily concerned with allocating what Calabresi called 'secondary' accident costs.[17]

He highlights Terence Ison's book, *The Forensic Lottery* and Patrick Atiyah's *Accidents, Compensation and the Law* as Commonwealth as contrasts to Calabresi's theoretical framework for evaluating accident law.[18] Ison, Cane writes, 'offered a practical proposal for replacing tort law with a no-fault system of compensation for 'diseases and violent injuries causing disablement and death'.[19] He goes on to explain how Commonwealth countries saw a wave of reforms that led to no-fault schemes in New Zealand and more limited no-fault schemes for specific issues (like automobile accidents) in other Commonwealth jurisdictions.

Australia, despite significant interest and reform efforts, has not followed New Zealand's example. Cane explains that Australian tort reformers fall into camps which he calls 'conservatives, radicals and moderates'.[20] Some conservatives, Cane argues, are compensationists who believe that tort law has allowed for the development of a 'fine balance … between the interests of injurers and the injured, and thus oppose reform of tort law'.[21] Other conservatives Cane calls economic rationalists, to whom 'the prime function of personal injury law is risk-management', and who oppose efforts to limit the range of damages available in tort on the basis that it would expose people to 'unacceptable threats to their personal health and safety'.[22] Moderates argue that either too much is spent compensating injured people, so damages should be reduced, or that tort law does not place enough weight on injured people's responsibility to avoid harm.[23] Radicals, with whom Cane aligns himself, push for no-fault schemes of various types.[24]

It is noteworthy that dominant tort theories (purposes) in both the US and Australia focus on cost allocation. This focus draws the attention of lawyers away

[16] John CP Goldberg and Benjamin C Zipursky, 'Torts as Wrongs' (2010) 88 *Texas Law Review* 917, 918; but see Gregory C Keating, 'Is There Really No Liability Without Fault?: A Critique of Goldberg & Zipursky' (2017) 15 *Jerusalem Journal of Legal Studies* 152.

[17] Peter Cane, 'Reforming Tort Law in Australia: A Personal Perspective' (2003) 27 *Melbourne University Law Review* 649, 653.

[18] ibid (discussing Terence Ison, *The Forensic Lottery: A Critique on Tort Liability as a System of Personal Injury Compensation* (Staples Press, 1967) and Patrick Atiyah, *Accidents, Compensation and the Law* (Weidenfeld and Nicholson, 1970)).

[19] ibid, 653.

[20] ibid, 651.

[21] ibid, 651.

[22] ibid, 651.

[23] ibid, 652.

[24] ibid, 651–52.

from questions of wrongfulness and toward questions of compensability, which in turn shapes the drafting of insurance policies. As will be discussed, these frequently exempt intentional torts from coverage, which can, in some cases, leave victims of child sexual abuse without a practical recourse.

With so many different theories of tort, it becomes important to consider how people bringing claims against the dioceses of Ballarat or Gallup and their lawyers understand the purpose of the systems. Tort law scholars may be concerned with the interaction between tort law and insurance premiums in society generally, but individuals considering whether to bring claims in tort are unlikely to consider the collective impact on insurance premiums, instead focusing primarily on their own circumstances.

In an article titled 'Harry Potter and the Trouble with Tort Theory', Scott Hershovitz describes how tort theory fails to account for the cost of litigation, including procedure and collateral effects of bringing claims. Among other things, Hershovitz considers a number of potential benefits to actions brought in tort that are not considered in much of the theoretical conversation.[25] First, he argues, bringing a claim can help a plaintiff achieve knowledge about the injury that the defendant had access to but would not otherwise have released. Second, the public nature of the dispute and judge's opinions contribute to the public discussion of what is right and what 'our' values should be. Third, the process of telling one's story in public is meaningful, especially when that telling is met with credence and recognition of an imposed wrong. Fourth, victims typically want a kind of vindication – knowledge that the person or entity they see as responsible for their pain is held accountable for it. There is a sense that a victim would not get the same satisfaction from holding the 'person who could have avoided the accident more cheaply' responsible for their injury if that is not the person the victim understands to have caused the harm.[26]

One plaintiffs' lawyer I interviewed, who represented a number of plaintiffs in cases against the Diocese of Gallup, described benefits much like those Hershovitz described when he explained to me how he encourages his clients. He said that he acknowledges that the process of bringing a civil claim is difficult, but that the process can be empowering and help them recast their self-identity. He said he tells his clients that

> [this] is about standing up for yourself and saying [to the Church] 'fuck you – you're not going to do this to me'. Be empowered, stop being a victim, start being a Survivor. Show people that you can fight and that you're not weak. I tell this to my clients because they're not weak, you know? It takes an incredible amount of courage for my clients to just to come into my office that first time and tell me about how a priest put his dick in my mouth.[27]

[25] Scott Hershovitz, 'Harry Potter and the Trouble with Tort Theory' (2010) 63 *Stanford Law Review* 67.

[26] ibid.

[27] Interview with anonymous plaintiffs' lawyer in 2015.

Important as the psychological benefit to standing up for oneself may be, and as consequential as the various other benefits Hershovitz discusses are, they are not generally described as part of the purpose of tort by theorists, nor are they the focus of lectures on tort in law schools. Practitioners occupy a sort of middle ground, having been taught about tort theory as a function of cost-allocation and burden-shifting, and drawing on that understanding as they present arguments for the benefit of clients who may understand the purpose of bringing a tort claim as standing up for themselves and holding accountable those who wronged them. The process requires lawyers to reframe questions of wrong and harm as questions of compensability, and implicitly acknowledge that tort does not provide a remedy for all harms. The lawyer's rough language in describing how he engages with his clients is evidence of this – part of his job is translating the language used by experts in legal systems back and forth into language familiar to people whose lives have been punctuated by addition, abuse and oppression. Without his acting in this role, his clients would struggle to understand and engage with the system.

III. Doctrine, or Theories of Liability

Tort law doctrine is expressed largely through theories of liability. Theories of liability connect wrongs to the defendant in a given case. The theories relevant to cases against dioceses alleging clerical child sexual abuse include both direct or indirect liability. When dioceses are held directly liable for abuse perpetrated by priests or religious, the theory of liability usually resembles one of the following: (1) negligence or recklessness in retaining priests or others who the organisation was or should have been aware were likely to abuse children in positions that, by their nature, facilitated the individuals' access to children; (2) failure to supervise employees and volunteers with access to children; (3) failure to report criminal behaviour to appropriate authorities; (4) concealing knowledge of abuse; or (5) abusive or wrongful tactics in response to allegations of sexual abuse. It is through these theories that organisations can be held directly liable. Indirect liability is typically theorised as vicarious liability (in the US this is often referred to as the doctrine of *respondeat superior*), through which the acts of an agent can be imputed to the principal.[28] This is justified because the agent or employee is presumed to be acting in furtherance of the goals of the principal or employer.

As the law has changed over time, theories of liability for child sexual abuse have been extended, reinterpreted or changed by law, usually to allow for more claims against organisations to go forward. These changes to law, like extensions of statutes of limitation discussed later in this chapter, are meant to address concerns

[28] See eg, Janna Satz Nungent, 'A Higher Authority: The Viability of Third Party Tort Actions against a Religious Institution Grounded on Sexual Misconduct by a Member of the Clergy (2002) 30 *Florida State University Law Review* 957; *Doe v Archdiocese of Portland*, 717 F Supp 2d 1120 (D Oregon, 2010).

that characteristics of child sexual abuse render it difficult for victims to prove their cases. The difference between vicarious liability and direct liability in this context is whether or not there is a theory that allows for recovery when the diocese did not know of the tendencies of their agent or employee to abuse. A principal who is vicariously liable for the wrongs of its agent is liable regardless of the principal's knowledge and/or behaviour. Claims of direct liability rely on the principal having some awareness of the abuse or its likelihood, and thus require plaintiffs to demonstrate not just the fact of abuse, but also the likelihood that the bishop knew or should have known that the individual was likely to abuse children. Direct claims also include those claims that allege intentional wrongdoing or negligence in responding to claims of abuse, including covering up or destroying evidence.

Each of the four jurisdictions where tort claims have been brought against either Ballarat or Gallup has a different approach to diocesan liability for child sexual abuse, and so they are discussed separately below. For a number of reasons, most tort cases against the dioceses of Ballarat and Gallup have largely either settled or been dismissed. When verdicts are reached and appealed, courts of appeal tend to focus on procedural issues, and no published decisions turn on the applicability of theories of liability against Ballarat and Gallup. Lawyers, for reasons of confidentiality, will not discuss the reasons their clients decide to settle cases, nor the advice that they provide them. The result is that, although these theories can be determinative of result for victims, their application occurs largely invisibly.

A. Victoria

In Australia, where the conservative project of tort reform has, as Cane discussed, not been widely adopted,[29] the Royal Commission explained that there are three 'legal bases for institutional liability for abuse currently available in Australia':[30] (1) negligence, based on the breach of a duty of care owed by the institution to a child in its care; (2) vicarious liability; and (3) a breach of a 'non-delegable duty to ensure that a third party takes reasonable care to prevent harm'.[31] The question of vicarious liability and non-delegable duties in the context of child abuse in institutional settings has a complicated history.[32] The Australian High Court in *New South Wales v Lepore* found in 2003 that any duty of care that institutions owe to children does 'not extend to illegal conduct or conduct where an employee was

[29] Cane (n 17) 653.

[30] Royal Commission into Institutional Responses to Child Sexual Abuse, *Consultation Paper: Redress and Civil Litigation* (January 2015) 33.

[31] ibid, 33.

[32] Allison Silink and Pamela Stewart, 'Tort Law Reform to Improve Access to Compensation for Survivors of Institutional Child Sexual Abuse' (2016) 39 *University of New South Wales Law Journal* 553, 558; see also Laura Griffin and Gemma Briffa, 'Still Awaiting Clarity: Why Victoria's New Civil Liability Laws for Organisational Child Abuse are Less Helpful Than They Appear' (2020) 43(2) *University of New South Wales Law Journal* 452.

pursuing a "frolic of their own"'.[33] In 2023, in *Prince Alfred College Inc v ADC*, the High Court determined that:

> Whether vicarious liability arises for an act of sexual abuse of a child that took place in a school or other institution, regard may be had to any special role the employer has assigned to the employee. Features of the employment such as authority, power, trust, control and the ability to achieve intimacy should be considered. Clearly a role embodying features of this kind may point to a strong connection between the employment and the wrongful act. The employment may be seen to provide more than a mere opportunity for the act to take place; it may provide the very occasion for it.[34]

As Allison Silink and Pamela Stewart explain, Survivors face 'considerable uncertainty as to whether a claim relying on vicarious liability will be successful or not under Australian law'.[35] This uncertainty incentivises settling claims before a final determination of law can be rendered, as the risks of bringing an unsuccessful claim, as will be discussed below, are quite high. This explains some of the dearth of written decisions in Australian law specifically relevant to tort claims against the Diocese of Ballarat.

The Royal Commission sought submissions from interested parties on issues regarding civil litigation.[36] It made many of those submissions public. Those made public are from a range of stakeholders, including individuals impacted by abuse or institutional responses to it; organisations providing legal, counselling, or other services to victims and their families; professional organisations of legal, mental health and social services providers; other government commissions of inquiry; and representatives of defendant institutions – including government and religious organisations. The Anglican Church of Australia's Royal Commission Working Group, for example, proffered that civil litigation cannot be reformed into the kind of redress system needed by victims, and that pastoral care would be more appropriate.[37] Other defendant-side and plaintiff-side advocates supported changing the law with respect to vicarious liability, arguing that vicarious liability should be imposed based on an 'enterprise risk' approach. The approach, 'which has been increasingly applied by the English and Canadian Supreme Courts to issues of vicarious liability in cases of institutional child sexual abuse … treats the creation of risk as a basis for the imposition of vicarious liability in cases of abuse'.[38]

[33] *New South Wales v Lepore* (2003) 212 CLR 511.

[34] *CCIG Investments Pty Ltd v Schokman* [2023] HCA 21 at 34 (citing *Prince Alfred College Inc v ADC* (2016) 258 CLR 134 at 152–53).

[35] Silink and Stewart (n 32) 558.

[36] Royal Commission into Institutional Responses to Child Sexual Abuse, Issues Paper: Civil Litigation (January 2015).

[37] Anglican Church, Submission No 11 for Issues Paper 5 'Civil Litigation' to Royal Commission into Institutional Responses to Child Sexual Abuse (6 December 2013) [5].

[38] Knowmore, Submission No 17 for Issues Paper 5 'Civil Litigation' to Royal Commission into Institutional Responses to Child Sexual Abuse (17 March 2014) 10.

B. New Mexico

In New Mexico, 'an employer is liable for the intentional torts of his employee if the torts are committed in the course and scope of his employment'.[39] In a case brought against New Mexico and out-of-state Catholic organisations, the New Mexico Supreme Court held in 2002 that

> the liability of a principal for the tortious act of an agent is the same as the liability of an employer for the tortious act of an employee. Such liability is grounded on the maxim 'respondeat superior,' and is to be determined 'by considering, from a factual standpoint, the question whether the tortious act was done while the employee ... was acting within the scope of employment'.[40]

In order to determine what acts are within the scope of employment, the New Mexico Supreme Court held that, 'employers who endow their employees with the means and authority to use force can be held liable for their employees' misuse of those instrumentalities and authority'.[41] Thus, whatever actions are implicitly authorised by a principal's placement of an individual in a position of power can be imputed to the principal. As a priest is placed by the diocese in a position of power, the fact a diocese did not authorise abusive behaviour cannot protect it from claims the priest misused his power.

C. Arizona

The Supreme Court of Arizona in 2012 clarified the test of vicarious liability under Arizona law, holding that the test turns on an employer's control or right to control the employee.[42] In Arizona:

> An employee's tortious conduct falls outside the scope of employment when the employee engages in an independent course of action that does not further the employer's purposes and is not within the control or right of control of the employer.[43]

Sexual abuse of children is clearly not within the job description of clergy or educators and is a clear violation of Catholic teachings. Cases in Arizona have accordingly only been able to progress on theories of direct liability, including breaching fiduciary duties to children in their care, negligent supervision, endangerment and various failures of reporting.[44]

[39] *McCauley v Ray*, 80 NM 171, 180 (NM 1968).

[40] *Tercero v Roman Catholic Diocese of Norwich*, 48 P 3d 50 (NM 2002).

[41] *Narney v Daniels*, 846 P 2d 347 (NM 1992).

[42] *Engler v Gulf Interstate Engineering, Inc*, 280 P3d 599 (Arizona, 2012); see also David Potts, 'Arizona Case Note: *Engler v. Gulf Interstate Engineering, Inc.* and the Role of Control in Vicarious Liability' (2012) 54 *Arizona Law Review* 1157, 1169.

[43] *Engler* 280 P3d (n 42) 602.

[44] See eg, Associated Press, 'Catholic Diocese of Phoenix Settles Sex-Abuse Claim' *Arizona Daily Star* (27 December 2006), tucson.com/news/catholic-diocese-of-phoenix-settles-sex-abuse-claim/

Cases in Arizona, therefore, usually require a showing that the person bringing the claim was not the first person abused by an individual – although the harm suffered by the first victim may not be measurably different from the harm suffered by a later victim. The burden-shifting focus of tort thus shapes the understanding of tort law in Arizona, where tort law theory has been interpreted to find it unjust to hold an employer accountable for an employee's abuse unless the employer can be proved to have knowledge that the employee had previously abused children. Bringing claims against the Diocese of Gallup can be more difficult, then, depending on where abuse occurred. Cases against the Diocese of Gallup in New Mexico would have an easier time proving the connection between the diocese and the harm suffered than those brought in Arizona. Indeed, a plaintiffs' lawyer in New Mexico told me that the question of third-party liability was rarely an issue in their matters, that legal issues were usually about whether the statute of limitations had run with respect to claims or the availability of records and the opportunity to conduct discovery with respect to documents that would support claims of direct liability.[45]

D. Navajo Nation

Navajo theories of tort are significantly more open to victims than either Arizona or New Mexico tort law theories. In *John Doe CB v Diocese of Gallup*, for example, the Gallup diocese and Franciscan orders were claimed to be vicariously liable for sexual abuse suffered at the hands of Chuck Cichanowicz in St Michaels, Arizona and Shiprock, New Mexico.[46] Both places are in the Navajo Nation. The complaint alleged direct liability on theories of negligence, including failing to warn, negligent supervision, premises liability and intentional theories of having 'aided and encouraged' or 'ratified' abuse itself when transferring the abuser to St Michaels after reports of his abusing children in previous parishes came to their attention.[47] All of these theories of liability were accepted, and the dispute about compensability centred on procedural issues of statutes of limitation and jurisdiction, as will be discussed below.

Of tort law applied in cases against the Diocese of Gallup, then, Navajo law allows for the most theories of liability connecting the diocese with harm suffered, and have not embedded the rights of the powerful in their limitation of theories

article_d86e391d-b6d2-5cba-9cf3-04732ed03043.html; Roman Catholic Church of the Diocese of Tucson, 'Third Amended and Restated Disclosure Statement Regarding Plan of Reorganization Dated May 25, 2005', Submission in *Re: Roman Catholic Church of the Diocese of Tucson*, 4-bk-04-04721-JMM, 25 May 2005; *Doe v Roman Catholic Church of the Diocese of Gallup, et al*, Complaint, CV 2013-361 (Arizona Superior Court, Coconino County, 28 May 2013).

[45] Interview with anonymous plaintiffs' attorney in 2015.

[46] See eg *John Doe CB v Diocese of Gallup et al*, Complaint, No WR-CV-208-09 (Navajo Nation District Court, District of Window Rock, Arizona, 12 May 2009).

[47] ibid, 9.

of liability in the ways that Arizona and New Mexico have. These differences in doctrine, with Arizona concerned more about not holding employers responsible when they cannot be proved to have acted in a blameworthy way and Navajo courts more concerned with ensuring those least able to avoid harm do not suffer without redress, and New Mexico somewhere between the two, have real impact on which cases can be brought, making *where* one was abused a key factor in determining whether or not a claim is likely to be successful.

IV. Procedure

Although a purely doctrinal approach to law might dismiss procedure as not central to 'substantive' legal issues, it is nonetheless a central aspect of how tort law is practised. I focus on three particular issues relevant to claims in tort brought against the dioceses of Ballarat and Gallup: statutes of limitation; jurisdiction; and the corporate organisation of a diocese under state law. As discussed in chapter two, doctrine is the applicable substantive law or 'merits' of a matter, while procedure governs how legal proceedings should be initiated, prosecuted and administratively managed.[48] In tort, 'nonmerits factors [often] overshadow the merits', skewing both the incentives and the outcomes in tort proceedings.[49] However, the distinction between the merits and nonmerits issues is not always a bright line, despite what Paul MacMahon calls 'rough agreement on what counts as procedure and what counts as substantive'.[50] I have included corporate law in this section because, although it is a doctrinal subject, its relationship to the subject matter of the cases brought against dioceses is widely seen as legalistic or process-oriented, and bears no relation to the question of whether abuse occurred or whether the diocese is connected to the abuser such that it should be held liable for the abuser's actions.

Only a fraction of the procedure applicable in these cases is specifically relevant to child sexual abuse. Time, the weight of precedent, and a reliance on facially neutral but complex procedural law have embedded the interests of powerful actors like the Church into law in Australia and the US. Some of these embedded procedures are remnants or contemporary iterations of the long histories of contestation between law and religion in the Western legal tradition discussed in chapter four. There are a range of laws embedded in the civil litigation process that protect religious organisations – some of which are intended to protect the free exercise of religion, but others

[48] Thomas O Main, 'The Procedural Foundation of Substantive Law' (2010) 87 *Washington University Law Review* 801, 810.

[49] Jonathan T Molot, 'How US Procedure Skews Tort Law Incentives' (1997) 73 *Indiana Law Journal* 59, 61.

[50] See, eg, Paul MacMahon, 'Proceduralism, Civil Justice, and American Legal Thought' (2012) 34 *University of Pennsylvania Journal of International Law* 545, 554, citing Cass R Sunstein, 'Incompletely Theorized Agreements' (1995) 108 *Harvard Law Review* 1733, 1735–36.

provide specific privileges to religious organisations, including the Church itself. The embeddedness of institutional interests can be identified in protections for religious organisations in law, including special tax status, clerical privileges, and corporate forms that accommodate governance structures unique to religious organisations.[51]

Statutes of limitation in the context of child sexual abuse are a classic example of how autonomous legal systems can prioritise rules over substantive justice, which ends up benefiting organisations. Statutes of limitation are meant to encourage people to bring claims rapidly and prevent evidence from growing stale, but their application in the context of child sexual abuse creates perverse incentives.

In both Australia and the US, statutes of limitation have been a key target of Survivor advocates. While such laws vary by jurisdiction, many jurisdictions, including all those in which cases have been brought against the dioceses of Ballarat and Gallup, have extended their statutes of limitation for child sexual abuse or have introduced exceptions to them.[52] The Royal Commission and the Victorian Law Reform Commission recounted how concerns with the application of statutes of limitation in Australia led to advocacy for new laws changing relevant limitations periods, which were ultimately enacted.[53] Marci Hamilton, arguing that statutes of limitation for child sexual abuse should be abolished entirely, has traced changes to statutes of limitation in states across the US.[54]

The impact of statutes of limitation is very tangible. Victims from Ballarat reported taking settlements from the diocese that did not reflect the gravity of their injury because 'short limitations periods [applicable at the time] meant they either had to take the compensation offered or receive no assistance'.[55] The limitations period in Victoria has been completely abolished. There are applicable statutes of limitation in Arizona, New Mexico and the Navajo Nation, all of which have been changed or interpreted to allow some, but perhaps not all, claims of child sexual abuse that would otherwise be barred from going forward.

In Arizona, the statute of limitations is generally two years from the date of the act giving rise to the cause of action, but in 1998, the Arizona Supreme Court endorsed a 'repressed memory doctrine', allowing claims to go forward where a victim's memory of sexual abuse had been repressed, asserting this doctrine to be 'appropriate given that the intentional act of the tortfeasor cause both the damage and the repression of memory'.[56] Thus, those victims in Arizona who could demonstrate that they had repressed memories of their abuse could bring claims.

[51] See eg, *Advocate Health Care Network v Stapleton*, 581 US 468 (2017).

[52] Limitation of Actions Amendment (Child Abuse) Act 2015 (Vic), s 1.

[53] See eg, Victorian Law Reform Commission, *Sexual Offences: Final Report* (Victorian Law Reform Commission, 2004) 84.

[54] Marci A Hamilton, *Justice Denied: What America Must Do to Protect Its Children* (Cambridge University Press, 2008) 9–15.

[55] Caroline Schelle, 'Ballarat Sexual Abuse Survivor Phil Nagle Hails New Compensation Rules' *The Courier* (14 June 2019), www.thecourier.com.au/story/6218005/its-a-great-day-ballarat-abuse-survivor-hails-new-compensation-rules.

[56] *Doe v Roe*, 955 P 2d 951, 960 (Arizona, 1998) (citing *Hewczuk v Sambor*, 803 F Supp. 1063, 1065 (ED PA, 1992)).

New Mexico, like Victoria, has changed its law legislatively. In 1995, New Mexico law was changed to allow actions for childhood sexual abuse to be commenced by the later of the victim's twenty-fourth birthday, or

> three years from the date of the time that a person knew or had reason to know of the childhood sexual abuse and that the childhood sexual abuse resulted in an injury to the person, as established by competent medical or psychological testimony.[57]

In 2017, it was changed again, this time to allow actions for childhood sexual abuse to be commenced by the later of the victim's twenty-fourth birthday, or

> three years from the date that a person first disclosed the person's childhood sexual abuse to a licensed medical or mental health care provider in the context of receiving health care from the provider.[58]

The courts of the Navajo Nation, bound by the Navajo Nation Code, 'utilize *Diné bi beenahaz'áanii* (Navajo Traditional, Customary, Natural or Common Law) to guide the interpretation of Navajo Nation statutory laws and regulation'.[59] Navajo law provides that, generally, personal injury actions must be filed 'within two years from the date [a plaintiff] discovered or should have discovered the nature, cause, and identity of the person causing the injury'.[60] However, the Supreme Court of the Navajo Nation held that in the context of child sexual abuse, because Native American children, 'as a "relatively powerless minority" may be expected to have acute effects of withdrawal and loss of contact with community when exposed to such abuse', the requirement that claims be brought within two years of the time that someone with 'reasonable diligence' must have discovered the link between the abuse and the injury suffered should be that of a reasonable person 'whose judgment is "altered in some way"' as a result of childhood sexual abuse.[61] Accordingly, in the Navajo Nation, claims can go forward when victims can demonstrate that the effects of the abuse prevented them from ascertaining the link between that abuse and their injuries.

In practice, although all of these jurisdictions have technically opened up the possibility of bringing claims past previously applicable statutes of limitation, the differences between the jurisdictions have significant ramifications. In Arizona, victims whose memory of abuse was not repressed, or who cannot sufficiently prove that it was by hiring a psychologist who will credibly testify to that repressed memory, are barred from bringing claims more than two years after the events. In New Mexico, victims do not need to prove what they remembered and when, needing only to provide testimony about when they first disclosed having been abused to a medical professional. In the Navajo Nation, the statute of limitations

[57] New Mexico Statutes § 37-1-30 (1995).

[58] New Mexico Statutes § 37-1-30 (2017).

[59] Title 7 Navajo Nation Code Courts and Procedure, § 204 A.

[60] *Doe BF v Diocese of Gallup, et al*, No SC-CV-06-10 (Navajo Nation Supreme Court, 9 September 2011).

[61] ibid.

is subordinated to the understanding that victims of child sexual abuse may suffer a range of obstacles to pursuing their legal rights. In Victoria, as the polity grew to sympathise with victims of child sexual abuse, the statute of limitations was abolished entirely. The movement to ensure statutes of limitations do no bar legitimate claims arising from child sexual abuse from going forward has made significant progress, but still, not all victims' claims can be brought.

Before any other determination, even before determining whether a statute of limitations applies, courts must make sure that they have jurisdiction to hear the cases before them. Courts may not move forward with respect to a case unless it is one that the court has the power to make decisions about. Among other things, courts cannot hear cases arising out of events that took place outside of the territorial boundaries of the state or locality which the court represents. The question of jurisdiction is of particular salience for victims bringing claims against the Diocese of Gallup, given the stark differences between law in Arizona, New Mexico, and the Navajo Nation.

As discussed above, victims abused by priests or religious within the borders of the Navajo Nation can do so under theories of direct and indirect liability, do not need to hire expert witnesses to testify as to whether or not they have repressed memories, and their disclosing having been abused to a doctor does not prevent them from being able to bring claims when they later connect the effects of that abuse with their cause. This might suggest that victims bringing claims in that jurisdiction are more likely to have success in bringing claims. However, the disfavoured status of Indigenous people embedded in US Constitutional law has effectively discounted the value of those claims and complicated the capacity of the Navajo Nation Supreme Court from making binding decisions about cases brought against non-Navajo persons (like the Diocese of Gallup) on Navajo land.

The US Supreme Court describes Native American nations as sovereign but dependent nations, meaning that they possess 'those aspects of sovereignty not withdrawn by treaty or statute, or by implication as a necessary result of their dependent status'.[62] This retained sovereignty includes the right to 'exercise some forms of civil jurisdiction over non-Indians on their reservations', including the adjudication of civil disputes stemming from a consensual relationship between the outsider and the tribe.[63] The extent of that jurisdiction under US federal law is less certain than suggested by *Wheeler*, but several victims have brought claims against the Diocese of Gallup, bolstered by the Navajo Supreme Court's claiming authority to make determinations in this space.

In *Doe BF*, a member of the Navajo Nation brought claims alleging sexual abuse by a Franciscan priest and naming the Diocese of Gallup and Franciscan orders as defendants. The Navajo Supreme Court held that it had jurisdiction despite the Catholic entities not being members of the Navajo Nation.[64] Before a decision was

[62] *United States v Wheeler*, 435 US 313, 323 (1978).
[63] *Montana v United States*, 450 US 544, 565 (1981).
[64] *Doe BF v Diocese of Gallup, et al* (n 60).

reached as to liability, it and two similar cases pending before Navajo courts settled out of court. The settlement kept the case from going forward past the discovery stage in the US district court to which it had been appealed and kept the issue of tribal jurisdiction from being determined by the US federal courts.

Had the *Doe BF* case not settled, it is not clear what the outcome would have been. A similar case brought by a member of the Choctaw Nation demonstrated the fragility of Indigenous courts' jurisdiction under US law, when the death of Justice Antonin Scalia likely prevented the US Supreme Court from stripping jurisdiction over non-Indigenous defendants from the Choctaw Nation's courts, although leaving the door open to the current, significantly more conservative, court to do so.[65] The power that the federal courts have to determine tribal jurisdiction calls into question the veracity of claims that Indigenous nations in the US have any real authority.[66] If Navajo courts are denied the authority to hold non-Indigenous persons and entities liable for wrongdoing committed on their land, Indigenous nations might legitimately question whether 'dependent' sovereignty is any kind of sovereignty at all.[67] Social disfavour of Indigenous people embeds itself in legal systems, shaping decision-making by Navajo plaintiffs who, rather than risk losing in a federal court on the basis of jurisdiction, might settle for an amount that is likely much less than what they would be entitled to through application of Navajo law.

For religious organisations like dioceses, common law systems have, over time, embedded many forms of protection and privilege. The Royal Commission's investigation into the response of the Sydney Archdiocese to the allegations of John Ellis drew the world's attention to one such embedding of privilege. Ellis, an altar boy who was abused by a priest in the 1970s, first sought redress from the Archdiocese through the Towards Healing programme.[68] Ellis later brought a claim in the civil courts of New South Wales, with respect to which the Court of Appeal ultimately held that there was no legal entity against which Mr Ellis's claim could proceed.[69] This ruling formed the basis for what came to be known as the 'Ellis Defence', which was widely criticised by Survivor advocacy groups and the Royal Commission itself.

[65] *Dolgencorp, Inc v Miss Band of Choctaw Indians*, 732 F 3d 409 (5th Cir 2013); see also Ed Gehres, 'Opinion Analysis: Dollar General, the Court's Longest Pending Case of the 2015 Term is a Four-Four Per Curiam Opinion' SCOTUSblog (25 June 2016), www.scotusblog.com/2016/06/opinion-analysis-dollar-general-the-courts-longest-pending-case-of-the-2015-term-is-a-four-four-per-curiam-opinion.

[66] Ed Gehres, 'Argument Analysis: Is Tribal Court Civil Jurisdiction over Non-Indians Truly a Constitutional Issue, or One of Settled Precedent?' SCOTUSblog (8 December 2015), www.scotusblog.com/2015/12/argument-analysis-is-tribal-court-civil-jurisdiction-over-non-indians-truly-a-constitutional-issue-or-one-of-settled-precedent.

[67] Anna V Smith, '"Win-Loss Is Still Pretty Bad": Tribes Falter at Supreme Court' Indianz.com (9 August 2018), www.indianz.com/News/2018/08/09/winloss-is-still-pretty-bad-tribes-falte.asp.

[68] Royal Commission into Institutional Responses to Child Sexual Abuse, *Case Study 08: Mr John Ellis's Experience of the Towards Healing Process and Civil Litigation* (March 2014).

[69] ibid.

The *Ellis* decision and the objections to it highlight the ways in which legal proceedings that focus on formal structures of law can render useless doctrine which is meant to provide avenue for legal redress. There was no active dispute about whether or not Mr Ellis had been abused, nor was there any active dispute about whether the abuse was the cause of suffering he described in his complaint, nor even a dispute about whether the priest who abused him had been under the control and administration of the Archdiocese and the Archbishop. Despite this, however, the court of appeals determined that there was no defendant against whom he could seek redress.[70] This result is emblematic of the kind of legalism that frustrates people – and as here, the particular legalistic or procedural rule is often subject to criticism and is sometimes eventually changed.

Judith Courtin quotes from Ellis's unsuccessful application to the High Court of Australia for leave to appeal from the decision of the Court of Appeal emphasising how the court's decision failed to provide substantive justice:

> If the Court of Appeal's decision is correct, then the … Church in NSW and the ACT has so structured itself as to be immune from suit other than in respect of strictly property matters for all claims of abuse, neglect or negligence, including claims against teachers in parochial schools … That immunity, they say, extends to the present day in respect of the parochial duties of priests. We say such an immunity would be an outrage to any reasonable sense of justice and we say it is wrong in law.[71]

This criticism is reflected in the submissions to the Royal Commission regarding civil litigation. Eleven of 13 submissions from plaintiff-side advocates called for a change in law such that institutions caring for children would always have an entity available to be sued for harms suffered by those children. Notably, of 10 submissions from defendant-side advocates and organisations, four similarly called for such a change, and only two defended the *status quo*. It was not fully abolished until 2019, when the law in New South Wales was changed to require an institution to nominate a defendant capable of responding to and paying for successful claims of abuse.[72]

Embedding protections for the powerful and barriers for disfavoured or more vulnerable groups through procedural law results in a legal system that consistently deprives litigants of substantive justice. It is characteristic of Nonet and Selznick's concept of autonomous law:

> Legality, understood as close accountability to rules, is the promise of autonomous law; legalism is its affliction. A focus on rules tends to narrow the range of legally relevant facts, thereby detaching legal thought from social reality. The result is legalism,

[70] *Trustees of the Roman Catholic Church v Ellis* (2007) 70 NSWLR 565.

[71] Judith E Courtin, 'Sexual Assault and the Catholic Church: Are Victims Finding Justice?' (PhD Thesis Monash University, 2015) quoting Transcript of Proceedings, *Ellis v The Trustees of the Roman Catholic Church for the Archdiocese for Sydney* [2007] HCA Mr Morrison, 16 November 2007).

[72] Michelle Brown, 'Catholic Church Ellis Defence Scrapped in "Momentous Day" for Abuse Survivors' ABC News (1 January 2019), www.abc.net.au/news/2019-01-01/catholic-church-ellis-defence-scrapped-from-new-years-day/10675890.

> a disposition to rely on legal authority to the detriment of practical problem solving. The application of rules ceases to be informed by a regard for purposes, needs, and consequences. Legalism is costly, partly because of the rigidities it imposes but also because rules construed *in abstracto* are too easily satisfied by a formal observance that conceals substantive evasions of public policy.[73]

Marc Galanter's classic essay, 'Why the "Haves" Come Out Ahead: Speculations on the Limits of Legal Change', details how wealthier participants in tort law systems with access to high-quality legal services find compliance with procedures easier, and those who engage repeatedly with the same system (typically large organisations who defend against multiple suits), tend to be much more accomplished at navigating procedural law for their benefit.[74] In cases brought against the dioceses of Ballarat and Gallup, we can see how procedural law benefits Church interests. Nonet and Selznick identified this kind of reframing of substantive justice issues as procedural questions as a defining characteristic of autonomous legal systems.[75]

We can also understand the importance of procedural law by considering the extent to which the focus of reform has been on changing procedural law to better accommodate victims interested in bringing claims. The changes to statutes of limitation and judicially created rules that allow victims to bring claims when they are capable of doing so have allowed many cases to go forward that may not otherwise have been. Similarly, while Mr Ellis was not successful in his claim or appeal, his story has led to a change in law and a new way of approaching liability for Church interests in Australia. It is notable that the procedural law that impacts the capacity of Indigenous legal systems to retain jurisdiction over claims arising within their territories is less visible as a problem related to clerical child sexual abuse, but it does demonstrate how a focus on rules of procedure (denying that Indigenous judicial systems have jurisdiction) over substance of their effects (this would effectively leave the plaintiffs without a forum to bring their claims) not just privileges the powerful, but also disadvantages some of society's most vulnerable.

V. Logistics

This chapter has considered how tort law theories – theories about tort's purpose and theories of liability that form tort law doctrine – shift concern away from harm of child sexual abuse and toward the relationship between abuser and employer. It has also considered how procedural law including statutes of limitation, jurisdictional limits, and corporate law have the effect of protecting the powerful

[73] Philippe Nonet and Philip Selznick, *Law and Society in Transition: Toward Responsive Law* (Routledge, 2001) 64.

[74] Marc Galanter, 'Why the "Haves" Come Out Ahead: Speculations on the Limits of Legal Change' (1974) 9 *Law & Society Review* 95.

[75] Nonet and Selznick (n 73) and fairness, rather than substantive justice 'are the first ends and the main competence of the legal order'.

from legitimate claims for accountability by vulnerable people. This section, on logistics, will consider other factors that can impact the capacity to bring a claim in tort. These logistics can include the emotional and financial difficulty of bringing claims, complications of rural life, and a general lack of legal and material resources. These issues impact the process for plaintiffs across the life of a case, including decisions about whether to bring a case, settle a case, and for how much.

First, as compared to most actions in tort, bringing a claim of child sexual abuse against a Catholic diocese is an emotionally, spiritually, socially, financially, and at times even physically difficult task. Consider oral testimony. The plaintiff's story has to be told in front of multiple people. In the US, depositions are a required part of the process, and so the story will have to be told multiple times.[76] Many of the people who are present at trial and in depositions are strangers, some of them being paid to argue that the plaintiff is lying, mistaken, or that acknowledged abuse does not warrant compensation. Also in the room is the most powerful man in a Catholic diocese – a man Catholic children are taught to revere as a living connection to the Divine. And this powerful man (and his predecessors) hired, supported, protected and continues to take the side of the abuser.

Compared to being injured in a car crash or suffering property damage (classic examples of tort actions), child sexual abuse is intensely traumatic, usually bringing deep feelings, including shame, fear and sadness. This is a serious barrier to people pursuing their claims. It requires incredible bravery to tell this kind of story out loud, much less in front of hostile parties, especially when those hostile parties are powerful religious leaders. Not only is this difficulty a deterrent to bringing actions, it also provides dioceses with significant leverage in negotiating settlement. A case's potential worth is diminished by the defendant's knowledge that few plaintiffs wish to testify.

Regardless of the amount of any settlement or recovery, the effects of abuse and the litigation process itself remain, and many victims may never feel truly at peace. Hardin-Burrola published an article in 2017 about a member of the Navajo Nation who brought a claim alleging abuse by a Franciscan brother working at St Michael Indian School.[77] When she asked the plaintiff's attorney 'if his client was satisfied with the settlement agreement', he responded:

> I do not believe victims of sexual abuse experience satisfaction when sexual abuse lawsuits are settled, … Nothing can ever be said or done to repair the scars caused by clergy sexual abuse. By resolving cases like this one, however, we hope it offers survivors of clergy sexual abuse some sense of closure and some sense of validation that the perpetrator is a confirmed sex offender who was allowed to prey upon innocent children.[78]

[76] See eg Michael J Legg, 'The United States Deposition – Time for Adoption in Australian Civil Procedure?' (2007) 31 *Melbourne University Law Review* 146.

[77] Elizabeth Hardin-Burrola, 'Clergy sex abuse case ending in settlement' *The Gallup Independent* (20 November 2017).

[78] ibid.

For those who bring claims, the discrepancy between what the lawyers think would have been just compensation and what victims usually settle their legal claims for reflects the limitations of tort as a system. Lawyers I interviewed expressed frustration at the low settlements their clients took, even as they understood and sympathised with their reasoning. The likelihood of a favourable outcome for claimants depends on, among other things, the victim/plaintiff's wherewithal to endure the process, and a calculation of likelihood of success given the realities of circumstance, available evidence, procedural law and applicable substantive law. Nonet and Selznick identified an emphasis on procedure as characteristic of autonomous law: 'Regularity and fairness, rather than substantive justice, are the first ends and the main competence of the legal order.'[79]

In addition to the emotional difficulty, there are financial and practical barriers to bringing claims. Before a victim begins an action in tort in common law countries like the US and Australia, a lawyer is almost always consulted and retained. For most victims, the prospect of paying fees to a lawyer during a suit would be prohibitive. In the US, most tort cases brought by individuals are typically taken on a contingency basis – so the lawyer will pay all fees upfront but will receive a percentage (usually between 20 and 40 per cent) of any recovery. In Australia, contingency fee arrangements are illegal, and so lawyers taking cases on a 'no win no fee' basis charge additional fees to compensate for the risk they take in providing the costs up-front to their clients.[80] Furthermore, unsuccessful plaintiffs in Australia are typically responsible for paying the costs of the defendant.[81] John Ellis, whose case is discussed above, was ordered to pay the costs of his bringing his case, which totalled over AUD650,000.[82] The purpose of these schemes is to encourage lawyers to only bring those claims that they believe have a good chance of winning, and to settle.[83] The result of incentivising lawyers to only take cases they believe are likely to result in a successful claim means that a lawyer's assessment of a potential client's emotional capacity may play a larger role in claims arising out of child sexual abuse than it does in less fraught kinds of cases. Lawyers' perception of the compensability of a potential victim's claim, then, is an initial barrier to a claim that operates invisibly, keeping claims from even being presented to a court.

In Australia, the story of John Ellis is often mentioned in connection with the scandal of child sexual abuse, and while it is important for the procedural question of corporate availability for suit, it also demonstrates how wealth facilitates access to justice. The case may have reached the Court of Appeal only because Ellis, unlike most people, had the wherewithal to litigate his case all the way through the

[79] Nonet and Selznick (n 73) 54.

[80] Stuart Clark and Christina Harris, 'The Push to Reform Class Action Procedure in Australia: Evolution or Revolution?' (2008) 32 *Melbourne University Law Review* 775, 788.

[81] ibid, 768.

[82] Royal Commission into Institutional Responses to Child Sexual Abuse (10 March 2014, Day 052) Statement of Counsel Assisting Gail Furness, C05302 [1-12].

[83] Cane (n 3) 282.

appeals stage. Most people settle. Ellis was a partner at a large, international law firm,[84] and had significantly more knowledge of the legal system, was in a stronger financial position, and benefited from more family and community support than would most any other Survivor. As a highly educated, relatively wealthy, married man with a sophisticated understanding of the legal system and access to some of the most skilled lawyers in New South Wales, he had advantages in bringing his claim that few other victims of clerical child sexual abuse have. That he nonetheless lost his case and suffered significant hardship in connection with the litigation is testament to the traumatic nature of both the abuse and the tort process itself.

Few in Ballarat and fewer still in Gallup have Mr Ellis's advantages. Inequity between classes and asymmetrical impact of rule enforcement on disfavoured groups within society is predicted in Nonet and Selznick's account of autonomous law.[85] The Victorian Aboriginal Child Care Agency's submission to the Royal Commission's call for consultation on redress and civil litigation highlights the way that, for people whose experience with the government and legal system has been as traumatic and abusive across centuries as it has been for Indigenous people, bringing a claim against a Catholic diocese involves considerations that people who have usually been able to rely on the system for substantive justice do not have:

> The 'system' is still experienced by many Aboriginal people as insurmountable and there is little point in putting yourself through the trauma of trying to have your word believed. VACCA acknowledges the trauma that those who have tried to have their sexual abuse and other childhood traumas including the trauma of removal and disconnection from land and culture addressed.[86]

Those who do trust in the state legal systems enough to bring a claim must also have access to legal services to advocate for their case. For people who live in urban or suburban regions, lawyers are not difficult to find. While low-income urban dwellers may lack resources to adequately evaluate or retain lawyers, rural residents face a lack of legal services in general. Both Arizona and New Mexico have low rates of lawyers for their state population as a whole, and the vast majority of those lawyers are concentrated in metropolitan areas like Phoenix, Albuquerque and Tucson, leaving few private attorneys in rural areas, and even fewer available to Indigenous people, who tend to live in some of the most remote areas of both states.[87] Those few private attorneys who work in rural areas tend to live in county seats, larger towns and relatively wealthier areas within rural counties.[88]

[84] Royal Commission into Institutional Responses to Child Sexual Abuse (n 82) C05288.

[85] Nonet and Selznick (n 73) 64.

[86] Victorian Aboriginal Child Care Agency Submission No 36 for Issue Paper 5 on Civil Litigation to Royal Commission into Institutional Responses to Child Sexual Abuse (17 March 2014) 7.

[87] See generally Lisa R Pruitt and Beth A Colgan, 'Justice Deserts: Spatial Inequality and Local Funding of Indigent Defense' (2010) 51 *Arizona Law Review* 219.

[88] My father was a lawyer practising in Navajo County from approximately 1984 to 1998 – first as a prosecutor assigned to crimes against children and those involving sexual assault, and then as a lawyer in private practice handling a range of domestic, civil and criminal matters. Growing up in that context

This means that people living in the most remote, poorest areas of the diocese, like those living in most of the Navajo Nation, have to drive hours just to meet with a lawyer. There is no public transportation. Not everyone has access to a dependable vehicle. Internet connectivity is expensive and may not even be available in poor, rural areas like the Navajo Nation.[89]

Another difficulty is social. Life in any rural area means a lack of anonymity. A plaintiff living in a city can usually go about their business and not be recognised by people who are aware of their having made allegations against a religious organisation. In a small town in a rural area, plaintiffs will not be able to maintain privacy as easily.[90] The lack of anonymity in Mildura, Victoria, for example, meant the entire community knew that police officer Ryan was challenging the Church. He tells of shopkeepers coming out when he walked by to threaten him over 'Bringing disgrace on our Church'.[91] For the lawyers, as well, the lack of anonymity complicates the prospect of taking on cases challenging powerful local institutions. A lawyer living and practising in one of the better-off town centres might be socialising with local authorities, including Church officials, on a regular basis, and 'These relationships can make it more difficult for a lawyer to be a zealous advocate because doing so may jeopardize some of these relationships.'[92]

Rural areas with sparse populations living far apart from one another can be host to a wide range of social and legal problems. Pruitt and Showman trace how distance, economics and a slew of other impediments to access to legal representation are common in rural areas of the American West, even as each place has unique characteristics that impact access to legal services in particular ways.[93] Pruitt and Colgan note that access to justice is particularly difficult for Indigenous people in the US, and argue that Arizona's system of funding justice services exclusively through county-based tax revenue creates significant disparities in access to justice for people in Navajo and Apache counties (the two which are part of the Diocese of Gallup and the two with the highest percentages of Indigenous people in the state) as compared to other rural counties in the state.[94] Between the lack of lawyers and the close-knit communities in Gallup it is perhaps not surprising that plaintiffs who brought cases against the diocese were represented by lawyers from

I knew that most of the lawyers in the county lived and had their offices in either the county seat of Holbrook or one of the relatively wealthy towns, like Pinetop-Lakeside.

[89] An 2019 *Salt Lake Tribune* article writes of optimism that schools (not residences) on the Navajo Nation might get broadband Internet in 2020. Zak Podmore, 'Broadband Internet Access Coming to Navajo Nation Communities in San Juan County' *The Salt Lake Tribune* (15 November 2019), www.sltrib.com/news/2019/11/15/broadband-internet-access.

[90] Lisa R Pruitt and Bradley E Showman, 'Law Stretched Thin: Access to Justice in Rural America' (2014) 59 *South Dakota Law Review* 466, 489.

[91] Denis Ryan and Peter Hoysted, *Unholy Trinity: The Hunt for the Paedophile Priest Monsignor John Day* (Allen & Unwin, 2013) 154.

[92] Pruitt and Showman (n 90) 490 (citations omitted).

[93] ibid, 528; see also Linda L Chezem, 'Public Health Law & Equal Access to Justice in Rural America' (2014) 59 *South Dakota Law Review* 529, 556.

[94] Pruitt and Colgan (n 87) 313–14.

larger cities outside the boundaries of the diocese. Of the three plaintiffs' lawyers listed by the bankruptcy court that represented claimants in the case, only one has an office in the diocese, and he is in Gallup, the largest town.

VI. Common Law of Tort, the Prototypical Autonomous Legal System

The rule of law project in the Western legal tradition was developed to counter the excesses of repressive law systems that dominated pre-enlightenment Europe (which in turn, were formed alongside of and in response to the development of canon law), and was developed as a part of these societies' slow transition from purely monarchical to more republican and democratic forms of government.[95] The rule of law is premised on the idea that all are equal before the law, that a person's position in society, including wealth or lack thereof, should not be a factor in the operation of law. The story of access to lawyers and courts in rural areas, especially in combination with poverty and existing social orderings that disadvantage Indigenous people, immigrants and other disfavoured groups reiterates the findings of critical and feminist theorists that this premise of equality cannot be trusted. Yet the gap between ideals of justice and their failure to manifest on the ground is not simply bad faith or hypocrisy. Instead, the interests of powerful entities are embedded in the structure of legal systems, while barriers multiply for weaker parties.

Max Weber pointed out a key paradox of the rule of law: the gradual accumulation of rules and procedures to temper repression and build up a more formal, rational and complex body of law results in structural advantages for formally rational and complex organisations over damaged citizens.[96] Autonomous law in Western society is the result of what Nonet and Selznick identify as an historic bargain: procedural autonomy for legal institutions in exchange for substantive subordination of those institutions to political will. It proclaims all are subject to law while facilitating a professional monopoly on legal proceedings and legitimated forms of justice. Autonomous law tames repression by maintaining a commitment to law as 'an instrument of social control' based on rules rather than values.[97] Courts remove themselves from the substantive formation of public policy in exchange for their capacity to hold political leaders and institutions to account to the law. As Nikki Godden-Rasul explained, referencing a substantial body of

[95] Harold J Berman, *Law and Revolution: The Formation of the Western Legal Tradition* (Harvard University Press, 1983) 543.

[96] Max Rheinstein (ed), *Max Weber on Law in Economy and Society* tr Edward Shils and Max Rheinstein (Harvard University Press, 1954) 228–29.

[97] Nonet and Selznick (n 73) 63.

feminist critiques of tort law systems, 'in practice, compensation through tort law in only an option for a very small proportion of sexual violence survivors':[98]

> Tort law primarily works to benefit and secure the status of white, middle-class, able-bodied men, evidenced by extensive feminist critiques which flesh out the human subject who is realised and idealised through tort law. This liberal legal person is 'rational, autonomous, self-contained, self-possessed, self-sufficient and formally equal before the law,' which does not represent members of social groups whose lives make most sense in relation to others and are shaped by systemic disadvantage, discrimination and violence. The conception of the human subject deeply entrenched in tort law doctrine informs the 'reasonableness' of behaviours and acts in negligence, the duties owed to one another, the types of harms which are most likely to be redressed.[99]

In Australia, the Court of Appeal's finding that the Archdiocese of Sydney did not exist in a form capable of being sued for abuse that occurred under the authority of a previous archbishop demonstrates how legal provisions embedded in law for the benefit of religious organisations complicate the connection between entity and harm that apply to organisations. In a US that has yet to come to grips with its dark history of genocide and cultural abuse in boarding schools for Indigenous people, Indigenous courts' power to hold Catholic organisations to account is uncertain. It is a hallmark feature of autonomous law that powerful interests are able to embed their advantages in law while those with less power cannot enforce their right which, in theory, should be protected.

A focus on procedural rather than substantive justice limits a legal system's value as a normative order, as we can see how rules as applied to cases brought in tort in Victoria, Arizona, New Mexico and the Navajo Nation render claims more or less compensable, based on factors unrelated to questions of whether or not the plaintiff suffered abuse at the hands of a diocesan agent or employee. Thus, even as particular contexts shape theories of tort, applicable doctrine and procedure, and the logistics of both practice and seeking justice in Ballarat and Gallup, the overall character of tort as a system across these contexts is largely autonomous. Context can shape the accessibility of law, and justice can be elusive. However, despite changing perspectives influencing the shape of tort law and making it easier to bring cases in many places, none of the tort law systems discussed here can be described as responsive, given the remaining difficulties and barriers to justice victims face. They are fundamentally autonomous legal systems.

[98] Nikki Godden-Rasul, 'Tort Law and Feminist Strategy: Lessons from Social Movement and Community Lawyering' (2025) *Social & Legal Studies* 1, 6.

[99] ibid, 5 (citations omitted).

6

The Royal Commission: A Quasi-Responsive System

I. Introduction

On 16 February 2016, Australian comedian Tim Minchin posted a song online titled 'Come Home (Cardinal Pell)'.[1] The song bluntly, comically and somewhat crudely calls for Cardinal George Pell to return to Australia to appear in person at the Royal Commission's hearing on Ballarat, labels Pell a 'goddamn coward' and expresses disbelief in Pell's claims of ignorance about priests' abuse of children as well as belief, support and admiration for victims. The song was published after the Royal Commission decided to allow Pell to appear via video link from the Vatican, where he was the Prefect of the Secretariat for the Economy, the third-highest role in Church hierarchy.[2] Pell had submitted evidence that a medical condition prevented him from flying, and although counsel appearing for victims noted the medical condition was relatively common and doubted the veracity of claims flying was a risk to Pell's health, the 'Commissioners [were] satisfied' that giving evidence by video link was acceptable.[3]

Public interest in the Royal Commission peaked with Pell's testimony, as the public's concern crystallised over stories of victims from Ballarat.[4] Over the course of the Ballarat Hearing, the live stream of proceedings on the Royal Commission's website was viewed almost 54,000 times.[5] Pell and Church officials were roundly criticised in the press.[6] Journalist Brigid Delaney commented that, 'The stories of

[1] Tim Minchin, 'Come Home (Cardinal Pell) – Tim Minchin' YouTube (16 February 2016), www.youtube.com/watch?v=EtHOmforqxk.

[2] 'What is George Pell's Job at the Vatican?' ABC News (29 June 2017), www.abc.net.au/news/2017-06-29/what-is-george-pells-job-at-the-vactican/8663256.

[3] Melissa Davey, 'George Pell Cleared to Give Sex Abuse Royal Commission Evidence by Video Link,' *The Guardian* (8 February 2016), www.theguardian.com/australia-news/2016/feb/08/george-pell-cleared-to-give-sex-abuse-royal-commission-evidence-by-video-link.

[4] Brigid Delaney, 'The Stories of the Broken Men of Ballarat Have Unleashed Compassion on a National Scale' *The Guardian* (2 March 2016), www.theguardian.com/commentisfree/2016/mar/02/the-stories-of-the-broken-men-of-ballarat-have-unleashed-compassion-on-a-national-scale.

[5] Royal Commission into Institutional Responses to Child Sexual Abuse, *Our Inquiry* (Commonwealth of Australia, 2017) [3.4.3].

[6] See eg, Melissa Davey, 'Commission Challenges Bishop's Claims He Was Unaware of Priest's Child Abuse' *The Guardian* (11 December 2015), www.theguardian.com/australia-news/2015/dec/11/commission-challenges-bishops-claims-he-was-unaware-of-priests-child-abuse.

the Ballarat men feel authentic and real. They connect with us. The same cannot be said for the testimony of Pell.'[7]

In his testimony from Rome, appearing via video link, Cardinal Pell's demeanour read as 'cut from cardboard'.[8] He chose his words carefully – likely in order to avoid perjuring himself or admitting fault. He said, when asked about Ridsdale, a serial abuser in the Diocese of Ballarat, 'It was a sad story and of not much interest to me.'[9] That statement came to be emblematic of Pell's response to the Royal Commission. Pell was later prosecuted for abusing two boys in Victoria, and was convicted and imprisoned. He was released after the High Court quashed his conviction in April 2020.[10]

This chapter will discuss the purpose of royal commissions in Australian society, the terms of reference that form the theory of the Royal Commission, the investigatory powers and flexible procedures which empower royal commissions, and the logistics that had an impact on the Royal Commission's efficacy. One of the Royal Commission's most responsive attributes lay in its capacity to establish a narrative of truth, something that the story of Cardinal Pell and the Ballarat Hearing helps to highlight. Minchin's 'pitch-perfect protest song' evidenced and channelled public anger with the Catholic Church and with Cardinal Pell as a symbol of Church leadership.[11] It also served as a demonstration of the efficacy of the Royal Commission in shaping the public narrative of clerical child sexual abuse, and the power of that narrative for victims. The song was linked to an online fundraiser. In six days, the fundraiser collected AUD203,065, at which point it was closed because it had collected almost thrice the amount required for its purpose of sending a group of victims from Ballarat to Rome to witness Pell's testimony in person.[12] Meshel Laurie, an Australian radio personality among the organisers of the fundraiser, wrote:

> [O]ur support for the survivors has come as a wonderful surprise to so many of them. They've told me repeatedly in the last week that they didn't think we in the wider community cared about them. They thought we didn't want to know about what happened to them, but your donations changed that. You've made them feel cared for and like what happened to them mattered to all of us. You've genuinely changed these people's lives. Never forget that.[13]

[7] Delaney (n 4).

[8] David Marr, 'We Learned About George Pell's Pain. But What About the Children' *The Guardian* (3 March 2016), www.theguardian.com/australia-news/2016/mar/03/we-learned-about-george-pells-pain-but-what-about-the-children.

[9] David Marr, 'George Pell Wasn't Much Interested in Stories of Abuse by Priests. Which was Lucky for His Career' *The Guardian* (1 March 2016), www.theguardian.com/australia-news/2016/mar/01/george-pell-wasnt-much-interested-in-stories-of-abuse-by-priests-which-was-lucky-for-his-career.

[10] Melissa Davey, 'George Pell: Australian Cardinal Released from Jail After High Court Quashes Child Sexual Abuse Conviction' *The Guardian* (7 April 2020), www.theguardian.com/australia-news/2020/apr/07/cardinal-george-pell-conviction-quashed-australia-high-court-freed-jail-appeal-upheld.

[11] Liam Viney, 'Tim Minchin's Come Home Cardinal Pell is a Pitch-Perfect Protest Song' *The Conversation* (18 February 2016), theconversation.com/tim-minchins-come-home-cardinal-pell-is-a-pitch-perfect-protest-song-54945.

[12] Michelle Nicol, 'Send Ballarat Survivors to Rome' Gofundme.com (17 March 2016), www.gofundme.com/f/sendballarattorome.

[13] ibid, update by Meshel Laurie, dated 20 February 2016.

II. Purpose of Royal Commissions

The Royal Commissions Act 1902[14] provides that the Governor General of Australia may issue letters patent in the name of the monarch, directing and authorising the establishment of an independent commission 'which relates to or is connected with the peace, order, and good government of the Commonwealth, or any public purpose or any power of the Commonwealth'.[15] Royal commissions in Australia are temporary, ad hoc 'instruments of investigation of executive government',[16] appointed and paid for by government and commissioned to perform specific tasks. Their 'primary function', Katie Wright explains, 'is widely acknowledged as learning lessons from past events to inform the future'.[17]

Nicholas Aroney explains that inquiries like royal commissions are typically either inquisitorial, investigative or advisory, although some inquiries have elements of all three.[18] The letters patent issued upon their appointment instruct the commission on the matters about which the Government has authorised it to investigate and report. As advisory bodies, royal commissions serve to 'marshal the facts and data needed for soundly based government decision-making'.[19] Since the growth of administrative and other government agencies providing a permanent source of data on which most governing relies, royal commissions have taken on roles including: to 'provide accountability, to allow wide public participation and to enrich the process of public policymaking'.[20]

Royal commissions are generally reserved for important social and political concerns. They are considered Australia's premier investigative mechanism, and have a reputation as independent, rigorous and effective:[21]

> The establishment of a royal commission attests to the gravity of the subject as governments reserve this elevated mode of public inquiry for the most weighty matters. Royal commissions carry the expectation of independence and rigorous inquiry and attract

[14] Although states and territories in Australia, as well as the Commonwealth Government, have legislation providing for royal commissions, for purposes of this discussion, references to royal commissions, except where specifically noted, will refer only to those appointed by the Commonwealth Government under the Royal Commissions Act 1902. See also Scott Prasser, 'When Should Royal Commissions be Appointed?' (2005) *Public Administration Today* 57, 57.

[15] Royal Commissions Act 1902.

[16] Susan Pascoe, 'The 2009 Victorian Bushfires Royal Commission: Lessons for the Conduct of Inquiries in Australia' (2010) 69 *The Australian Journal of Public Administration* 392, 393.

[17] Katie Wright, 'Remaking Collective Knowledge: An Analysis of the Complex and Multiple Effects of Inquiries into Historical Institutional Child Abuse' (2017) 74 *Child Abuse and Neglect* 10, 11.

[18] Nicholas Aroney, 'The Constitutional First Principles of Royal Commissions' in Scott Prasser and Helen Tracey (eds), *Royal Commissions & Public Inquiries: Practice & Potential*, (Connor Court Publishing, 2014) ch 2.

[19] Scott Prasser and Helen Tracey, 'History, trends and key issues – the story so far …' in Scott Prasser and Helen Tracey (eds), *Royal Commissions & Public Inquiries: Practice & Potential* (Connor Court Publishing, 2014) 5.

[20] ibid, 5.

[21] Janet Ransley, 'Public Inquiries into Political Wrongdoing' in Scott Prasser and Helen Tracey (eds), *Royal Commissions & Public Inquiries: Practice & Potential*, (Connor Court Publishing, 2014) ch 4.

> high levels of media and community interest. This level of independence renders royal commissions risk for government as they cannot be controlled once they are created.[22]

Michael Eburn and Stephen Dovers identify three characteristic features of Australian royal commissions.[23] First, despite being called for by the Government and having powers established by statute, they are commissioned by the Governor-General in order to foster the perception that they are independent.[24] Second, royal commissions enjoy significant coercive authority, including the ability to summon people to appear and testify and produce documents, and the power to compel such appearance and production, even when issues of privilege or the right to avoid self-incrimination would otherwise interfere.[25] The strength of Australian royal commissions to compel disclosure is notable even among other countries that follow the Westminster model and employ royal commissions.[26] Third, hearings are usually public and witnesses 'may be examined and cross-examined by counsel assisting the commission as well as counsel who have been granted leave to appear to represent the interests of parties who may be affected by the outcome of the inquiry'.[27]

Although the practice of royal commissions may appear similar in many respects to the practice of law in other legal systems, it has unique attributes. Whereas most legal systems do not conduct their own research, the public hearings were only the tip of the iceberg of information available to commissioners investigating institutional responses to child sexual abuse. The Royal Commission, 'had an extensive policy and research program that drew upon the findings made in public hearings and information from private sessions, as well as generating new evidence through research' and deliberation with experts.[28] Royal commissions are typically chaired by senior legal professionals while the other commissioners are experienced senior professionals from fields relevant to the subject of the inquiry,[29] and the Royal Commission was no exception.[30] The chair, the Honourable Justice Peter McClellan AM, was a Judge of the Court of Appeal in New South Wales, and the other commissioners were senior leaders from law, police, public service, psychiatry and politics.[31]

Royal commissions are valued in Australia because of the perception that they are independent and trustworthy investigatory mechanisms.[32] Janet Ransley

[22] Pascoe (n 16) 393 (citation omitted).

[23] Michael Eburn and Stephen Dovers, 'Learning Lessons from Disasters: Alternatives to Royal Commissions and Other Quasi-Judicial Inquiries' (2015) 74 *Australian Journal of Public Administration* 495, 496.

[24] ibid, 496.

[25] ibid, 496.

[26] Prasser (n 14) 58.

[27] Eburn and Dovers (n 23) 496 (citing Scott Prasser, 'Royal Commissions in Australia: When Should Governments Appoint Them'? (2006) 65 *Australian Journal of Public Administration* 28, 31–32).

[28] Royal Commission into Institutional Responses to Child Sexual Abuse, *Final Report: Our Inquiry* (December 2017).

[29] Prasser (n 14) 58.

[30] Royal Commission into Institutional Responses to Child Sexual Abuse (n 28).

[31] ibid.

[32] See eg, Ransley (n 21).

points to independence as the 'key criterion' underlying the 'perception that royal commissions … are a superior type of investigation'.[33] Royal commissions must be seen as especially independent and trustworthy in order to overcome any cynicism about their origins. Trust has two sides: perception of trustworthiness; and trustworthiness itself. Independence is a valued characteristic of royal commissions, but there is no certainty that this independence or the knowledge the process produces will have policy impact. Public policy scholar Scott Prasser explains that governments establish royal commissions for 'politically expedient reasons such as to show concern about an issue, give an illusion of action, show responsiveness to a problem, co-opt critics, reduce opposition, delay decision-making and reassert control of the policy agenda'.[34] As the rest of this chapter discusses in more detail, royal commissions do not have the capacity to effect any changes to law, policy or regulation, ultimately undermining their authority. They can only issue recommendations. They are limited by their terms of reference. Despite these weaknesses, most of the Royal Commission's recommendations were implemented, and it produced a mountain of data and research on a wide range of related issues, creating a public narrative of truth and support for victims that served its purpose.

III. Terms of Reference: A Royal Commission's Doctrine

Then-Prime Minister Julia Gillard announced the Royal Commission on 12 November 2012, and its terms of reference were issued on 11 January 2013.[35] This happened after, and perhaps because of, a call for a royal commission by the *Newcastle Herald* and an appearance on a popular television programme from then Detective Chief Inspector Peter Fox. Both the *Herald* call and Fox's appearance centred on clerical sexual abuse in community settings rather than abuse of children in residential 'care' facilities.[36] The call and appearance drew media attention to rates of suicide among victims of sexual abuse by Catholic priests, including some prominent members of Australian society.[37] This context may have

[33] ibid.

[34] William Budiselik, Frances Crawford and Donna Chung, 'The Australian Royal Commission into Institutional Responses to Child Sexual Abuse: Dreaming of Child Safe Organisations?' (2014) 3 *Social Sciences* 565, 571 (quoting Prasser (n 14) 34).

[35] *Royal Commission into Institutional Responses to Child Sexual Abuse* (Terms of Reference, as amended November 2014).

[36] Katie Wright and Shurlee Swain, 'Speaking the Unspeakable, Naming the Unnameable: The Royal Commission into Institutional Responses to Child Sexual Abuse' (2018) 42 *Journal of Australian Studies*, 139, 140.

[37] Joanne McCarthy, 'John Pirona's Suicide in 2012 Was an "Important Cog" that Led to a Royal Commission, Said His Father' *Newcastle Herald* (20 October 2018), www.newcastleherald.com.au/story/5706527/too-much-pain-the-family-tragedy-behind-a-royal-commission-and-national-apology.

contributed to the terms of reference being restricted to investigating sexual abuse, as opposed to child maltreatment more broadly, even as the scope of institutions being investigated was broadened to include residential facilities 'caring' for indigent, immigrant, disabled, Indigenous or orphaned children as well as institutions interacting with children in community settings.

The terms of reference directed the Royal Commission to examine how institutions had responded to child sexual abuse. It was charged with investigating systemic failures and with making recommendations for policy, practice and legal reform. It was also tasked with making recommendations as to how the effects of abuse could be alleviated and how victims could receive justice. The letters patent authorising the Royal Commission made clear that child sexual abuse in institutional contexts is a systemic problem that required an interdisciplinary, well resourced and well-planned research agenda in order for the country to come to grips with it.[38] As with most public inquiries, it was at once concerned with both the past and the future. A central focus was learning lessons from people's experiences of institutional child sexual abuse and institutional responses to allegations or instances of child sexual abuse. The common refrain, articulated by Gillard when announcing the inquiry, was that it was meant to 'ensure that what happened to children in the past could never be allowed to happen again'.[39]

Frank Golding called attention to the disappointment among those who were brought up in 'institutional out-of-home Care (OOHC) in Australia',[40] when the Royal Commission's terms of reference were issued with a narrow focus on sexual abuse. Care leavers, whose advocacy and efforts were critical to the eventuation of the Royal Commission, had hoped that the investigation would consider not just sexual abuse, but also 'the physical suffering, the emotional starvation and the cold absence of love, of tenderness, of care', for which Prime Minister Kevin Rudd had apologised in 2009.[41] Indeed, those hopes were raised when Gillard announced the Royal Commission. She specifically referenced Rudd's apology in her announcement.[42] Golding, Kathleen Daly, and others have critiqued the Royal Commission and the related national redress scheme for unsatisfactory results for care leavers and others with lower social status as children.[43] Golding's account of how organisations like CLAN lobbied intensively for the Royal Commission after

[38] Royal Commission into Institutional Responses to Child Sexual Abuse, Letters Patent.

[39] Wright and Swain (n 36) 144.

[40] Frank Golding, '"Problems with Records and Recordkeeping Practices Are Not Confined to the Past": A Challenge from the Royal Commission into Institutional Responses to Child Sexual Abuse' (2019) 20 *Archival Science* 1, 1 (explaining that 'The term "Care" is problematic; hence, it is often capitalised (as in this paper) or used in ironic quotation marks').

[41] ibid, 4.

[42] ibid, 4.

[43] Kathleen Daly, 'Inequalities of Redress: Australia's National Redress Scheme for Institutional Abuse of Children' (2018) 42 *Journal of Australian Studies* 204. The term 'care leavers' generally refers to those who had been raised in out of home 'care' facilities of one sort or another.

receiving Rudd's apology, however, speaks to Australians' belief in the power of royal commissions.[44]

In comparison to most royal commissions, the Royal Commission was longer, conducted more hearings, commissioned more research, interviewed more people, made available more evidence, and captured more of the public's attention. It worked hard at providing emotional support and communicating care for victims. The commissioners understood their project to include being cognisant of the trauma experienced by victims of child sexual abuse. The Royal Commission sought to be trauma-informed and to actively seek the participation of people who might be left out in other legal systems.

Daly critiqued the Royal Commission's terms of reference limiting the focus to child sexual abuse and the redress scheme that the Commission proposed, which was (mostly) implemented through legislation.[45] She argued that the scheme should have distinguished between those who suffered in 'care' settings and those who were abused in community settings in order not to disadvantage care leavers.[46] She pointed to the other kinds of abuse that children in residential facilities, orphanages, homes, detention centres and similar facilities suffer – physical, emotional and cultural – and how this abuse was not addressed in the proposed scheme, in which the scale of severity was determined almost solely by degree of sexual contact, thus minimising experiences of trauma and abuse in residential settings.[47] Daly also highlighted a report prepared for the Royal Commission showing significantly lower payments to care leavers (average AUD30,000) than non-care leavers (average over AUD50,000) through the Towards Healing protocol, despite evidence care leavers suffered 'a higher severity of abuse', and argued that this disadvantage was likely to continue with the individualised assessment put forth by the Royal Commission:[48]

> Children grew up in 'total institutions', that is, batch living of a large group of 'inmates', controlled by a small supervisory staff. The major spheres of life (sleeping, playing, working) were all in 'the same place and under the same single authority'. Survivors recall a 'dehumanizing institutional environment', one of being 'totally at the mercy' of staff with no one to turn to. They lived in 'a constant fear of sexual abuse [and were subject to] deprivations of food and schooling, forced labour, and medical neglect', alongside physical and sexual abuse.[49]

Golding described the Royal Commission's terms of reference as embodying the perception of sexual abuse as the 'core transgression of innocent childhood', and described how the narrow focus took public attention away from care

[44] Frank Golding, 'Sexual Abuse as the Core Transgression of Childhood Innocence: Unintended Consequences for Care Leavers' (2018) 42 *Journal of Australian Studies* 191, 193.

[45] Daly (n 43).

[46] ibid, 205–06.

[47] ibid, 211–12.

[48] ibid, 206.

[49] ibid, 9.

leavers and centred it on children who had been abused in community settings.[50] The assessment framework enacted by Parliament contemplated payments of AUD5,000 in recognition of non-sexual abuse and AUD5,000 in recognition of a victim's being 'institutionally vulnerable'.[51] Awards for sexual contact ranged from AUD5,000 for 'exposure abuse' to AUD70,000 for 'penetrative abuse'.[52] Defining recovery amounts by reference to the degree of sexual contact while offering relatively small amounts in recognition of other forms of abuse sends the message that physical, emotional, cultural, spiritual and other forms of abuse, exploitation and neglect in closed institutional settings was acceptable for the lower-status children who resided in them even as it (rightly) establishes that a single instance of sexual abuse is unacceptable.

The Royal Commission heard from a number of community representatives, including those who argued that the Commission's recommendations should depart from the terms of reference and recommend redress for those who suffered other kinds of abuse in institutional contexts, and acknowledged that the approach they would take 'will disappoint a number of those who have participated in our consultation processes to date'.[53] The Royal Commission made clear, however, that they did

> not accept that out Letters Patent allow us to consider redress for those who have suffered physical abuse, neglect or emotional or cultural abuse if they have not also suffered child sexual abuse in an institutional context. Also, we do not accept that our Letters Patent allow us to consider redress for all of those who were in state care, who were child migrants or who are members of the Stolen Generations, regardless of whether they suffered any child sexual abuse in an institutional context.[54]

Thus, the Royal Commission acknowledged that there were serious justice issues that impacted care leavers, and that significant constituencies believed that they could and should include more than just sexual abuse in their consideration, but they considered themselves to be bound by the terms of reference, which they understood to bar a broader investigation, and concluded they had no power to consider topics not within their defined remit.

Ben Mathews, who called the terms of reference 'prudently drawn' shortly after their announcement, suggests that the particular harms related to the violation of taboos inherent in child sexual abuse are good reasons to treat child sexual abuse separately from other kinds of abuse.[55] Whether this justifies being treated separately in redress schemes is a normative argument – but it does not appear to be the

[50] Golding (n 44) 198.
[51] National Redress Scheme for Institutional Child Sexual Abuse Assessment Framework 2018.
[52] ibid.
[53] Royal Commission into Institutional Responses to Child Sexual Abuse, *Redress and Civil Litigation Report* (Commonwealth of Australia, 2015) 102.
[54] ibid, 6.
[55] Ben Mathews, 'Royal Commission Faces Challenges But Provides an Opportunity for Change' *The Conversation* (14 January 2013), theconversation.com/royal-commission-faces-challenges-but-provides-an-opportunity-for-change-11576.

Royal Commission's argument. By rooting their reasoning in the powers delegated to the Commission without making a normative argument, one can surmise that the Commissioners were not convinced that sexual abuse is 'the core transgression of childhood', requiring of separate treatment from other kinds of abuse, but were convinced that they were bound by their terms of reference.

IV. Truth-Telling: The Theory of the Royal Commission

The Royal Commissions Act 1902 provides royal commissions with significantly more coercive power than other legal systems,[56] at least with respect to production of evidence. Royal commissions have the power to acquire any documentary, physical or testimonial evidence that might exist and to require the testimony of any person in Australia.[57] The Act contemplates that royal commissions will appoint counsel to question witnesses appearing before them, and provides that this counsel, and counsel representing parties in interest, 'may, so far as the Commission thinks proper, examine or cross-examine any witness on any matter which the Commission deems relevant to the inquiry'.[58] By bringing to light all evidence commissioners and staff can identify, giving parties the opportunity to test that evidence in public, and ensuring as many points of view are heard as the commission deems relevant, a royal commission can, having earned public trust, establish a credible narrative of truth about an issue of public concern.

Australian royal commissions stand out among government inquiries for their strong powers to compel testimony, documents and other kinds of evidence.[59] Most legal proceedings can require the production of evidence, but royal commissions have power to compel production of evidence that is exempt in other legal systems.[60] A lawyer can be compelled to testify about matters otherwise subject to legal privilege.[61] People may not refuse to testify, produce a document or thing, or answer a question, even if doing so would incriminate that person or make someone subject to a penalty.[62] A spouse can be compelled to testify against their spouse.[63] Other statutory privileges, like the confidential professional relationships privilege, the religious confessions privilege, and the exclusion of evidence arising

[56] Nicholas Aroney, 'A Power "Singular and Eccentrical": Royal Commissions and Executive Power after Williams' (2014) 25 *Public Law Review* 99, 115.

[57] Royal Commissions Act 1902.

[58] ibid.

[59] Prime Minister and Cabinet Legislation Amendment (2017 Measures No 1) Bill 2017, 9 August 2017, Sch 5 – Royal Commissions.

[60] Australian Law Reform Commission (ALRC), *Making inquiries: a new statutory framework, Report 111* (October 2009).

[61] ibid, 17.11 (citing Royal Commissions Act 1902 (Cth), s 2(5)).

[62] *Sorby v Commonwealth of Australia* (1983) 46 ALR 237 (Gibbs CJ).

[63] ALRC (n 60) (citing *S v Boulton* (2006) 151 FCR 364, 387 (Black CJ dissenting)).

from a settlement of a dispute are not applicable in royal commissions.[64] Hearsay and opinion evidence is not excluded from the kinds of evidence a royal commission can consider.[65] The few limitations on the royal commission's coercive powers include: that statements made by a witness to a royal commission cannot be used against them in other proceedings; manufacturing secrets;[66] and that confidential matters can be withheld from the public to protect stakeholder or public interests where the commission deems necessary.[67]

In its *Interim Report*, delivered in 2014, the Royal Commission explained that, in order to 'bear witness to the abuse and trauma inflicted on children who suffered sexual abuse in an institutional context', the commissioners saw both public hearings and private sessions as necessary – one a more formal, public affair, aimed at establishing a public record, and the other a private, supportive setting aimed at ensuring they hear the stories of as many people as possible.[68] In response, Parliament passed legislation amending the Royal Commission Act to 'permit evidence to be given in "private sessions" "to facilitate the Commission's receipt of information from persons directly or indirectly affected by child sexual abuse in a manner less formal than a hearing"'.[69]

Testimony in private sessions is not formally considered 'testimony', and there is no threat of perjury in making a statement in a private session. Victims telling their stories did not have to be concerned that not remembering details, or not being able to prove the truth of their statements would subject them to any kind of consequence.

Shurlee Swain described the Royal Commission as being one of a group of inquiries that are 'marked by a shift in focus from the policy makers to the victims whose testimonies constitute the greater part of the evidence'.[70] Earlier inquiries are better 'understood as part of the process of establishing and then refining the various systems that provided "care" for children outside their families', or 'inquiries that respond to a particular crisis, investigating causes and suggesting remedies', which she called 'damage control'.[71] Although the Royal Commission was initiated under the same authorising legislation as earlier investigations, its chief purpose – 'to ensure that what happened to children in the past could never be allowed to happen again'[72] – reflects its place as a part of what Jeffrey Olick describes as an age of regret:[73]

[64] ibid, 17.127.
[65] ibid, 16.73 fn 85.
[66] ibid, 250; Royal Commissions Act 1902 (Cth), s 6DD.
[67] ALRC (n 60) ch 1.
[68] Royal Commission into Institutional Responses to Child Sexual Abuse, *Interim Report* (June 2014).
[69] Royal Commissions Amendment Bill 2013, s 1.4.
[70] Shurlee Swain, *History of Australian Inquiries Reviewing Institutions Providing Care for Children, report for Royal Commission into Institutional Responses to Child Sexual Abuse* (October 2014).
[71] ibid.
[72] 'Transcript: Read the PM's Full Statement on the Child Sex Abuse Royal Commission' *Newcastle Herald* (12 November 2012), www.theherald.com.au/story/969662/transcript-read-the-pms-full-statement-on-the-child-sex-abuse-royalcommission.
[73] Jeffrey K Olick, *The Politics of Regret: On Collective Memory and Historical Responsibility* (Routledge, 2007) 12.

> The practices of individualizing accusations of sexual abuse, discrediting witnesses and minimizing reporting in the interests of public morality were successful only while inquiries looked to experts rather than victims for the answers to the problems they were addressing. The inquiries since the late 1980s, which have actively sought survivor testimony, have broken open such silences. While residents of children's institutions had in the past been invited to give evidence before inquiries, their testimony was always corrupted by their status. The shift in focus is linked to the apology movement that has become increasingly evident across the Western world in the aftermath of World War II. Initially a function of recognizing and remembering the Holocaust, apologies have since spread to the impact of war, racial discrimination and, more recently, social wrongs.[74]

The Royal Commission's policy and research programme drew on information disclosed in public hearings, private sessions and written accounts. They heard from academics, policymakers and government representatives, non-governmental organisations, regulatory and advisory bodies, advocacy groups, and the general public through issues papers, consultation papers, roundtables, expert consultations, community forums, and public and private hearings. It published 11 issues papers, receiving (and making public) 621 submissions in response. It published five consultation papers about which 410 submissions were received and made public. It held seven public and 28 private roundtables, 44 commissioner-led community forums, and nine consultations with young people (three of which took place in youth detention centres).[75] The international journal *Child Abuse & Neglect*,[76] the Australian journal of Christian theology *St Mark's Review*[77] and the *Journal of Australian Studies*[78] all published special editions focused on the Royal Commission, and prominent journals in other disciplines published articles about the Royal Commission or relying on its findings.[79]

The Royal Commission was actively concerned with working in a culturally safe and appropriate manner with Aboriginal and Torres Strait Islander communities across Australia. They may not have always been successful in avoiding retraumatising people,[80] but there was significant effort and thought put into each step of the process. The Final Report explained that the Commission

> connected with a range of stakeholders in these communities including Elders; community members; land councils; Stolen Generations groups; Aboriginal health; legal

[74] Swain (n 70) 9–10.

[75] Royal Commission into Institutional Responses to Child Sexual Abuse (n 5) [3.3].

[76] (2017) 74 *Child Abuse & Neglect*.

[77] (2018) 245 *St Mark's Review*.

[78] (2018) 42 *Journal of Australian Studies*.

[79] See, eg, Kim Oates, 'The Royal Commission into Child Sexual Abuse: A Beginning, Not an End' (2018) 54 *Journal of Paediatrics and Child Health* 221; Keith L Kaufman et al, 'Recommendations for Preventing Child Sexual Abuse in Youth-Serving Organizations: Implications From an Australian Royal Commission Review of the Literature' (2019) 34 *Journal of Interpersonal Violence* 4199.

[80] Jane Bardon, 'Sexual Abuse Survivor Falls Through the Cracks, as Lawyers Accuse Governments and Institutions of Playing Hardball' ABC News (2 December 2018), www.abc.net.au/news/2018-12-02/child-sex-abuse-royal-commission-retta-dixon-redress-survivors/10573132.

> and children's services; and other Aboriginal and Torres Strait Islander community organisations, to obtain permission and build support for our work. We also worked with survivor groups from particular institutions, and held survivor gatherings or consultations in a number of regional and remote communities. Our Aboriginal staff were critical to reducing barriers to engagement and building trust.[81]

This concern was also reflected in its research agenda. The Royal Commission's Aboriginal Knowledge Circle collaborated with expert researchers to produce reports on Aboriginal and Torres Strait Islander children and child sexual abuse in institutional contexts.[82] One such report describes the ways that Indigenous children have been uniquely vulnerable to predation since the beginning of the settler-colonial project in Australia and concludes with its repeating Indigenous peoples' calls to be 'directly involve[d] … in any and all decisions that affect them and the lives of their families'.[83]

In addition to its thoughtful approach to serving Indigenous communities, the Royal Commission also employed culturally relevant and practical means to communicate effectively and compassionately with incarcerated people, people living with disabilities, children and young people, immigrant communities, older people, people experiencing homelessness and other vulnerable groups across Australia.[84] CLAN leader Leonie Sheedy praised the warmth and personal kindness she received from McClellan and Royal Commission staff, crediting them with earning the trust of her organisation's membership, and comparing them favourably to other legal authority figures:

> And one of our 80-year-old members said to him, 'What should we call you Sir?' … he said, 'You call me Peter'. And then he stayed with us in that garage for hours, answering all of our questions. How many judges have done that?[85]

With multiple means of electronic and personal connection, the Royal Commission's efforts to be informative, responsive and sensitive to community need were evident. These efforts were appreciated, as indicated by the standing ovations and loud applause that the commissioners and counsel assisting received in their final sitting and positive treatment in news and opinion articles.[86] Even those who

[81] Royal Commission into Institutional Responses to Child Sexual Abuse (n 5) [3.4.2].

[82] Telethon Kids Institute, 'Aboriginal and Torres Strait Islander Children and Child Sexual Abuse in Institutional Contexts' Report for the Royal Commission into Institutional Responses to Child Sexual Abuse (July 2017).

[83] ibid, 44.

[84] ibid, 44.

[85] Melissa Davey, '"They Had Nowhere to Hide": Abuse Survivors Praise Commission for Shaking Institutions' *The Guardian* (1 April 2017), www.theguardian.com/australia-news/2017/apr/01/nowhere-to-hide-abuse-survivors-praise-commission-shaking-institutions.

[86] Michael Salter, 'Royal commission provides a vital blueprint for justice for sex abuse victims – now it's time to act' The Conversation (15 August, 2017), theconversation.com/royal-commission-provides-a-vital-blueprint-for-justice-for-sex-abuse-victims-now-its-time-to-act-82491; Helen Pitt, 'Royal Commission's message to Australia' *The Sydney Morning Herald* (14 December 2017), www.smh.com.au/national/royal-commissions-message-to-australia-20171214-h04fin.html.

criticised the Royal Commission in other contexts wrote positively of its acting to benefit all former residents of government or religious institutions and going beyond their mandate in their advice with respect to records and record-keeping to ensure that their recommendations would benefit a wider population.[87]

The Royal Commission's research agenda was interdisciplinary, mixed-method and extraordinarily broad in scope.[88] It made major contributions to knowledge relevant to child abuse across disciplines. Aside from the unparalleled quantitative data and deep well of qualitative data made available to researchers, research produced new knowledge about the best ways to support children's testimony in court,[89] new understanding of stigma constituted in institutional settings,[90] new knowledge about patterns of reporting and convictions after delays in reporting child sexual abuse[91] and new insight into the influence of organisational culture on incidence of child sexual abuse.[92] But the Royal Commission did not just collect a library of evidence and fuel academic insight. It also sought expert and stakeholder opinion on the evidence in order to advise organisations and policy makers, and to change cultures across institutions and Australian society. To do this, it worked to weave the various sources together into a coherent narrative and slate of recommendations for changes to law, public policy, organisational policy, regulatory agendas and norms of interaction within child-serving organisations across Australia. Sarah Morton argues that the Royal Commission's efforts at translating the evidence and crafting recommendations for changes show promise as a model for reform in other areas of social life.[93]

Criminologist Michael Salter praises the Royal Commission for serving as a 'transitional space' between personal trauma and public understandings of child sexual abuse and thereby making new understandings and social change possible.[94] He brings up its non-adversarial and flexible procedures, crediting them with providing material for interspersing personal narratives alongside narratives of law or policy. Weaving together the personal with the legal in this way allowed the Royal Commission to serve as a 'transitional mechanism' that can be both

[87] Golding (n 40) 6–7.

[88] Sarah Morton, 'Getting Evidence into Action to Tackle Institutional Child Abuse' (2017) 74 *Child Abuse & Neglect* 111, 111–12.

[89] Becky Earhart et al, 'Judges' Delivery of Ground Rules to Child Witnesses in Australian Courts' (2017) 74 *Child Abuse & Neglect* 62.

[90] Kathleen McPhillips, 'Traumatic Isolation: Institutional Stigma and the Australian Royal Commission into Institutional Responses to Child Sexual Abuse' (2018) 20 *Health and History* 75.

[91] Judy Cashmore, Alan Taylor and Patrick Parkinson, 'The Characteristics of Reports to the Police of Child Sexual Abuse and the Likelihood of Cases Proceeding to Prosecution After Delays in Reporting' (2017) 74 *Child Abuse & Neglect* 49.

[92] Donald Palmer and Valerie Feldman, 'Toward a More Comprehensive Analysis of the Role of Organizational Culture in Child Sexual Abuse in Institutional Contexts' (2017) 74 *Child Abuse & Neglect* 23.

[93] Morton (n 88) 113.

[94] Michael Salter, 'The Transitional Space of Public Inquiries: The Case of the Australian Royal Commission into Institutional Responses to Child Sexual Abuse' (2020) 53 *Australian and New Zealand Journal of Criminology* 213, 213.

'personally and politically meaningful'.[95] Salter argues that this creates spaces for interaction between 'traumatized and non-traumatized systems of meaning' and a public discourse imbued with emotional depth.[96] The theory of justice through truth-telling filtered through the Royal Commission's use of procedure to ensure participation of people across Australian society.

V. Procedure of the Royal Commission

Alongside enrolling a professional cadre of judges, lawyers, counsellors and investigators, the Royal Commission designed procedures and collected evidence in ways that furthered the system's purpose in trauma-informed ways. Victims were provided with a variety of means by which they could tell their stories, express their opinions and otherwise engage with the process:

> A trauma-informed approach was adopted to the conduct of private sessions and surrounding processes. This meant we had to be aware of the diverse and far-reaching impacts of childhood trauma on survivors. We engaged people in ways that affirmed their experiences and responses while minimising interactions or processes that could increase their trauma.[97]

In private and public sessions, the Royal Commission received testimony of thousands of victims of sexual abuse. It sought and received comment from victims' advocates, experts, institutional representatives, past and present leaders, teachers, psychologists, other professionals and the public on a range of issues, including redress schemes, working with children checks, and institutional programmes for redress and accountability, receiving over 23,900 pieces of correspondence.[98] Many outside experts, concerned citizens, activists, family members and victims submitted reports and responses to calls for submissions to advise and contribute to the Royal Commission.

Like other royal commissions, the Royal Commission also had an adversarial component, especially in the public hearings. Watching the hearings live and reading transcripts of hearings I could not attend, the compassion and consideration counsel assisting the Royal Commission showed to victims who testified and the sharp rigour with which they treated senior (and formerly senior) officials in Catholic organisations are both notable. As Ian Bryce explains, 'Witnesses giving testimony include some accused of abuse (many are in jail) or (more often) accused of covering up abuse. Typically they get pressed and question somewhat aggressively by tenacious Council Assisting – it's good to see them squirm.'[99] At hearings

[95] ibid, 219.
[96] ibid, 226.
[97] Royal Commission into Institutional Responses to Child Sexual Abuse (n 5) 28.
[98] ibid.
[99] Ian Bryce, 'Child Abuse Royal Commission – a Personal Perspective' (2017) 126 *The Australian Humanist* 20, 20.

I attended, people there, some of whom told me they were victims, commented on their appreciation for seeing former officials like Brother Paul Nangle, who had been headmaster at St Patrick's College in Ballarat, challenged by authoritative Senior Counsel on his statements about not knowing or suspecting that children in his charge were being abused.[100]

As discussed above, the privilege against self-incrimination is not applicable in royal commissions, and while self-incriminatory testimony is not admissible against the speaker in a later proceeding, there is no limit on the use of testimony and evidence against any person or entity other than the speaker. Officials are aware that their testimony could be used against Church organisations, even if not against them personally. The testimony of notorious abuser Gerald Ridsdale highlights this dynamic. Having already admitted to more than 100 crimes against children and giving his testimony from prison, he maintained that he did not know or could not remember who knew about his abuse, why he was moved from parish to parish, and what diocesan officials supervising him did when they learned of his crimes. Officials and others who see their loyalty to the Church as paramount looked for ways to protect the Church, even when they had given up hope of the Church's protecting them in return. It is clear that he was seen as a hostile witness, who needed to be cajoled into admitting wrongdoing.[101] This is apparent in how questions were composed as well as in terms of the kind of testimony that the questions were designed to elicit. Treating Catholic officials with suspicion, combined with warm and supportive treatment of victims and Survivor advocates, added to a narrative that connected the Australian public's concern with victims and directed anger at the Church and its representatives.

Although many prosecutions were initiated as a result of the Royal Commission, the testimony provided to the Royal Commission primarily served as data to understand child sexual abuse in institutional settings as a social problem, and helped the Royal Commission to consider institutional accountability as a political problem. The trove of evidence and data provided by victims, witnesses, academics, researchers and advocates collectively formed the basis on which counsel assisting and the commissioners would test the evidence put forward by officials and others defending institutions that had failed the children in their charge. Commissioners gave institutional parties about whom negative conclusions were drawn the opportunity to respond, but also expressed serious concerns about the truthfulness of testimony of senior Catholic officials. The findings were devastating for the Church's reputation. Although observers had previously expressed their frustration at officials' testifying that they did not recall events or denials of awareness of

[100] See also Chris Johnston, 'Ballarat Christian Brothers headmaster "can't recall" abuse' The Age (23 February 2016), www.theage.com.au/national/victoria/ballarat-christian-brothers-headmaster-cant-recall-abuse-20160223-gn1kf1.html.

[101] Frank Brennan, 'Cardinal Pell, his lawyers and the Royal Commission' Eureka Street (22 November 2015), www.eurekastreet.com.au/article/cardinal-pell--his-lawyers-and-the-royal-commission.

abuse,[102] the Royal Commission's findings made clear that the commissioners had seen through protestations about memory and found the officials' lacking, thus affirming the feelings and perceptions of observers and victims alike.[103] The Royal Commission's focus on truth-telling allowed it to be flexible in how it collected evidence, using different kinds of evidence for different (and sometimes limited) purposes, in order to help the commissioners develop an holistic understanding of the social problem, and this depth of knowledge that they acquired and discussed in giving their findings carried significant weight with the Australian public.

VI. Logistics of the Royal Commission

There are significant practical benefits attributed to the Royal Commission. The wealth of data, research and knowledge that the Royal Commission collected and made available to researchers, policymakers and the public has informed Australian public discourse and policy relevant to institutional child sexual abuse. Its recommendations are largely endorsed by experts, and commenters are optimistic that successful implementation of the recommendations is likely to reduce rates of child sexual abuse in the present and future, increasing the likelihood that victims are believed and helped, and improving the quality and efficacy of that assistance. Most of its recommendations for organisations and governments have been adopted by governments and child-facing institutions across Australia.

The Royal Commission ultimately issued 400 recommendations for different Australian institutions, which are collated and presented in its final report.[104] These recommendations were broad in scope and ambitious in reach. It had recommendations for the federal Government, including the establishment of a national office for child safety, the development of a national framework to prevent child sexual abuse, and the creation of a portfolio overseeing policy relevant to childhood. It had recommendations for state and territory governments, including the adoption of policies and creation of agencies aimed at child protection, to take care to implement child protection policies in places of detention and other institutions engaged in child-related work, and to implement training and other programmes, in consultation with communities, to create the kind of cultural change required to truly protect children. It also had recommendations for non-government organisations, including the Catholic Church and other religious institutions. Among these was a recommendation that the rite of confession be modified to permit

[102] Konrad Marshall, 'Cardinal George Pell: Ballarat reacts to testimony characterised by memory loss' The Age (29 February 2016), www.theage.com.au/national/victoria/cardinal-george-pell-ballarat-reacts-to-testimony-characterised-by-memory-loss-20160229-gn65yi.html.

[103] Royal Commission into Institutional Responses to Child Sexual Abuse, *Report of Case Study No 28: Catholic Church Authorities in Ballarat* (Commonwealth of Australia, 2017).

[104] Royal Commission into Institutional Responses to Child Sexual Abuse, *Preface and Executive Summary* (Commonwealth of Australia, 2015).

(or require) a priest receiving a confession from someone who has abused a child or children to report the confession to secular authorities. This caused controversy in Australia and among Catholics around the world.[105]

The Royal Commission's recommendations were praised by experts in child protection like Joe Tucci and Monique Bom of the Australian Childhood Foundation, who approved of its demonstration of deep understanding that institutional child sexual abuse is more likely when: (1) 'those with power over children are not questioned or sanctioned'; (2) 'when that power is unchecked and perceived to be all pervasive'; and (3) 'when justice for the most vulnerable is replaced with institutional self-protection'.[106]

The Royal Commission's final report included a list of developments to law and policy across Australia that were put in place during the life of the Royal Commission in response to its previously released findings.[107] These included changes to law related to statutes of limitation, the duty of institutions to provide a safe environment for children, and provide litigants with a proper defendant, which meant abolishing the Ellis Defence. They also included new legislation implementing reportable conduct schemes, child safe standards, and modernised and simplified rules related to criminal sexual offenses relating to children.[108] New policies have been adopted by institutions across Australian social life: sporting, schools, religious organisations, scouting, medical facilities and residential care.[109] People were prosecuted as a result of evidence revealed to the Royal Commission. 'As of 31 July 2017, [the Royal Commission] had made 2,552 referrals to police, and police had laid charges in a number of cases.'[110] Pell himself was the subject of a prosecution that drew intense interest from the Australian public.[111]

Many of the practical outcomes attributed to the Royal Commission are likely to inure to the benefit of children and society today, and thus go beyond any form of redress or retribution that the other legal systems considered in this book are capable of. Real change and a better future for children is at the heart of what most victims want. Victims and experts largely agree that nothing can completely

[105] Olivia Colombo, 'Perspective: Seal of Confession Laws' *The Torch* (27 November 2019), bctorch.com/2019/11/27/perspective-seal-of-confession-laws; Frank Brennan, 'Circumscribing the Seal of the Confessional' *Eureka Street* (20 August 2018), www.eurekastreet.com.au/article/circumscribing-the-seal-of-the-confessional; Michael A Peters, 'Child sexual abuse: The final report of the Australian Royal Commission into institutional responses to child sexual abuse' (2019) 51 *Educational Philosophy and Theory* 233.

[106] Joe Tucci and Monique Blom '"These Were Terrible Years. No Love or Kindness, No Safety or Warmth". Reflections on the Outcomes of the Royal Commission into Institutional Responses to Child Sexual Abuse in Australia' (2019) 20 *Journal of Trauma Dissociation* 373, 377.

[107] Royal Commission into Institutional Responses to Child Sexual Abuse, *Volume 17: Beyond the Royal Commission* (Commonwealth of Australia, 2017).

[108] ibid.

[109] ibid.

[110] ibid, 45.

[111] Simon Buchen SC, 'The Acquittal of Cardinal George Pell' *Law Society Journal Online* (17 January 2023), lsj.com.au/articles/the-acquittal-of-cardinal-george-pell.

heal the trauma of child abuse or redress its harm, and thus a focus on effective prevention of future abuse is imperative. Prevention is an impact that matters. In this, the Royal Commission may prove itself to be the most responsive of the legal systems studied in the book. It has made actual improvement in the area those most impacted says is most important.

VII. Responsive or Autonomous: Evaluating the Royal Commission

Thus far, this chapter has presented a hopeful image of the Royal Commission – flexible procedures and a purposive approach allowed it to be attentive and responsive to the needs of Australia's diverse communities, and its narrative power shaped how the Australian public understands the problem of child sexual abuse in institutional settings. But the Royal Commission does have two significant weaknesses as a legal system. First, there is a remaining perception of inequity of treatment for people who suffering from abuse (of many kinds) while in the 'care' of state or religious organisations. Second, a royal commission has no authority to change policy – its power is limited to making findings and recommendations. The Royal Commission refused to even make recommendations on subject matters they understood as outside of their terms of reference.

Nonet and Selznick describe deference to authority and strict interpretation of the limits of delegated power as a defining feature of autonomous law:

> [Autonomous law], concerned with legal purity, keeps its distance from the political order and adheres to the rules without assuming responsibility for the consequences of enforcement. Repressive and responsive law are more interested in outcomes, and hence are more ready to deploy political resources.[112]

The reluctance to step outside defined limits to pursue substantive justice is a characteristic of autonomous law – keeping strictly to defined limits in order to maintain independence, and thereby, legitimacy.

Autonomous law roots may also be reflected in the Royal Commission's lack of power to ensure their recommendations get taken up. Royal commissions across sectors have issued well-researched reports with reasonable recommendations for addressing the problems identified in their terms of reference and seen those recommendations fail to be made into law or adopted as policy. Prasser and Tracy point out that royal commissions' work has been disregarded for over a century, including the very first royal commission on where to locate Australia's capital.[113] That commission recommended Albury and Tumut, just over 300 kilometres

[112] Philippe Nonet and Philip Selznick, *Law and Society in Transition: Toward Responsive Law* (Routledge, 2001) 93.

[113] Prasser and Tracey (n 19).

from where Canberra now sits.[114] In recent decades, Australians have seen royal commissions investigate Indigenous deaths in custody,[115] corruption in political arenas, public officials' response to bushfires, and a number of other important issues. Despite well-researched reports detailing recommendations for changes to law, policy or regulatory approaches, only some of the recommendations have been implemented.[116]

Royal commissions have never been understood to require parliamentary action, as Aroney summarises Brennan J's explanation:

> [W]hile the findings of a royal commission do not (and legally cannot) have direct legal consequences for any person's rights, duties or liabilities, they do have every potential to move the Executive to exercise its other undoubted powers in some form of governmental or ministerial response, such as the prosecution of an individual for an alleged commission of a crime or the introduction of a Bill into Parliament.[117]

When the Royal Commission was established, there was a great deal of hope about its potential, and when the Royal Commission issued its Redress Report and proposed scheme, outside of the equity concerns expressed within the Care-leaver community, it received broad praise. Timothy Jones wrote that:

> The commission constitutes the most sophisticated and thorough investigation yet into abuse within the Catholic Church globally. Its recommendations are breathtakingly bold. They provide the most comprehensive pathway so far, to redress and prevent abuse in an institution that has had endemic and catastrophic failures in this area.[118]

All state, territory and federal governments, and the major churches involved, have signed up for an official redress scheme, but the scheme (the 'Redress Scheme') that went into effect is not exactly what was recommended. It has been criticised for, among other things, capping the amount that can be awarded to a victim at a lower amount than recommended by the Royal Commission and denying financial compensation to victims convicted of certain crimes. Survivor advocacy groups criticise this restriction, pointing to the high rates of children abused in care, saying that if the officials in whose care children were placed had protected them from sexual and other forms of violence, the children may not have later committed crime.[119] This is particularly troubling given the 722 private sessions

[114] ibid.

[115] Thalia Anthony, 'Deaths in custody: 25 years after the royal commission, we've gone backwards' *The Conversation* (13 April 2016), theconversation.com/deaths-in-custody-25-years-after-the-royal-commission-weve-gone-backwards-57109.

[116] But see, Prasser (n 14) 639.

[117] Nicholas Aroney 'A Power "Singular and Eccentrical": Royal Commissions and Executive Power after Williams' (2014) 25 *Public Law Review* 99, 99 (citing *Victoria v Australian Building Construction Employees' and Builders Labourers' Federation* (1982) 152 CLR 25, 158–62 (Brennan J)).

[118] Timothy W Jones, 'Royal Commission Recommends Sweeping Reforms for Catholic Church to End Child Abuse' The Conversation (15 December 2017), www.theconversation.com/royal-commission-recommends-sweeping-reforms-for-catholic-church-to-end-child-abuse-89141.

[119] 'Child sex abuse redress scheme to cap payments at $150,000 and exclude some criminals' ABC News (26 October 2017), www.abc.net.au/news/2017-10-26/sex-offenders-to-be-excluded-from-child-abuse-redress-scheme/9087256.

held with Survivors in prisons, who could legitimately have expected that sharing their stories might mean that people (including themselves) would eventually have a means of redress. Although the Royal Commission listened to victims and heard their voices, without political will, if legislatures and courts fail to act on any of its recommendations, victims might reasonably ask what purpose it serves to be heard.[120]

Despite the best of intentions, the Redress Scheme's implementation has also fallen well short of Survivors' hopes. An independent review conducted in 2021 found that 'a significant and urgent reset' of the Redress Scheme was required.[121] A parliamentary inquiry in 2024 warned that, with a significant backlog and a surge in applications, 'Unless changes are made, some survivors could miss out on redress.'[122]

Royal commissions play an important, highly politicised role in Australian public life with the power to shape public opinion, influence legislative decision-making, and the potential to inspire tangible changes in legal and social orders across Australia. With few fixed features other than a remarkably strong subpoena power and the Government's role in appointment and defining terms of reference, they have been instituted to investigate the concerns of the day since Australia's federation. The authorising and governing legislation leaves appointed commissioners a great deal of flexibility in organising and conducting investigations, reflecting an understanding that royal commissions may investigate such a wide variety of topics that flexibility is desirable. Royal commissions often are tasked with investigating powerful entities, even though, as ad hoc mechanisms, they have little doctrine or procedure that carries through from one commission to the next.

Unlike the other systems discussed in this book, the Royal Commission is not meant to address the particular circumstances of individual actors, but to investigate and make recommendations for the problems of a society. Its purpose is political in the sense that it is intended to produce recommendations for changing policy, polity, people and institutions, in addition to a narrative of truth. The Royal Commission's final report reflects its view that the problem of child sexual abuse in institutional settings is structural and pervasive, that its impacts across society are profound, and that redressing harm, reforming legal process, helping victims, identifying risk factors, changes in policies and practices to prevent abuse, and other efforts to improve the future will take significant and sustained effort and

[120] Kathleen Daly and Juliet Davis, 'National Redress Scheme for child sexual abuse protects institutions at the expense of justice for survivors' The Conversation (7 March 2019), www.theconversation.com/national-redress-scheme-for-child-sexual-abuse-protects-institutions-at-the-expense-of-justice-for-survivors-112954.

[121] Robyn Kruk, *Final Report: Second Year Review of the National Redress Scheme*, www.nationalredress.gov.au/sites/default/files/documents/2024-08/final-report-second-year-review-national-redress-scheme.pdf.

[122] Christopher Knaus, '"Dangerous Crunch Point": Risk Abuse Survivors Will Be Denied Justice Due to Delays in Australia's Redress Scheme' *The Guardian* (27 November 2024), www.theguardian.com/australia-news/2024/nov/27/dangerous-crunch-point-abuse-survivors-risk-being-denied-justice-due-to-delays-in-australias-redress-scheme.

investment by stakeholders across society. Its recommendations, and the diverse array of actors and institutions called upon to institute change reflects a nuanced and comprehensive approach to a complex problem.

Responsiveness is so linked with flexibility that it bears repeating that flexibility alone is not sufficient. Responsiveness requires responsible, discriminate and selective forms of flexibility.[123] 'A responsive institution is not just flexible, it centres the normative and counter-domination impulses essential to its integrity while taking account of new forces in its environment.'[124] The Royal Commission's capacity to adapt its procedures to collect evidence in ways that respond logically to the incentives of different stakeholders demonstrates its purpose-centred and adaptive approach. The Royal Commission's responsiveness is a product of a broad purpose to improve Australia's response to child sexual abuse in institutional settings and intentional accommodation of people who might otherwise face challenges in engaging with a legal system. The stated intent of using the coercive and legal authority of a royal commission for the benefit of victims forms the basis the Royal Commission's commitment and capacity to counter defined forms of domination. Its discriminate and responsible approach to gathering sufficient evidence to test the truthfulness of officials while making efforts to protect victims from unnecessary trauma in providing their evidence demonstrates the purposive approach that suggest the Royal Commission was, at least, incipiently responsive.

[123] Nonet and Selznick (n 112) 77.
[124] ibid, 77.

7

Chapter 11: A Quasi-Responsive System

I. Introduction

Between July 2004 and December 2024, 28 Catholic dioceses, eight archdioceses and four religious orders in the US filed for protection under Chapter 11 of the US Bankruptcy Code (together, the 'Diocesan Debtors'), all of them seeking to use the process to help them manage debt arising from claims related to child sexual abuse.[1] One of these is the Diocese of Gallup, which filed for Chapter 11 protection in the Bankruptcy Court for the District of New Mexico in November 2013.[2] At the time the diocese filed, there were 13 lawsuits pending against the diocese, some before Arizona courts, and others in Navajo courts. Some of these were about to enter into a trial phase. Another is the Franciscan Friars of California, which had operated many of the schools where Apache and Pueblo children were abused, and which filed in the Northern District of California on 31 December 2023, halting then-ongoing litigation in California, Arizona and New Mexico.[3]

Local journalist Elizabeth Hardin-Burrola commented that, in its timing, the Diocese of Gallup's filing was like other Diocesan Debtor cases: 'When a diocese is coming very close to a court date, they tend to file for bankruptcy because it stops all the lawsuits against it, and that's exactly what happened.'[4] Robert Pastor, a plaintiffs' lawyer who brought many of the cases against the diocese, agreed, saying that Bishop Wall, 'has done what we see all the other bishops do – they run to bankruptcy perhaps seeking financial protection, but more importantly, protection from the discovery process'.[5]

[1] 'Bankruptcy Protection in the Abuse Crisis' BishopAccountability.org, www.bishop-accountability.org/bankruptcy.htm; Marie T Reilly, 'Catholic Dioceses in Bankruptcy' (2019) 49 *Seton Hall Law Review* 871, 'Appendix A: Case Information'.

[2] Chapter 11 Petition, *In re: Roman Catholic Church of the Diocese of Gallup, a New Mexico Corporation Sole* (United States Bankruptcy Court District of New Mexico, No 13-13676-t11, 12 November 2013).

[3] Chapter 11 Petition, *In re: Franciscan Friars of California, Inc*, No 23-41723 (Bankr ND Cal), 31 December 2023).

[4] 'Dark Canyon Part Nine: The Diocese of Gallup' KSFR (14 December 2017), www.ksfr.org/dark-canyon.

[5] Mary Wisniewski, 'America's Poorest Diocese Set to File for Chapter 11 Bankruptcy Amid Sex Abuse Claims' NBC News (4 September 2013), www.nbcnews.com/news/us-news/americas-poorest-diocese-set-file-chapter-11-bankruptcy-amid-sex-flna8C11071499.

Bishop Wall, in a declaration filed on the first day of the bankruptcy proceeding, tried to stave off criticism.[6] First, he deflected blame for child sexual abuse by arguing abuse occurred in the decades before his tenure – 'Many of the claims related to acts that occurred in the 1950's, 1960's and 1970's' – and explaining how programmes the diocese adopted in more recent years work to reduce the likelihood of future abuse or increase the chances of it being discovered and reported.[7] Wall also put forward the diocese's relative poverty and emphasised the programmes it provides to communities within its boundaries, explaining that, 'the services provided by the Diocese to the communities within its geographic territory are particularly important given the number of parishioners who are living below the poverty level'.[8] Wall also argued that, contrary to the opinions of Pastor and Hardin-Burrola, the diocese's purpose in filing was to

> reach a resolution that will take into account the important interests of all these constituencies and provide compensation to those harmed, provide counselling and spiritual services to those who have been harmed and still allow the Diocese to continue ministering to those within its community.[9]

These arguments are typical of Diocesan Debtors across the US. Facing criticism that filing for bankruptcy protection is a means of avoiding responsibility for child sexual abuse, the Archdiocese of Milwaukee said it filed so that it could ensure equitable treatment among victims and 'allow the Church to move forward on stable financial ground, focused on its Gospel mission'.[10]

A former priest now advocating for Survivors discounts arguments such as Wall's and the Archdiocese of Milwaukee's, commented that whatever they say, filing for bankruptcy is meant to protect the assets of the dioceses:

> [T]he Bankruptcy Code, like all matters of civil law, has been used as a shield and a sword by Roman Catholic bishops … [so] the only reason they would employ bankruptcy is because it was to their benefit. So even if it was the best pastoral option for survivors, they would only do it if it was best for them, personally. This is not for the people. This has never been about Survivors, they only thing they choose is self-defense.[11]

The discrepancy between bishops' claims to be filing bankruptcy in order to treat victims fairly and critics' observations that the filing allows dioceses to avoid facing victims in a court of law seems irreconcilable. Indeed, the equitable purposes bishops are claiming may seem entirely unlikely to victims who have dealt with obstruction from bishops in the lawsuits that precipitated the filing.

Like the other legal systems studied in this book, Chapter 11 has its own philosophical underpinnings, its own processes and procedures, its own way of

[6] 'Declaration of Bishop James S. Wall in Support of Chapter 11 Petition and First Day Motions' *In re Roman Catholic Church of the Diocese of Gallup*, No 13-13676 (Bankr DNM, 12 November 2013).

[7] ibid, [VI.C-E.].

[8] ibid, [VI.F.].

[9] ibid, [VI.I.].

[10] *Listecki v Official Committee of Unsecured Creditors*, 780 F 3d 731 (7th Cir, 2015) (citation omitted).

[11] Interview with anonymous advocate, 2015.

resolving conflicts, and its own logics and logistics. Like other systems, it also exists in relationship with other legal and social orders, outside of which it cannot be understood. The Diocesan Debtors would never have filed bankruptcy if not for their liability in tort, and the plans developed and implemented through the bankruptcy process are generally funded through insurance policies, and the intricacies of insurance law impact the Diocesan Debtor cases in a range of ways. However, unlike tort or even insurance law, bankruptcy law is not usually thought of as something with much relation to wrongdoing or responsibility for personal harms.

As with the previous three chapters of this book, each of the following sections will discuss an aspect of Chapter 11. Section II will discuss the twin purposes of bankruptcy in the US system, and how Chapter 11, designed to respond to the complexities of corporate failure, has become a place for dioceses to address their liability for child sexual abuse. Section III, on theories of bankruptcy, reviews literature on Chapter 11, with a focus on how flexibility and consensus-building are embraced by those who argue for Chapter 11 to have a normative agenda toward equity and substantive justice. Section IV combines the discussion of doctrine and procedure. Insolvency processes, including Chapter 11, can resemble administrative processes, and it is difficult to disentangle doctrine and procedure. But the section will discuss how Chapter 11 facilitates collective action and shifts stakeholder incentives, allowing for realignment of interests. It will also discuss what a relational theory of bankruptcy reveals about Chapter 11 as a legal system. Following that will be a discussion of logistics in Chapter 11, including how and when claims are submitted, and the non-monetary provisions that the Diocesan Debtors have agreed to. The chapter will conclude with a discussion of Chapter 11's incipient responsiveness – a conclusion that, at the outset, might seem surprising!

II. Purpose of Chapter 11

A means of addressing unsustainable debt is necessary in any economic system that allows for credit, and systems for addressing debt have existed across social, geographic and cultural boundaries for most of recorded history.[12] Bankruptcy in the US is said to have two primary purposes: (1) to give severely indebted persons the opportunity for a 'fresh start', allowing for renewed economic activity; and (2) to ensure that creditors are treated equitably.[13] The Bankruptcy Code, codified as Title 11 of the United States Code, sets out a number of different chapters that allow individuals and organisations to liquidate, restructure and shed debt, or accomplish numerous other goals.[14] This chapter will focus on Chapter 11,

[12] See eg Theodore C Albert, 'The Insolvency Law of Ancient Rome' (2006) 28 *California Bankruptcy Journal* 365.

[13] See eg *Grogan v Garner*, 498 US 79 (1991); *Local Loan Co v Hunt*, 292 US 234 (1934).

[14] *Bankruptcy Code*, 11 USCS prec § 101; but see Katherine Porter and Deborah Thorne, 'The Failure of Bankruptcy's Fresh Start' (2006) 92 *Cornell Law Review* 67.

under which all of the Diocesan Debtors have filed for protection. Chapter 11, titled 'Reorganization', is principally used by corporations to restructure debts and emerge again in a healthier financial position.[15] Restructuring through Chapter 11 'has no single template but typically involves the refinancing and discharge of debt, sale of certain lines of business, entity reconfiguration, and changes in management and personnel and firm governance'.[16]

Chapter 11, as a system for corporate reorganization, establishes judicial oversight over the process through which heterogenous claims against a debtor corporation from all jurisdictions where the debtor may operate are resolved. This avoids inefficiencies, increasing the potential for the corporation to emerge from Chapter 11 as a going concern while maximising the potential recovery for all stakeholders. Stakeholders include any party with an interest in the debtor or the estate, such as: (1) secured creditors, who may hold liens on real or personal property; (2) unsecured creditors, some of which may hold priority claims, including bondholders, trade creditors, banks, victims in tort (like the Survivors in the Diocesan Debtor cases), employees, taxing authorities, government licensing or regulatory bodies; (3) holders of equity interests in a corporate debtor; (4) the US Trustee, tasked with overseeing the administration of bankruptcy cases, (5) the attorney general of a state in which a debtor charitable organisation is chartered; (6) in the Diocesan Debtor cases, parishioners; and (7) the debtor and related parties, among others. Each stakeholder has their own interests – their ability to pursue their interests in bankruptcy depends on both non-bankruptcy and bankruptcy law. Within each group of stakeholders, there are varying degrees of priority, some of which are set out in the Bankruptcy Code, and others by private agreement or other applicable law. Chapter 11 is designed to facilitate the negotiation and implementation of an all-encompassing plan of reorganization, solving problems of market failure by anticipating complexity and providing opportunities for collective action by otherwise vulnerable stakeholders.

The Diocesan Debtors are examples of mass tort bankruptcies, which were not contemplated by the people who drafted the Bankruptcy Code, but have become a well-known type of corporate reorganization. Mass tort bankruptcies are filed by corporate entities that, but for tort liability, would not be in financial trouble. Although Chapter 11 might be said to have developed a jurisprudence of mass tort, the focus of this jurisprudence is on procedure. Most mass tort bankruptcies are resolved with the creation of trusts to which the debtor and its insurers contribute money. Trusts are administered and claims paid out to tort victims by trustees appointed through the stakeholder-approved plan. Award amounts are based on a matrix agreed to through the plan process. The prototypical mass tort case is an asbestos manufacturer. Section 524(g) of the Bankruptcy Code, added after the first cases of asbestos manufacturers, provides that companies facing claims related to

[15] Bankruptcy Code (n 14) § 1101 et seq.

[16] Kathleen G Noonan, Jonathan C Lipson and William H Simon, 'Reforming Institutions: The Judicial Function in Bankruptcy and Public Law Litigation' (2019) 94 *Indiana Law Journal* 545, 548.

asbestos may use the process to transfer their liabilities and channel all future claims to a trust.[17] It provides that the bankruptcy court can issue 'channelling injunctions' shielding non-debtor third parties from suit, including insurance companies that contribute to the trust. Although section 524(g) is, by its terms, applicable only to cases involving asbestos, the process has been extended to a number of other contexts.[18] Medical device manufacturers like the AH Robins Corporation, maker of the Dalkon Shield, pharmaceutical companies like Purdue Pharma and other corporations responsible for mass tort have been approved to create trusts to address their liability while shielding future operations from ongoing claims and litigation.[19] Like other mass tort cases, in every Diocesan Debtor case that has a confirmed plan, the plan sets up a trust funded by the diocese and its insurers from which victims are paid after their claims are reviewed and assessed by a trustee.[20] The trusts are set up in largely the same ways as trusts are set up in other mass tort cases.

Both purposes of bankruptcy, the fresh start and equitable treatment of creditors, are generally served by preservation and maximisation of value in Chapter 11 cases. By separating a profitable business from liability that would deter any new investment and, ultimately, leave all stakeholders worse off, mass tort processes preserve the value of an ongoing business while maximising the total financial recovery available for the entire community of tort victims. However, bankruptcy scholars Jonathan Lipson and Pamela Foohey critique an over-emphasis on value preservation[21] as Chapter 11's purpose, arguing that the US Supreme Court, in *Czyzewski v Jevic Holding Corp*, endorsed a bankruptcy jurisprudence in which process is as important as outcome – that participation and procedural integrity are key factors in the ensuring the equitable treatment of creditors.[22] Chapter 11, Foohey argues, 'is designed to produce negotiated settlements rather than litigated judgments'.[23] This view would cast the process by which decisions are made as critical to Chapter 11 purpose as a fresh start and equitable treatment for creditors are for bankruptcy generally.

III. Theories of Bankruptcy

Since the 1990s, two competing camps have dominated the literature on theories of bankruptcy: proceduralists and traditionalists.[24] These two groups have different

[17] See eg Stephen J Carroll et al, 'Asbestos Litigation' (RAND Institute for Civil Justice, 2005) ch 6.

[18] See, eg, *Menard-Sanford v Mabey (In re AH Robins Co)* 880 F 2d 694 (4th Cir, 1989).

[19] Peta Spender, 'Blue Asbestos and Golden Eggs: Evaluating Bankruptcy and Class Actions as Just Responses to Mass Tort Liability' (2003) 25 *Sydney Law Review* 223.

[20] See eg Marie T Reilly, 'Catholic Dioceses in Bankruptcy' (2019) 49 *Seton Hall Law Review* 871.

[21] Pamela Foohey, '*Jevic*'s Promise: Procedural Justice in Chapter 11' (2018) 93 *Washington Law Review Online* 128, 129 (discussing Jonathan C Lipson, 'The Secret Life of Priority: Corporate Reorganization After *Jevic*' (2018) 93 *Washington Law Review* 631.

[22] ibid, 129.

[23] ibid, 134 (quoting Jonathon C Lipson, 'The Shadow Bankruptcy System' (2009) 90 *Boston University Law Review* 1609, 1620).

[24] Susan Block-Lieb, 'The Logic and Limits of Contract Bankruptcy' (2001) 2 *University of Illinois Law Review* 503, 508–09.

views about the relative importance of the fresh start and equitable treatment of creditors as the purposes of bankruptcy. Proceduralists would say the value at stake in bankruptcy is the functioning of the overall economy, and conclude that the equitable treatment of creditors should be the primary goal, while traditionalists would point to norms of forgiveness and rehabilitation, and tend to focus more on the fresh start. Proceduralists, often affiliated with the law and economics movement, argue that the purpose of bankruptcy should be efficiency and wealth maximisation. They argue the 'fresh start' concept should not apply to corporate debtors, and generally discount the importance of the normative ideal of forgiveness in connection with business activity.[25] Traditionalists tend to see Chapter 11 proceedings as rehabilitative and centred on preserving the value of a business as a going concern, and they defend the process as pragmatic and adaptable in furthering those purposes. One traditionalist view of bankruptcy sees it as a normative mechanism offsetting the harsh downsides of a free-market system.[26] This view lends itself well to the image of debtors who cannot pay their debts as penitents seeking absolution through sacred ritual. But traditionalists argue that the efficiency and equity of bankruptcy processes is also better for broader society. The Bankruptcy Code, to traditionalists, is intended to give stakeholders the flexibility to pursue pragmatic and equitable solutions tailored to each debtor's particular circumstances.[27]

Critics of Chapter 11 often point to the flexibility that traditionalists exalt to argue that it allows the process to be drawn out, disadvantaging creditors who must wait years before receiving a fraction of what they are owed.[28] Now-Senator Elizabeth Warren argued that this flexibility combined with the participatory nature of decision-making in Chapter 11 is, on the contrary, an effective way to maximise the value of a troubled firm and distribute that value fairly among disparate groups of stakeholders.[29] She pointed to evidence that corporate restructuring through the Chapter 11 process: (1) is relatively efficient at sorting those firms for which a financial restructuring is possible from those for which it is not; (2) facilitates a restructuring process, encouraging efficiency and value preservation; and (3) is at least as good, if not better, for most creditors, than a more rigid process that strips control of firms from managers and enforces a strict absolute priority rule.[30] She argued that flexibility and encouragement of consensus-building in the Chapter 11 process incentivises cooperative and mutually beneficial behaviour among stakeholders.[31]

[25] Douglas G Baird, 'Bankruptcy's Uncontested Axioms' (1998) 108 *Yale Law Journal* 573, 576–77.

[26] David A Skeel, Jr, 'Vern Countryman and the Path of Progressive (and Populist) Bankruptcy Scholarship' (1999) 113 *Harvard Law Review* 1075, 1119.

[27] See eg, Harvey R Miller and Shai Y Waisman, 'Is Chapter 11 Bankrupt?' (2005) 47 *Boston College Law Review* 129, 146–50.

[28] See eg, Lynn M LoPucki, 'The Trouble with Chapter 11' (1993) *Wisconsin Law Review* 729, 747–49.

[29] Elizabeth Warren, 'Bankruptcy Policymaking in an Imperfect World' (1993) 92 *Michigan Law Review* 336, 344–73.

[30] Elizabeth Warren, 'The Untenable Case for Repeal of Chapter 11' (1992) 102 *Yale Law Journal* 437.

[31] ibid.

Proceduralists, on the other hand, 'envision[] bankruptcy law as a set of rules approximating the contractual terms to which, at the time credit is extended, a creditor and debtor would agree should govern in the event of the debtor's insolvency'.[32] This is called the contract theory of bankruptcy. The contract theory of bankruptcy is linked to the idea of the 'creditors' bargain', which posits that best way to understand the purpose of bankruptcy is finding resolutions that would 'mirror the agreement one would expect the creditors to form among themselves were they able to negotiate such an agreement from an *ex ante* position'.[33] Bankruptcy serves these interests when it is primarily understood as a means of 'ensur[ing] that fights among creditors and other investors of capital do not accelerate a firm's liquidation'.[34]

A contract theory of bankruptcy has little to say about tort creditors like victims in Diocesan Debtor cases. Robert Rasmussen and David Skeel would address this by privileging tort claimants ahead of consensual creditors, even if that increases the cost of credit in the market, because 'it [would] force[] corporations to take into account the injuries their behavior imposes on third parties'.[35] Tort claimants should represent, for Rasmussen and Skeel, an exception to the general rule of 'deference to private contracting'.[36] 'Economic theories of bankruptcy … require that the state establish the appropriate treatment of nonconsensual creditors and that this rule cannot be altered by contract.'[37] In practice, however, tort claimants are typically treated as unsecured creditors, with the same priority as trade creditors, and any punitive damages treated with lower priority still. As Kathleen Noonan and colleagues note, Chapter 11 'often glosses over differences in the normative salience of the underlying conduct giving rise to claims'.[38]

Not every theorist falls cleanly into one group or the other – there is diversity among bankruptcy theorists and scholars.[39] Some argue that both proceduralists and traditionalists are missing the point – that corporate reorganisation is not moved by academic theories alone but by the realities of the situations, including legal manoeuvring.[40] This third perspective might be seen as a call for a new legal

[32] Robert K Rasmussen, 'An Essay on Optimal Bankruptcy Rules and Social Justice' (1994) 1 *University of Illinois Law Review* 1, 1.

[33] Thomas H Jackson, 'Bankruptcy, Non-Bankruptcy Entitlements, and the Creditors' Bargain' (1982) 91 *Yale Law Journal* 857, 860.

[34] Baird (n 25) 578.

[35] Robert K Rasmussen and David A Skeel, Jr, 'The Economic Analysis of Corporate Bankruptcy Law' (1995) 3 *American Bankruptcy Institute Law Review* 85, 87.

[36] ibid.

[37] Rasmussen (n 32) 19, citing Robert K Rasmussen, 'Debtor's Choice: A Menu Approach to Corporate Bankruptcy' (1992) 71 *Texas Law Review* 51, 67.

[38] Kathleen G Noonan, Jonathan C Lipson and William H Simon, 'Reforming Institutions: The Judicial Function in Bankruptcy and Public Law Litigation' (2019) 94 *Indiana Law Journal* 545, 564.

[39] See eg, Jonathan C Lipson, 'Debt and Democracy: Towards a Constitutional Theory of Bankruptcy' (2007) 83 *Notre Dame Law Review* 605.

[40] Karen Gross, 'A Response to J.J. White's Death and Resurrection of Secured Credit: Finding Some Trees but Missing the Forest' (2004) 12 *American Bankruptcy Institute Law Review* 203, 213; George W Kuney, 'Hijacking Chapter 11' (2004) 21 *Emory Bankruptcy Developments Journal* 19, 30.

realist (NLR) approach to bankruptcy scholarship – one that considers doctrinal, purposive, theoretical, procedural and practical aspects of bankruptcy systems. Bankruptcy lawyers in practice need to understand and engage with legal theories, the structures of the Bankruptcy Code and Federal Rules of Bankruptcy Procedure, the economic and business realities their clients face, their clients' understandings of the process, and the logistics of practice. One of the key points of agreement between traditionalists, this third perspective and elite corporate restructuring professionals is the value of flexibility of process.[41] Flexibility is so central to the practice that it is even noted in an obituary for a high-profile, elite corporate restructuring lawyer.[42]

IV. Chapter 11 Doctrine and Procedure

A. Collective Action and Shifting Incentives in Chapter 11

A bankruptcy case is initiated by the filing of a petition in the bankruptcy court. The instant that a bankruptcy case is filed, nearly all kinds of proceedings ongoing or contemplated against a debtor are stayed, or paused.[43] This is the effect of the 'automatic stay'. If a creditor, regardless of jurisdiction or forum, attempts to collect or otherwise act on a pre-petition debt, any such act is void or voidable, and bankruptcy judges may hold creditors in contempt or even award punitive damages for wilful violations.[44] This is what Hardin-Burrola and Pastor were referring to when expressing frustration with the pending cases against Gallup being halted – plaintiffs go from being in control of tort proceedings they brought to being potentially subject to serious penalties for taking any action against the diocese, including before the court in which their claims are pending.

It is understandably frustrating for Survivors not to be able to present their arguments in the forum of their choice. However, the substance of the law applicable to their claims does not change. Claims arising under statutory, contract, tort or other regimes are still governed by those regimes, although the bankruptcy plan in Chapter 11 determines the way the claims will be addressed. Once the debtor/tortfeasor has filed for bankruptcy, instead of continuing with their claims in state court, creditors file claims with the bankruptcy court. Creditors with any kind of

[41] Skeel (n 26). Skeel's tribute to Vern Countryman (one of the giants in American bankruptcy law) examined the history of how this alignment came to be and explained why it is an unusual alignment.

[42] Michael J de la Merced, 'Harvey R. Miller, Renowned Bankruptcy Lawyer, Dies at 82' *New York Times* (27 April 2015), www.nytimes.com/2015/04/28/business/harvey-r-miller-renowned-bankruptcy-lawyer-dies-at-82.html.

[43] Bankruptcy Code (n 14) §362.

[44] ibid, §362(k); *In re Shamblin*, 890 F 2d 123, 125 (9th Cir, 1989); *In Re Schwartz*, 954 F 2d 569, 572 (9th Cir, 1992); but see Bankruptcy Code (n 14) § 362(d).

claim against a debtor that relates to pre-petition activity have the right to submit a claim – whether that claim is of a determined amount or is contingent, whether the claim is acknowledged or disputed, and whether or not the creditor has filed a lawsuit time of filing. A claim's validity is determined under state law, while bankruptcy law controls its collectability.[45]

Filing for protection under Chapter 11 effects a shift in the balance of power between stakeholders.[46] While formally the duties of a corporation's directors and managers do not change, a debtor may no longer take any action outside of the ordinary course of business without approval of the bankruptcy court.[47] As the process continues toward the ultimate goal of confirming a plan of reorganization, creditors in a position to have some, but not all, claims paid have a particular kind of leverage. If the plan proposes to change the rights of any class of creditors or stakeholders, it requires their consent in order to move forward.[48]

'The genius of bankruptcy reorganization law is that it provides incentives for debtors and their creditors, notwithstanding their disparate interests, to reach a voluntary agreement on the terms of the restructuring.'[49] By limiting the extent to which a plan proponent can divide classes of claims and requiring consent from impacted parties, the Bankruptcy Code impacts parties' relative power – incentivising stakeholders to consider and reconsider the bargaining positions and settlement possibilities available. Unlike a typical civil case, in which parties are either plaintiffs or defendants, and therefore adversaries, in a Chapter 11 case the various stakeholders have interests that may align, or not, with other stakeholders in what might best be described as a game of three (or even four) dimensional chess.

Understanding themselves to be 'courts of equity', bankruptcy courts have the discretion to be open to creative solutions to the problems facing stakeholders, and most judges strongly encourage parties to find common ground through whatever solution might best suit their needs. The process of proposing and confirming a plan of reorganization draws on the perspective of the various stakeholders – they can pursue their goals according to their own incentives and interests, including forming new alliances or purchasing positions that allow for additional input in decision-making.

The shifting balance of power, in a typical case, works to benefit a creditor (or group of creditors) known as the 'fulcrum',[50] whose votes on a plan of reorganization are most crucial to its confirmation.[51] One strategy of professional distressed

[45] See eg *United States v Whiting Pools, Inc*, 462 US 198 (1983).

[46] Lipson (n 23) 1632.

[47] Bankruptcy Code (n 14) § 363.

[48] ibid § 1126(c).

[49] Steven L Schwarcz, 'Sovereign Debt Restructuring: A Bankruptcy Reorganization Approach' (2000) 85 *Cornell Law Review* 956, 959.

[50] See eg, Sam Badawi and Matthew Rose, 'Considerations for Holders of the Fulcrum Claim in a Chapter 11 Proceeding' (2022) 36 *Insights: The Corporate & Securities Law Advisor* 25.

[51] Jonathan C Lipson, 'Governance in the Breach: Controlling Creditor Opportunism' (2010) 84 *Southern California Law Review* 1035, 1039.

investors is to invest in multiple tranches of securities in companies in financial straits in order to ensure they obtain the fulcrum security.[52] If they ultimately hold sufficient amounts of a fulcrum security, they enjoy a particular leverage over a debtor seeking to confirm a plan of reorganization – and if the strategy works, the investors will own all or a significant percentage of stock in the company going forward, having purchased it for the price of the fulcrum security and the professional services required to navigate the Chapter 11 case.[53]

Plan confirmation requires the affirmative vote of a majority (two-thirds in amount and one-half in number) in a class of claimants whose claims are impaired by the plan.[54] The primary constituencies whose acceptance of a plan structure the plan proponent[55] will seek are those holding fulcrum securities – especially those who might be willing to accept something other than cash in return for their support for the plan. A creditor class that is partially in the money may be willing to accept stock, bonds or other interests, or to otherwise be willing to accept something other than cash to compensate for claims not being paid in full on the date on which they are owed. Creditors and other stakeholders who know that they would be paid in full or who know they will receive nothing have less of an incentive to negotiate, and less influence over the plan's confirmation.

In the Diocesan Debtor cases, we can see that Chapter 11 changes leverages. It shifts the interests of dioceses, insurers and victims. For dioceses themselves, they are likely to ultimately pay less to each Survivor/claimant through a plan of reorganization than they otherwise would have been required to pay if all, or even some portion, of the Survivors were to bring successful civil claims. They also avoid dragging out the bad optics of constantly opposing Survivors in litigation as the cases come forward. Instead, the bankruptcy proceeding allows them to resolve all the claims against them, gives them leverage to convince insurance companies to make large contributions, and changes the tone and purpose of the applicable law. All of this in addition to the court not spending any time considering whether or not the claims are true, or even if the diocese was negligent.

Insurance companies are incentivised to settle in mass tort Chapter 11 cases by the prospect of establishing a finite cap on the amount they owe, a channelling injunction prescribing future claims on the policies held by the dioceses, and no longer being obligated to pay for litigation defence. Because bankruptcy offers finality in exchange for a single cash payment, insurance companies are incentivised

[52] ibid.

[53] Michelle M Harner, 'Trends in Distressed Debt Investing: An Empirical Study of Investors' Objectives' (2008) 16 *American Bankruptcy Institute Law Review* 69, 70 (citing Jonathan M Landers, 'Reflections on Loan-to-Own Trends' (2007) 26 *American Bankruptcy Institute Law Review* 1 and 44–46 and 'The Vultures Take Wing: Investing in Distress' *The Economist* (31 March 2007) 77–78); Lipson (n 23) 1632.

[54] Bankruptcy Code (n 14) § 1121.

[55] While most plans are proposed by debtors, once a period of exclusivity expires (or is terminated for cause), creditors and other stakeholders are allowed to propose plans, often plans that compete with the debtors. Bankruptcy Code (n 14) § 1121.

to contribute a significant sum to fund a trust. Insurance companies benefit from not funding litigation and arguing about coverage on a case-by-case basis.

Creditors' committees, controlled by Survivors in the Diocesan Debtor cases, are critical to securing votes to confirm a plan, and therefore have a fair degree of leverage in negotiations on the terms of the plan, especially compared to the leverage a single plaintiff would have in an individual tort action. Individually, this may seem rights-insensitive, but collectively and pragmatically, it improves average outcomes for Survivors and shifts limited resources away from contestation and transaction costs and toward compensation payments while allowing Survivors to insist on enforceable non-monetary concessions (discussed below).

In tort cases brought by Survivors against Catholic organisations, specific knowledge produced can impact whether future cases will be covered by insurance policies. The mere threat of an unfavourable factual finding can have important effects on stakeholder behaviour – institutions take measures to avoid those findings, even at cost of money or reputation. In Gallup, the diocese filed for bankruptcy shortly before trials began in cases where the fundamental issue was the diocese's level of knowledge about a priest's tendency to abuse. A jury or judge's factual finding that the diocese knew or should have known that Charles Hageman was likely to be abusing children would have limited the ability of the diocese to resist future claims, and potentially lead to punitive damages. It might also have impacted their insurance coverage. This sequence of events might be interpreted as the diocese seeking to avoid a determination of fact not just unfavourable to their legal position, but one which risks their insurance coverage. The diocese's reluctance to release records of its priests, preferring to protect its records at the cost of other priorities in negotiating a settlement, could support this interpretation. By filing for bankruptcy protection, the diocese of Gallup was able to avoid a full accounting of its knowledge about the priests who abused children within the diocese. The avoidance of scandal surely plays a role in the diocese's desire to avoid a full accounting, but it is important to also consider how insurance shapes litigant incentives.

The resolution of disputes between dioceses and insurance companies by bankruptcy courts was crucial to confirming plans in the Tucson, Fairbanks, Oregon Jesuits, Wilmington, St Paul and Minneapolis, and Gallup cases, among others. In Gallup, the most notable insurance issue arose around New Mexico Property and Casualty Insurance Guaranty Association's (NMPCIGA) role as an appointed receiver in the liquidation of the Home Insurance Company, which had issued policies to the Gallup diocese between 1965 and 1977. NMPCIGA is an entity created by New Mexico law to ensure payment and avoid financial loss to claimants or policyholders as a result of the insolvency of an insurer. NMPCIGA argues that the relevant policies did not cover 'bodily injury that is either expected or intended by the insured'.[56] Pointing to complaints and claims that the diocese

[56] 'New Mexico Property and Casualty Insurance Guaranty Corporation's Statement in Connection with November 10, 2015 Status Conference' *In re Roman Catholic Church of the Diocese of Gallup*, No 13-13676-t11 (Bankr DNM, 9 November 2015).

'knew or should have known' of the abusive tendencies of Hageman and others, NMPCIGA argued that the policies do not cover harms incurred when the diocese knew or should have known of habitual offending.

The local *Gallup Independent* published an editorial using arguments grounded in Christian theology[57] and pointing to NMPCIGA's argument about not covering claims when the diocese knew or should have known of the abuse as 'a classic example of why the public frequently views both lawyers and insurance companies with similar distaste'.[58] In civil cases, insurance companies are generally less vocal or visible, as they tend to pay for litigation defence, and their interests (in denying liability and, if there is liability, paying as little as possible), align with those of the defendant. The Diocesan Debtor cases not only realign insurance company interests by incentivising them to settle and put a finite limit on liability. They also make the companies' participation more visible than it is in civil litigation.

In Gallup, the parties ultimately settled, with NMPCIGA paying USD1,850,000 in exchange for a channelling injunction in the plan of reorganization.[59] The victims also received a priority claim of USD3,750,000 in the Home Insurance Corporation's liquidation proceeding, the proceeds of which would flow to victims through the trust. Whether the public criticism influenced the settlement, or a simple cost–benefit analysis that settling was in each stakeholder's best interest, the Chapter 11 process did sever the mutuality of interest between the insurer and the debtor, and led to new incentives for all stakeholders. This does not mean the insurer's interests are necessarily aligned with those of victims, but it realigns the playing field. Chapter 11 is not a binary, zero-sum contest. It is a multi-stakeholder-negotiated process where stakeholders' interests are realigned in ways that allow for new alliances or strategies to be sought or employed.

In the Diocesan Debtor cases, not only do we see Survivors, as a group, having a key role in the process through the statutory committee, but by severing the interests of insurers and debtors/tortfeasors, instead of a two-party contest between an individual Survivor and the diocese backed by an insurance company, we see a three-party negotiation. All parties are incentivised to conclude the process as soon as possible to avoid lawyers' fees – the insurance companies because they pay for their own attorneys, the debtor/diocese because they pay for their own and the committee's lawyers, and the committee because the more spent on lawyers, the less available for recovery. All parties are also incentivised to ensure that the plan is at least minimally fair to all parties with a vote in the process – it would be a waste of time to promote a plan that has no chance of being confirmed. In general, so long as most stakeholders act in good faith, a Chapter 11 plan is only confirmed when most stakeholders agree that they would be better off, or in the same position, under the

[57] Editorial, 'Taking the low road in diocese bankruptcy' *Gallup Independent* (23 November, 2015) (citing *Proverbs* 22:22, 'Do not exploit the poor because they are poor and do not crush the needy in court').

[58] ibid.

[59] 'Exhibit H to Plan of Reorganization' *In re Roman Catholic Church of the Diocese of Gallup*, No 13-13676-t11 (Bankr DNM, 21 April 2016).

plan than they would be if the debtor were to be liquidated. This does not mean that all stakeholders are happy with the plan, but that they agree it is preferable to other options available in the circumstances.

Survivors in Diocesan Debtor cases usually, as a collective, hold the fulcrum position – and the opportunity to negotiate a creative settlement as a part of the plan. This is a kind of substantive legal responsiveness that puts Survivors in a position where they have power that matters. In Chapter 11, the plan negotiation and confirmation process incentivises stakeholders to work together to find ways of resolving their disputes. It is not uncommon for creative solutions to emerge through this process.

In a typical bankruptcy case of a for-profit corporation, a creditor holding the fulcrum security might opt for stock, convertible debt, security interests or some form of compensation other than cash or a simple promise to pay cash. This is the goal for distressed debt investors, who want to end up with a controlling equity stake in return for their discounted investment in risky bonds. In a mass tort proceeding involving a for-profit company, the plan can provide for all equity of the ongoing company to be held by the trust funding victim recovery, so tort victims, as a group, are essentially the new owners of the company.[60] In the Diocesan Debtor cases, of course, many of these creative forms of compensation are not available. Dioceses and religious orders do not have stockholders, and Survivors are not likely to be interested in any security interests they might have to offer. Further, because most victims' claims are not yet expressed in a fixed amount owed (the amount owed is in dispute and contingent on settlement or judicial resolution), the compensation scheme must anticipate a process of evaluating victim claims. Victims, therefore, can be anticipated to exert what power they may have to shape the form of claims evaluation and to find alternate forms of compensation, in addition to pushing for larger contributions to the trust established for their benefit. The confirmed plans in Diocesan Debtor cases all include non-monetary forms of compensation, and reports about the confirmation processes evidence that committee members were pushing for these measures.[61] These non-monetary forms of compensation will be discussed below in section C.

B. Lessons Learned: Relationality and the Diocesan Debtor Cases

Lipson's 'Bargaining Bankrupt: A Relational Theory of Contract in Bankruptcy' describes a theory of bankruptcy that accounts for concerns about relationships

[60] See generally Meredith Edelman, 'Corporate Moral Insolvency: Lessons from Purdue Pharma' (2024) *Griffith Law Review* 1.

[61] Stephanie Innes, 'Diocese Abuse Victims Speak as Bankruptcy Case Nears End' *Arizona Daily Star* (+ 10 July 2005); Elizabeth Hardin-Burrola, 'Diocese to Accept Liability, Apologize?: Reorganization Plan Includes Amends for Sex Abuse Victims' *The Gallup Independent* (14 May 2016).

between more and less powerful actors.[62] Basing his argument on Ian MacNeil's relational theory of contract, he called this a relational theory of Chapter 11, arguing that bankruptcy judges should pay attention to the relationships among the relevant parties as they consider whether settlements should be approved, and notes that a relational theory of contract in bankruptcy would 'ask courts to focus on' agreements between creditors, investors, and debtors (or other parties) made at the expense of weaker stakeholders.[63] A relational theory of contract calls for contract terms to be understood in terms of the social, cultural and political context in which they are agreed, and that this understanding should impact their interpretation as well.[64] Relational contract theory sees ongoing relationships between actors as inherently relevant to considerations of whether discrete instances, whether breaches or settlements, are fair.[65] In adapting that theory to situations involving violence and disparate power relationships, Tamara Kuennen argues for giving decision-makers the authority to override stakeholders' decisions when a relational analysis indicates that the less-powerful party is being coerced.[66]

Lipson points to relational concerns with 'interpersonal relations across many dimensions, including bargaining leverage, the effect of contracting on third parties, and the efficacy of formal versus informal legal mechanisms',[67] and argues that these concerns are under-theorised in the corporate reorganization context. He suggests that a relational theory of corporate restructuring would consider the 'repeat players',[68] including distressed investors, bankruptcy professionals and bankruptcy judges, and the important roles they play in Chapter 11 cases. A relational theory of Chapter 11 would take into account the advantages that repeat players and professionals gain through experience and ongoing relationships as well as how the Chapter 11 process impacts relationships of power between debtors, creditors and other stakeholders. A relational perspective is also in line with an NLR approach to understanding law in that both are concerned with how processes actually work as well as broader social goals.

The Chapter 11 bar is small, and smaller still is the group of professionals who work on mass tort proceedings. The professionals involved in the Diocesan Debtor cases tend to be repeat players from a small number of law firms, accounting firms and other professionals. These professionals understand how to use the flexibility of the Bankruptcy Code to benefit their clients, but also seek to maintain their

[62] Jonathan C Lipson, 'Bargaining Bankrupt: A Relational Theory of Contract in Bankruptcy' (2016) 6 *Harvard Business Law Review* 239, 275.

[63] ibid, 275.

[64] ibid, 244.

[65] Tamara L Kuennen, 'Private Relationships and Public Problems: Applying Principles of Relational Contract Theory to Domestic Violence' (2010) *Brigham Young University Law Review* 515, 596.

[66] ibid, 596.

[67] Lipson (n 62) 269.

[68] See eg Marc Galanter, 'Why the "Haves" Come Out Ahead: Speculations on the Limits of Legal Change' (1974) 9 *Law & Society Review* 95.

reputations within the small community of repeat players in major bankruptcy cases. They have learned a great deal about the particularities of child sexual abuse and religious organisations in bankruptcy. Among them are lawyers from Pachulski Stang Ziehl & Jones LLP, a well-respected boutique corporate restructuring firm which has acted as counsel for the committees of creditors in 17 of the Diocesan Debtor cases. Dioceses, Survivors and insurers all have access to counsel with specific knowledge about the relevant issues and who have developed relationships with each other. In the 20 years since dioceses started filing bankruptcy, the relationships between professionals have, in at least some cases, helped facilitate consensual settlements. Survivors and their counsel learned to ask for administrative, procedural or otherwise non-financial kinds of relief, including time to tell their stories in court. Professionals' experience with other Diocesan Debtor cases has taught them that 'providing Survivors with a voice early in the case will build trust in the Court, the process, and enhance prospects for a timely and fair global settlement that Survivors can support'.[69]

Not all of the lessons have benefited Survivors. Dioceses learned to separately incorporate parishes under state law, to support assertions that the property parishes used belong to those parishes and avoid the property being used to fund recoveries. When the first few dioceses filed for bankruptcy in 2004–2007, litigation on questions of whether property belonged to dioceses or parishes was frequent and the subject of a number of discussions in law reviews.[70] Between 2006 and 2012, many dioceses across the US began to reconfigure their corporate status and move assets to other corporate entities, prompting some critics to argue that these manoeuvrers were cynical attempts to avoid paying victims of child sexual abuse.[71] Parishes are separately incorporated in most Diocesan Debtor cases filed after 2007. Later cases, like that of the Archdiocese of Milwaukee, saw litigation about whether or not transfers of property made in the years before the bankruptcy filing were fraudulent transfers made for the purpose of defeating creditors legitimate claims against the estate.[72]

[69] The Official Committee of Unsecured Creditors' Motion to Authorize a Status Conference for the Presentation of Survivor Statements, *In Re The Roman Catholic Bishop of Sacramento*, No 24-21326 (USBC ED California) Docket 924, 2.

[70] See eg Mark E Chopko, 'An Overview on the Parish and the Civil Law' (2007) 67 *The Jurist* 194; Catharine Pierce Wells, 'Who Owns the Local Church? A Pressing Issue for Dioceses in Bankruptcy' (2004) 29 *Seton Hall Legislative Journal* 375; Jo Renee Formicola, 'The Further Legal Consequence of Catholic Clerical Sexual Abuse' (2007) 49 *Journal of Church and State* 445; Nicholas M Gaunce and Robert Luther III, 'Deliver Us From Evil: Why Bankruptcy Judges May Properly Rely on the Free Exercise Clause & RFRA to Protect Church Property from the Grasps of Tort-Creditors' (2008) 43 *Valparaiso University Law Review* 641; Christina Davitt, 'Whose Steeple Is It? Defining the Limits of the Debtor's Estate in the Religious Bankruptcy Context' (2005) 29 *Seton Hall Legislative Journal* 531.

[71] Jack Lyons, 'Diocese Come Under Scrutiny as they Change Legal Structures' Crux (23 January 2020), www.cruxnow.com/church-in-the-usa/2020/01/dioceses-come-under-scrutiny-as-they-change-legal-structures.

[72] *Listecki v Official Committee of Unsecured Creditors*, 780 F 3d 731 (7th Cir, 2015).

C. Bar Dates, Non-Monetary Provisions and the Logistics of Chapter 11

In Chapter 11 cases, courts establish a 'bar date' before which claims against the estate arising from any time before the 'petition date' (the day the bankruptcy case was filed) must be filed or be barred from being enforced. Mass tort cases sometimes have provisions for people who have a claim based on events that happened pre-petition but which, for some reason, cannot be submitted before the bar date. In some Diocesan Debtor cases, people who were abused pre-petition, but whose claims are tolled or otherwise cannot be brought before the bar date, are represented by a future claims representative. Despite this representative, those who do not file claims by the bar date will usually not be entitled to the same recoveries as those who do.

The process of filing a claim in bankruptcy is much simpler and less emotionally fraught than bringing a lawsuit. The claim form does not require the claimant to provide much detail other than the existence of a claim, any required live testimony is before a limited audience, and the adjudication process is significantly less formal. That being said, the bar date period is relatively short, and the diocese is unlikely to be aware of all the people who have a claim against it, and so giving public notice and informing people of what they need to do if they have a claim is important. Bankruptcy courts usually require debtors to directly inform anyone who the debtors have reason to believe might have a claim, as well as posting advertisements in newspapers, in public places, and sometimes on the radio or Internet, but it is likely that some percentages of victims are never made aware of the requirement that they must file a claim with the bankruptcy court before the bar date and lose their opportunity. Even if they are made aware of the bar date, some may not have the resources or capacity to determine that the bar date applies to them, obtain the correct form, fill it out properly and return it to the bankruptcy court before the bar date. While bankruptcy makes some of the logistics of seeking compensation easier than tort, it does not eliminate logistical difficulties entirely. And the timing of the bar date makes compliance with the remaining logistical requirements especially critical.

Given what we know about the nature of child sexual abuse, we can assume that not all victims who might hold claims have come forward in any of the Diocesan Debtor cases. Some of these are people who were made aware of the bar date and yet, for whatever reason, have not come forward. Others are aware that they were abused but not aware that they had a claim, or not aware of the bar date, or not aware of how the bankruptcy filing and bar date affected their rights. Some, of course, have their own reasons to not pursue claims.

In Gallup, notice was provided directly to those already participating in a legal process involving the diocese, and to those who the diocese had reason to believe might have a claim. Public notice was provided by purchasing advertising in or issuing press releases to regional and local publications, purchasing advertising on local radio stations that broadcast in English, Navajo and Spanish, and by posting physical notices in 'certain locations that are located in the extremely remote areas, but may be close to one of the Parishes, including such locations as public health centers, post offices, and all Navajo Chapter Houses'.[73] When the diocese filed, there were 13 tort actions pending against it. By the time the bankruptcy case ended, there were claims filed on behalf of 57 people, most of whom never previously filed a claim in any other forum.[74] Despite any flaws with the notification process, it is reasonable to conclude that at least some of the 44 people who submitted claims to the bankruptcy court but never brought a tort action might have only come forward because the diocese filed for Chapter 11 protection.

In May 2024, Hardin-Burrola wrote to me of her concerns about the Franciscan Friars case, which had filed on the last day of 2023 in California. She was concerned that, although she knew the religious order had been responsible for a number of abusers sent to the White Mountain Apache Reservation, she had not seen much information about the case.[75] Checking the docket showed that the judge had set 19 July 2024 as the bar date, and while notice was to be posted in relevant counties in Arizona and New Mexico, and public notice in some local newspapers, there was no provision to send notice to any of the Indigenous peoples on whose land abusers had worked – not to the White Mountain Apache Tribe or any of six other nations that might be impacted. I advised her to reach out to the United States Trustee, the lawyers representing the Franciscans and the lawyers representing the committee of unsecured creditors. On 3 July, 2024, *The National Catholic Reporter* published her article in which she noted how the lack of notice to Indigenous governments and newspapers that serve local communities on and near reservations 'seemed particularly jarring' as the USCCB had, on 14 June, released a 'Pastoral Framework for Indigenous Ministry' that acknowledged a 'need for "healing and reconciliation" between Native communities and the church'.[76] She wrote:

> Just days after the bishops' document was released and NCR posed those questions, an attorney for the Franciscans advised the court they would be requesting additional public notice for the seven tribes, along with an extended bar date deadline of Aug. 30.[77]

Without Hardin-Burrola's familiarity with the places and patterns of abuse in and around the Diocese of Gallup and her willingness to call attention to a lack of

[73] Motion for an Order Fixing Time for Filing Proofs of Claim, Approving Claim Forms, and Approving Manner and Form of Notice, *In re Roman Catholic Church of the Diocese of Gallup*, No 13-13676-t11, 15.

[74] Elizabeth Hardin-Burrola, 'Diocese of Gallup to File Bankruptcy: Mounting Clergy Sex Abuse Legal Claims Spark Chapter 11 Reorganization' *The Gallup Independent* (3 September 2013) 1 and 5.

[75] Personal communication from Elizabeth Hardin-Burrola to Meredith Edelman.

[76] Elizabeth Hardin-Burrola, 'Franciscan Friars of California Ask to Extend Abuse Claim Deadline' *National Catholic Reporter* (3 July 2025), www.ncronline.org/news/franciscan-friars-california-ask-extend-abuse-claim-deadline.

[77] ibid.

notice, the bar date might never have changed, and any number of victims might not have been notified of the proceeding at all.

In addition to financial recoveries, every Diocesan Debtor case that has a confirmed plan of reorganization has non-monetary provisions included in that plan. These provisions are different in each case, but among them are requirements for private and public apologies, the institution of educational and other programmes intended to help prevent future abuse, funding of therapy or other mental health services, public disclosure of records related to abusive priests, changes to policy and public statements of regret. Some of these public statements include very specific requirements. In the plan confirmed with respect to the Diocese of Wilmington Delaware, for example, the bishop was required to issue a written statement of gratitude for Survivors who have spoken about abuse suffered as minors.[78]

Non-monetary agreements in plans, while they carry the trappings of the kind of remedy many victims are seeking, do not carry the moral condemnation that comes with a criminal conviction or a determination of liability in a civil action. In Gallup, the judge allowed victims to speak at the confirmation hearing, where they spoke of the pain and harm that had come their way because of being abused and then ignored by priests and leaders in the diocese.[79] But the judge's rulings confirming the plan and closing the case centred on whether or not the requirements of the Bankruptcy Code had been met and not the abuse that caused the liability and, ultimately, the bankruptcy filing.

None of the plans in the Diocesan Debtor cases has exactly the same list of non-monetary provisions as any other, but, over time, the list has tended to grow, with later plans usually including most or all of the provisions in earlier plans, and sometimes new provisions. This is evidence of responsiveness. Despite their differences, most of the plans include requirements such as: that the bishop (or other highest authority in the organisation) personally provide apologies to Survivors; that bishops travel to parishes where abusive priests worked in order to listen to Survivor stories and make public apologies; that schools and parishes post plaques condemning abuse; and that diocesan printed materials (websites, magazines, bulletins and similar outlets) include acknowledgement of abuse and responsibility-taking, publish Survivor testimonies and provide information on accessing diocesan and outside resources.

Over time, progress has been made in getting Diocesan Debtors to produce their records, an issue of contention in many cases. At the confirmation hearing for the Diocese of Gallup's plan of reorganization, Survivors, including members of the creditors' committee, explained that they reluctantly supported the plan, deeply disappointed that Gallup diocese had not agreed to release personnel

[78] Diocese of Wilmington, 'Non-Monetary Settlement Undertakings' (2019), www.cdow.org/non-monetary-settlement-undertakings.

[79] Elizabeth Hardin-Burrola, 'Bishop Apologizes: Bankruptcy Judge Confirms Reorganization Plan' *The Gallup Independent* (22 June 2016).

records.[80] As discussed in chapter one, the Archdiocese of Santa Fe agreed in 2022 to create an 'Abuse Document Archive' at the University of New Mexico, and this was hailed as 'a unique part of the settlement agreement negotiated by a panel of survivor representatives and not called for by similar settlements in other states'.[81] Two years later, a 'publicly available university archive of accused priest files and related abuse documents' was one of a list of 11 non-monetary provisions agreed to by the Archdiocese of New Orleans and the committee of unsecured creditors representing Survivors in its bankruptcy case.[82]

In Chapter 11, once a plan is confirmed, the bankruptcy court typically retains jurisdiction until all the terms of the plan are implemented. This means that the court has the power to directly enforce non-monetary provisions made part of a plan.[83] In an action in tort, an agreement to non-monetary terms in a settlement is essentially treated as a contract between two parties, and so a victim arguing that a diocese violated the terms would generally have to initiate a new lawsuit in order to enforce its terms. Disputes about the sufficiency of the Diocesan Debtors' implementation of the non-monetary provisions can, in theory, be resolved more efficiently than disputes about the implementation of a settlement agreements in most other contexts.

In practice, the efficacy of the non-monetary agreements has varied significantly, and in Gallup, some observers argued that bad faith of the diocese undermined the agreements' value to Survivors. A member of the creditors' committee explained that the Diocese had taken aggressive postures, strongly resisting every attempt to get it to take responsibility. 'We were hitting the wall. There was this huge resistance for any little thing that came up. Whether it was one filing, whether it was a paper, whether it was a definition, or a timeline. We were fighting the Church at every turn.'[84]

The plan in Gallup required, among other things, that:

> The Bishop will personally visit each operating Parish or Catholic school in which abuse is alleged to have occurred or where identified abusers served, with a schedule to be published at least thirty (30) days in advance of each meeting (including by posting on the Diocese's website, posting in the Parishes, publishing in the Parish bulletins, publishing in the Voice of the Southwest, and by reasonable notice to all Tort Claimants of any such meetings), inviting all known survivors of abuse in that Parish or geographical area to attend and shall provide a forum/discussion during his visit to address questions and comments. The Diocese shall provide a telephone number and email address for parties to contact on a confidential basis in order to schedule a meeting.

[80] ibid.

[81] Phaedra Haywood, 'Judge OKs Archdiocese of Santa Fe Settlement of $121Million in Clergy Abuse Cases' *Santa Fe New Mexican* (29 December 2022).

[82] Pachulski Stang Ziehl & Jones, 'Archdiocese and Official Committee of Unsecured Creditors Agree to Nonmonetary Provisions' (7 November 2024), www.pszjlaw.com/newsroom-news-436.html.

[83] See eg *Gomes v Roman Catholic Church of the Dioceses of Tucson* (*In re Roman Catholic Church of Diocese of Tucson*), BAP No AZ 07-1409 (9th Cir BAP, 2008).

[84] 'Dark Canyon' (n 4).

> The Bishop shall be available upon reasonable notice to have a private conference with any Tort Claimant or any other person that informs the Diocese that he or she was sexually abused by clergy, religious or employees of the Diocese.[85]

Although these and other requirements appeared similar to those in other plans, they did not contain deadlines by which they were required to be accomplished. Fighting the committee at every step had given the diocese the power to decide its terms for complying with the non-monetary provisions.

A few months after the plan was confirmed, on 28 September 2016, *The Gallup Independent* published an editorial criticising Bishop Wall for not attending a panel discussion held at a local theatre in Gallup after a screening of the movie *Spotlight*, and noting that the bishop had yet to begin complying with the requirement to hold healing services.[86] '[B]y skipping the invitation, Gallup's bishop missed a perfect opportunity. He missed the opportunity to show the public he truly is a courageous spiritual leader, worthy of the position he holds.'[87] The diocese's director of communications responded in the same issue, explaining the bishop had attended a retreat during the week before the event, and was busy with 'administrative duties' on the day of the event.[88] The first of the required healing services was held in November 2016 at the cathedral in Gallup.[89] This was not the end of concern in Gallup with the diocese's compliance with non-monetary provisions of the plan. Through 2017, the diocese announced and postponed several healing services:

> One service in February was postponed for more than a year because of an "oversight" by the bishop's staff, which scheduled the service on the same evening as the bishop's Mardi Gras fundraiser. The fundraising party was a top priority, and clergy abuse survivors were a low priority.[90]

In November 2017, Hardin-Burrola invited me to attend one of the healing services, 'to see how the bishop reads from his notebook in a monotone voice'.[91] I attended a service in Shiprock, in the Navajo Nation, which consisted of Bishop Wall and a local priest reading prepared statements, some singing of religious hymns and scripted prayer. After the service, the bishop was available in a small room for people to speak with him privately. *The Gallup Independent* published an editorial on 20 April 2018, reflecting on the healing services 'held at nearly 40 Catholic parishes across the diocese in Arizona and New Mexico'.[92] It criticised

[85] 'Exhibit R to Plan of Reorganization' *In re Roman Catholic Church of the Diocese of Gallup*, No 13-13676-t11, (Bankr DNM 21 April 2016).

[86] 'Editorial and Letter to the Editor Response' *The Gallup Independent* (28 September 2016).

[87] ibid.

[88] ibid.

[89] Elizabeth Hardin-Burrola, 'Diocese to Begin Services for Sexual Abuse Survivors Saturday' *The Gallup Independent* (17 November 2016).

[90] Editorial, 'The Gallup bishop's upside-down priorities' *The Gallup Independent* (31 August 2017).

[91] Email from Elizabeth Hardin-Burrola to Meredith Edelman (8 November 2017), 'Re: Gallup Independent Nov. 2, 2017 Editorial: Hard lessons, truths for Sisters of the Blessed Sacrament'.

[92] Editorial, 'Diocese's healing services reflect a slipshod bishop' *The Gallup Independent* (20 April 2018).

Wall for offering religious services rather than a 'forum/discussion during his visit', as had been required by the plan.[93]

V. The Incipient Responsiveness of Chapter 11

Selznick described autonomous law as rule-centred, while 'Responsiveness begins with *outreach and empowerment*.'[94] Autonomous systems rely on doctrine to maintain the separation between law and politics, whereby decision-making is reduced to a process of analysing events according to defined rules. Responsive law should not have rigid, inflexible doctrine – it should be purposive and flexible, and substantive justice, rather than rigid conformance with black-letter law, should be the driving motivation of decision-making:[95]

> The capacity of law to deliver justice depends on the range of interest it acknowledges. All must have effective (as well as formal) access to the legal system, and the law must be open to new claims of right. In this century we have seen substantial movement in both directions. Labor and civil rights legislation; legal services for the poor; environmental and consumer protection: all have greatly expanded the reach of justice.[96]

Bankruptcy judges overseeing mass tort cases, including the Diocesan Debtors, have sometimes commented that Chapter 11 is a poor fit for responding to corporate wrongdoing. Chapter 11 is a process for corporate reorganization, and bankruptcy courts do not have the authority to make factual findings about misconduct underlying the claims in tort that precipitate a mass tort bankruptcy. The bankruptcy court has no legal authority to condemn the wrongfulness of a religious organisation placing people they knew were likely to abuse children in positions of authority. Chapter 11 is designed to facilitate stakeholders' negotiated restructuring of a corporation which, despite the lack of vindication for victims, creates opportunities for participation by realigning the relationships and incentives of various corporate stakeholders. Chapter 11 places Survivors in a position where, collectively, they have real leverage in decision-making. Furthermore, the relationships developed and lessons learned by professionals with experience from multiple Diocesan Debtor cases has led to positive developments. Although the bankruptcy judges might be right that Chapter 11 is a poor fit for addressing corporate wrongdoing, the forum does allow for collective action, and in the Diocesan Debtor cases, this has meant enforceable agreements to apologise, implement policy changes and disclose records. A poor fit might still demonstrate possibilities for how a better fitting system might function.

[93] ibid.
[94] Philip Selznick, *The Moral Commonwealth: Social Theory and the Promise of Community* (University of California Press, 1992) 465.
[95] Selznick (n 94) 467–70.
[96] ibid, 465.

Chapter 11's promise comes from bankruptcy's inclusive, negotiated process for decision-making, which resembles Selznick's description of responsive law, even as its embedded purposes decidedly do not conjure a fulsome vision of substantive justice for victims of corporate wrongdoing. Bankruptcy law's dual goals of a fresh start for debtors and equitable treatment for creditors, while frequently in tension with each other, are both largely justified in terms of public policy and overall economic benefit. The nearly exclusive focus on economic concerns means that bankruptcy courts are ill-equipped to address moral accountability, and many believe the process allows corporations who access it to avoid meaningful justice. Unlike the Royal Commission, the commencement of the diocese of Gallup's bankruptcy proceeding was met by dismay from those in the Survivor movement who heard of it. People saw it as a way of trying to avoid responsibility. Chapter 11 is designed to absolve corporations of financial debt, not hold them accountable for having allowed abusers to prey on vulnerable children or any other kind of corporate wrongdoing.

Nevertheless, the proliferation of bankruptcy cases resulting from mass tort, whether asbestos manufacturers, medical device companies, energy companies, pharmaceutical companies, scouting and sporting organisations, or the Diocesan Debtors themselves has led to the development of a jurisprudence of mass tort. Between this jurisprudence and Chapter 11's existing processes for creditors, there are real advantages in Chapter 11 for tort victims. As victims in a mass tort case occupying the 'fulcrum' position, Survivors in the Diocesan Debtor cases have leverage to secure both financial and non-monetary concessions. By severing the interests of insurance companies and the dioceses they issued policies to, multi-party negotiation and more creative settlement arrangements become possible, often to the benefit of victims.

Bankruptcy law may be pragmatically driven toward something resembling substantive justice, but it is hardly the emotionally intelligent justice that attends to victim vindication that would characterise a truly responsive system. This system designed to forgive financial debt is not necessarily well-equipped to apportion moral condemnation. Although religious ideas of forgiveness may underly bankruptcy theory, forgiveness is reconfigured from a moral emotion to a financial fact. Heather Strang's research shows that apology only matters when it is perceived as 'sincere apology',[97] and the criticisms of Bishop Wall's required healing services make clear his apologies were not perceived as sincere by everyone. A forced apology is likely to be perceived as less sincere than a gift of apology that is volunteered out of a sense of remorse. Masses of healing may not contribute as much to true healing when victims know they are compelled by order of a bankruptcy court, or when they are conducted in ways that undermine victim healing. Although the process may have facilitated agreement on a plan, it may have done so at the cost

[97] Heather Strang and Lawrence W Sherman, 'The Practice of Restorative Justice: Repairing the Harm: Victims and Restorative Justice' (2003) *Utah Law Review* 15.

of victims having their day in court, of hearing an authority condemn the actions of a wrongdoer. Settlement may have come at the cost of moral accountability.

At the end, bankruptcy law is purposive, and while it demonstrates some responsive characteristics in facilitating constructive and participatory decision-making, its purposes include a fresh start for the debtor and the equitable division of property among creditors, not the establishment of a narrative of truth or the allocation of responsibility for grievous harm. A more responsive system, with the production of justice as a purpose, would concern itself with establishing a narrative of truth and to find ways of repudiating anti-social or harmful behaviour – it would provide victims with their day in court and the potential of vindication.

8

Lessons on Responsive Law and Corporate Accountability

I. Summary of Book and Introduction to Chapter

Selznick argued that 'justice requires a responsive legal order'[1] and that responsiveness requires legal systems to be purposive in seeking substantive justice. There are a number of ways one might compare or analyse legal systems and how they approach dispute-resolution and other social or legal problems. One might consider rates of compensation for victims, rates of case resolution or measures of stakeholder satisfaction.[2] These kinds of studies consider, essentially, the outputs of legal systems. My focus is on the character of legal systems. Chapter two introduced my framework to evaluate legal systems as repressive, autonomous or responsive, based on Nonet and Selznick's articulation of those three concepts.[3] It explained how purpose, theory, doctrine, procedure and logistics – different aspects of legal systems –serve as variables within the framework. Purposes of legal systems and the legal theories that bring these purposes to life are artefacts of social orderings, developed over time as products of public imagination, professional reasoning and the interests of powerful stakeholders. Doctrine is not static, but drafted, changed and interpreted by people living within social orders. Procedure and the logistics of practice are the work and creation of lawyers and judges, while the logistics of pursuing or defending actions are deeply dependent on social and physical positioning of actors within social orders. The framework for responsive law I have developed in this book is designed to take these different aspects into account in order to determine the overall character of legal systems. This final chapter will add to the theory of responsive law and refine the framework based on the learnings of chapters three to seven.

[1] Philip Selznick, *The Moral Commonwealth: Social Theory and the Promise of Community* (University of California Press, 1992) 463.

[2] See eg Magdalena Flatscher-Thöni, Andrea M Leiter and Hannes Winner, 'Pricing Damages for Pain and Suffering in Court: The Impact of the Valuation Method' (2013) 10 *Journal of Empirical Legal Studies* 104; Frank Cross and Charles Silver, 'In Texas, Life is Cheap' (2006) 59 *Vanderbilt Law Review* 1873; Walter Simmons and Rosemarie Emanuele, 'Male and Female Recoveries in Medical Malpractice Cases' (2004) 62 *Review of Social Economy* 83.

[3] Philippe Nonet and Philip Selznick, *Law and Society in Transition: Toward Responsive Law* (Routledge, 2001).

As I introduced the different aspects of legal systems in chapter two, I used corporate criminal liability as an example to help me define each aspect and demonstrate how the framework operates. I found that corporate criminal liability results in seriously disparate treatment for humans and corporations, a kind of dual-law system. Criminal legal systems have been used to prosecute abusers and many individuals have been imprisoned, but criminal legal systems are largely not holding the corporations that enabled abuse accountable. To the extent that criminal legal systems' capacity to label a corporation a criminal is meant to communicate their subjectivity to law, then the silence of criminal legal systems with respect to corporations that put known abusers in positions of power over children undermines that claim.

Applying the framework as I introduced it, I found that corporate criminal liability resembles a repressive regime – dioceses and other corporations are part of a privileged and protected class of subjects. Corporate violence is only sometimes cognisable through criminal legal systems, and even then, the range of consequences to which they might be subject is limited, especially as compared to the range of consequences and punishments the same criminal legal systems routinely impose on human beings.

Chapter three introduced Ballarat and Gallup as dioceses (and corporations) that each have long histories of enabling abuse. Both have also engaged with multiple legal systems in relation to those histories. Chapters four, five, six and seven discuss canon law, tort, the Royal Commission and Chapter 11 bankruptcy in turn, legal systems these dioceses have engaged with but which are fundamentally different from each other. Using the responsive law framework, the chapters evaluate the capacity of legal systems to address diocesan accountability for abuse through doctrine and procedure, as well as how the purpose, theory and logistics of legal systems impact that capacity. These chapters demonstrate how, in order to understand the overall character of a legal system, we need to move beyond a dichotomy between law on the books and law in action and attend to the multiple aspects of legal systems. This final chapter takes lessons from chapters three to seven to revisit Nonet and Selznick's responsive law theory, testing its limits and incorporating feminist and critical scholarship to advance the theory by demonstrating how victims and other stakeholders' participation in decision-making can, for corporate wrongdoing, address what Nonet and Selznick identified as a risk of responsive law.

II. Corporate Accountability, Responsive Law and Legal Systems

A. Purpose and the Risk of Responsiveness

Nonet and Selznick drew on giants of nineteenth- and twentieth-century legal theory, describing autonomous law as 'suffused with a spirit of constraint', limiting the power of legal systems to make political change in exchange for the power to enforce law against even political leaders.[4] They describe responsive law as an ideal, a way of pushing autonomous legal systems toward more substantive justice. This ideal is, in their writing, one sought by many legal reformers, but which carries with it inherent risk.[5] Citing criticism of an 'activist Warren Court', pushing aside precedent in response to social change and political forces, they caution that opening the doors to political forces might result in a legal system losing 'the ability to moderate the role of power in society; it regresses to repression':[6]

> There is indeed a tension between openness and fidelity to law, and that tension poses the central problem of legal development. The dilemma is not unique to law: All institutions experience a conflict between integrity and openness. Integrity is protected when an institution is strongly committed to a distinctive mission or can be held accountable to that mission by external controls. Committed institutions, however, become wedded to their perspectives and ways of doing things; they lose sensitivity to their environment. Accountability is most readily maintained when performance can be measured by determinate standards; at the same time, the demand for accountability fosters insecurity and a search for bureaucratic havens where responsibilities are narrowly defined and easily met. In other words, accountability breeds formalism and retreatism, rendering institutions rigid, incapable of coping with new contingencies. Openness, on the other hand, presumes wide grants of discretion, so that official conduct may remain flexible, adaptive, and self-corrective. But responsibilities are more elusive when they lose precision, and there is a risk that commitments will be diluted as flexibility is sought. Hence, openness degenerates readily into opportunism, that is, unguided adaptation to events and pressures.[7]

The Royal Commission was successful, in large part, because the commissioners were, in Nonet and Selznick's terms, competent. As discussed in chapter six, I believe that the Royal Commission was quasi- (but not fully) responsive. I suspect that Nonet and Selznick would have described it as responsive without the qualification.

The Royal Commission's commitment to the production of knowledge, to providing opportunities for victims to be heard, and to making actionable, useful recommendations designed to have real impact on society was made manifest through their careful, respectful and well-received body of work. The Royal Commission's authority to devise its own procedural rules in accordance with its understanding of the most efficient and effective way to gather, synthesise and report on data and evidence allowed for a remarkably broad and deep inquiry into social, organisational, institutional, psychological, theological, criminological and historical understandings of child sexual abuse. Its very nature as an ad hoc commission also exemplifies the risk of responsive law that Nonet and

[4] ibid, 69.
[5] ibid, 73.
[6] ibid, 74–76.
[7] ibid, 76.

Selznick discuss: political forces can be oppressive or liberating. While the Royal Commission was able to respond to many of the victims' interests and needs as well as triggering governments and institutions around Australia to adopt policies and practices that research suggests will reduce incidence of child sexual abuse, it was able to do so because the political forces behind its initiation and the individual commissioners appointed to carry out its work were genuinely committed to the purposes identified in the terms of reference.

Survivor advocacy groups identify truth-telling, the importance of being believed and a recognition that they were wronged as key interests of many individuals who have suffered clerical child sexual abuse:

> Whilst SNAP welcomes the direction from Pope Francis to end the 'secrecy' rule on child sexual abuse in the Catholic Church, the broad cultural habitus of the Catholic Church still, in the view of many of our members, emphasises 'duty' to avoid 'scandal' and the disgrace, shame and dishonour that such 'scandal' brings on the Church. Hence the institution's 'good image and reputation' in the public square is considered more important than the evil perpetrated and the resultant suffering for victims.
>
> Our members report how this secretive culture is deeply harmful and is, in fact, another form of abuse. They note the importance of openness, honesty and transparency in both their individual healing journeys and in the redress of the faith-based institution(s) responsible for their abuse.[8]

This desire for validation is also reflected in academic literature.[9] The Royal Commission has been widely praised for, among other things, changing the scope of the public conversation in Australia. Survivors report feeling validated, and even those who did not participate in the Royal Commission report positive feelings knowing that there is a public narrative establishing the wrongfulness of child sexual abuse and increasing the likelihood of victims being believed.[10] Strang and Sherman's empirical conclusions about symbolic reparation being more important than material reparation to most victims across types of crime give context to the importance of these feelings to victims.[11]

Michel Foucault's paradigm-shifting work, laying bare the relationships between knowledge and power, and the importance of the production of truth and knowledge as part of larger systems of social control, demonstrates how regimes of power are inextricably linked to systems designed to pursue knowledge production.[12] This

[8] Witness Statement of the Survivors Network of those Abused by Priests (SNAP) in Aotearoa New Zealand, Statement no WITN0377001 (28 April 2021) 22–23, www.abuseincare.org.nz/assets/Uploads/Statement-of-the-Survivors-Network-of-those-Abused-by-Priests-in-Aotearoa-New-Zealand-for-the-Faith-based-Redress-hearing.pdf.

[9] See eg Robyn Holder, *Just Interests: Victims, Citizens and the Potential for Justice* (Edward Elgar Publishing, 2018).

[10] Melissa Davey, '"It Was Us Against Everyone": How Abuse Survivors Will Keep Pushing for Change' *The Guardian* (14 December 2017), www.theguardian.com/australia-news/2017/dec/14/it-was-us-against-everyone-how-abuse-survivors-will-keep-pushing-for-change.

[11] Heather Strang and Lawrence W Sherman, 'Repairing the Harm: Victims and Restorative Justice' (2003) *Utah Law Review* 15.

[12] Michel Foucault, *Power*, tr James D Faubion (Allen Lane, 2001).

helps to explain some of the Royal Commission's success. The Royal Commission, initiated by the Prime Minister and Governor-General of Australia, devoted significant public resources and attention to the project of producing a narrative of truth and creating a break with the past. The truths determined by canon and tort law, the narratives established by the Royal Commission, and limited fact-finding bankruptcy courts can conduct all produce different kinds of knowledge. The narrative power of the Royal Commission changed hearts and minds across Australian society, and resulted in real change to law and policy.[13] My assessment of the Royal Commission as quasi-responsive rests in no small part on its capacity for narrative-building and impact on the broader society. And bankruptcy's lack of capacity to weave such a narrative is a large part of its not being fully responsive.

But the Royal Commission's recommendations left to Parliament and the Australian state governments whether they would provide victims with a resolution, including the implementation of a redress scheme, or make policy changes. In this case they did, although that has not always been true for other royal commissions. Ultimately, whether or not the Royal Commission empowered victims rests on what it means to be empowered. If it means to feel respected as a citizen whose concerns are taken seriously, then commissions of inquiry like the Royal Commission may indeed empower victims. But, if it means the power to effectuate some tangible change, whether the payment of damages, delivery of an apology, gesture of contrition, or to compel some disclosure or other act, royal commissions cannot empower victims directly.

The Royal Commission harnessed the power of the state to compel disclosure of institutional records, which is a demand of most victims and largely serves their interests, but power to initiate or compel material redress remained in the hands of the state and the Church, and victims' voices were steps removed from the rooms where decisions were really made. Whether or not victims' interests are centred through the process is, in Nonet and Selznick's terms, a question of the competence of legal institutions. In the Royal Commission's case, it (and its commissioners, counsel assisting and staff) were competent, and even virtuous, but Nonet and Selznick's point – that the flexibility and purposive nature of responsive processes could be co-opted by repressive forces, – reveals a real weakness of royal commissions as legal systems.

B. Bringing Responsive Law into Conversation with Feminist Theories of Knowledge Production

Nonet and Selznick argue that responsive law should 'perceive[] social pressures as sources of knowledge and opportunities for self-correction';[14] that responsive

[13] See eg Jodi Death, *Governing Child Abuse, Voices and Victimisation: The Use of Public Inquiry into Child Sexual Abuse in Christian Institutions* (Routledge, 2017) ch 6.

[14] Nonet and Selznick (n 3) 77, emphasis in original.

law is only possible if 'purpose can be made objective enough and authoritative enough to control adaptive rule making'.[15] Feminist theorist Sandra Harding's critique of 'the view from nowhere' argues that 'Knowledge is always socially situated', and so researchers should seek to produce a stronger kind of objectivity; a kind that actively seeks to understand social orders from multiple perspectives, especially those of marginalised persons and communities.[16]

Responsive law, as a theory, can benefit from adopting Harding's view of knowledge production. Nonet and Selznick argue that

> political movements' use of legal systems to pursue social goals constitutes a kind of increased participation in legal systems that pushes them toward being more responsive by bringing 'new bases of support to the development and implementation of public policy.[17]

Their vision of responsive law presumes judges and juries should remain at the centre of legal systems, imbued with authority to shape law through their determinations. So long as judges are understood as decision-makers, their competence is a key factor to the outcome of a legal proceeding. In order for a legal system to be truly responsive, decision-making processes must rest on deep knowledge of legal problems from all perspectives, especially those of marginalised or vulnerable stakeholders. Kimberle Crenshaw's work on intersectionality reveals how different types of oppression can intersect in ways that impact individuals' capacity and willingness to interact with legal systems, and the capacity of legal professionals to understand the perspectives of people experiencing multiple forms of oppression.[18] Centring jurists in legal processes leaves marginalised and vulnerable people at the mercy of the system's competence in gathering and representing the perspective 'from below'.[19]

Consider what the comparison between Ballarat and Gallup helps to demonstrate about the problem of clerical child sexual abuse. The similarities between Ballarat and Gallup highlight the distinctions between the two dioceses, calling attention to how overlapping patterns of social and political domination can both increase likelihood of abuse and limit access to justice. These are unique places, with historical, social and political realities that impact the way child sexual abuse by Catholic priests and religious occurred, how it has been litigated, and what people in those places want and expect from legal systems.

In Ballarat, sectarianism and the Catholic community's insulation within the larger community created conditions that allowed a group of men with power

[15] ibid, 77.

[16] Sandra Harding, *Objectivity and Diversity: Another Logic of Scientific Research* (University of Chicago Press, 2015) 158. I was sorry to hear of her passing as I submitted the manuscript for this book.

[17] Nonet and Selznick (n 3) 97.

[18] Kimberle Crenshaw, 'Demarginalizing the Intersection of Race and Sex: A Black Feminist Critique of Antidiscrimination Doctrine, Feminist Theory and Antiracist Politics' (1989) 1 *University of Chicago Legal Forum* 139.

[19] Harding (n 16) 40.

to ignore and subjugate the needs of vulnerable children, such that even when a police officer sought to investigate an abusive priest, the officer lost his job and the priest continued to abuse.[20] Yet, in more recent years, through media investigations, the intervention of a state-level investigation, and then the Royal Commission itself, public opinion shifted toward belief in Survivors and disapproval of the Church's response to them. Ballarat's relative wealth contributed to its visibility as an 'epicentre' of clerical child sexual abuse, where brave and committed Survivors worked across decades and ultimately changed perspectives, law and policy. The Royal Commission produced data that informs a wealth of research on best practices to protect children. Changes to law and new policies in public and private institutions have followed the Royal Commission and offer hope that fewer children will suffer abuse now and in the future. A Redress Scheme was implemented to compensate victims. Public sympathy and support for Survivors was tangible and widespread.

Gallup, with a history of successive colonisations and a population largely living in poverty, is a place where many children are and have been extraordinarily vulnerable to predation, and where there are many high hurdles that a Survivor seeking legal redress must overcome. Although the Diocese of Gallup's bankruptcy case resulted in payments for more Survivors than might otherwise have been paid, and in a number of non-monetary concessions, the diocese's power and influence in the local community, combined with a relative lack of interest by the wider public, allowed the diocese to provide half-hearted apologies, leaving many unsatisfied. As discussed in chapter seven, when the Franciscan Friars filed their bankruptcy case in California, the religious order failed to provide proper notice to tribal authorities, despite being aware that its friars were responsible for abusing children across 'Arizona, California, Idaho, Missouri, New Mexico, Nevada, Oregon, Utah and Washington', including, as Elizabeth Hardin-Burrola reported,

> at least 25 friars with at least one ministry assignment in Arizona or New Mexico. Thirteen of those friars served at least one assignment on a Native American reservation or within a tribal community – the Colorado River Indian Tribes, Gila River Indian Community, Pascua Yaqui Tribe, San Carlos Apache Tribe, Tohono O'odham Nation and White Mountain Apache Tribe in Arizona, and the Mescalero Apache Tribe in New Mexico.[21]

It is remarkable that it took a journalist reaching out to the legal professionals working on the case for these sovereign nations to be provided with the information they needed to inform their citizens of the bankruptcy filing and the importance of the bar date. I cannot conceive of a good explanation for how the

[20] Denis Ryan and Peter Hoysted, *Unholy Trinity: The Hunt for the Paedophile Priest Monsignor John Day* (Allen & Unwin, 2013).

[21] Elizabeth Hardin-Burrola, 'Franciscan Friars of California Ask to Extend Abuse Claim Deadline' *National Catholic Reporter* (3 July, 2024), www.ncronline.org/news/franciscan-friars-california-ask-extend-abuse-claim-deadline (quoting and citing filings from the bankruptcy case).

governments and newspapers that serve Indigenous communities were left off the list for public notice of the Franciscans' bankruptcy filing.

Autonomous law is characterised by a veneer of equality – that the outcome in cases with the same 'facts' should be the same. But no two cases can truly be the same. Ballarat and Gallup surely are not. Every situation is unique, even as they may share characteristics. The autonomous law premise of objectivity – that the best person to make decisions about right outcomes is always emotionally removed from the situation and without a personal interest in its outcome – has its limits, and responsive law should push back against that assumption. The Survivors of Ballarat have become visible advocates for justice, and Nonet and Selznick might argue that their participation in legal systems and their advocacy for the Royal Commission demonstrates overall responsiveness of the Australian legal order. But, when considered alongside Gallup, we are reminded that the community of victims of clerical child sexual abuse is much larger than the visible community of Survivors, and that those who are less visible are also much more likely to face intersecting forms of domination related to race, class, gender and other social, economic or political oppression.

The level of self-help that the community of Survivors from Ballarat has demonstrated is remarkable – their decades of advocacy and work have brought about real change. But this cannot be expected of all victims of corporate wrongdoing. Corporations are designed to allow for economic activity at scale, and thus, by their nature, can have an impact on large groups of people – and more often than not, victims of corporate wrongdoing are members of marginalised communities.[22] They cannot be expected to exercise the level of self-help that Survivors from Ballarat did. A legal system cannot be said to be responsive unless it is proactive about stakeholder participation – unless it facilitates participation for all.

A responsive system, in Nonet and Selznick's theory, would be open to listening to the perspectives of a wide range of stakeholders. The limits of this version of responsive theory, especially in the context of corporate wrongdoing, is that it tends to leave out those who are least capable of advocating for themselves through formal legal systems; those who require support to voice their claims. When corporate wrongdoing targets marginalised communities, the barriers between those communities and legal systems can protect powerful corporations and leave victims without recourse. As the 'father of environmental justice' Robert Bullard commented:

> We know there is nothing free about free enterprise; there are costs and externalities born by a system where the greatest wealth is generated from the greatest exploitation.

[22] See eg Ángel Eduardo Rivera, 'Contested Necrocapitalism: Indigeneity Versus Extractivism in Northern Canada' in Ariadna Estévez (ed), *Necropower in North America: The Legal Spatialization of Disposability and Lucrative Death* (Palgrave MacMillan, 2021) 129–50; Sandya Hewamanne and Nigel South, 'Women and the Structural Violence of "Fast-Fashion" Global Production: Victimisation, Poorcide and Environmental Harms' in Emma Milne et al (eds), *Gendering Green Criminology* (Bristol University Press, 2023) 148–69.

> And when you look at how those things intersect, it shows you how this whole Western culture perceives nature as something to be exploited and dominated. … Communities are viewed in the same context. When certain lands are seen as exploitable, the people that happen to be living there are viewed as expendable. Hence the genocide of Native people and the exploitation of slaves. At the same time, pollution is seen as just a byproduct of moving to the highest level of the economy. Smoke, air pollution, water pollution … that is the smell of progress. When it comes to waste, waste will flow along the path of least resistance. Historically, this means places near populations that have 'less value' and have less political clout to resist. And you end up having places that are 'sacrifice zones,' zones that are viewed as expendable when it comes to the environment, population, and health. When laws and regulations are built with this mindset, you end up assigning a value to those locations, and somehow that is where the waste and other externalities go.[23]

When it comes to corporate wrongdoing, a responsive system must do more than be willing to listen to Survivors who can advocate for themselves. It must be proactive about identifying victims of corporate wrongdoing, facilitating their fulsome participation in legal processes and preventing future wrongdoing.

The Royal Commission and Chapter 11 demonstrate different ways that systems can be proactive about identifying victims and facilitating their participation. The Royal Commission was proactive in collecting data about the problem of child sexual abuse in institutional contexts. It commissioned research, held public hearings, evaluated data, listened to, and vindicated, victims in ways both private and public. The process was designed to give victims a chance to speak and be heard, and the commissioners paid careful attention to what they said. One of their very first acts was to give people options about how they wanted to present their stories. While the process of public hearings was controlled by the commissioners and counsel assisting, individuals could submit their stories via private testimony, as a written statement, or in digital format, including through artwork sent to the Message to Australia. Between accepting letters and other submissions, including anonymous ones, travelling around the country for private hearings, and interviewing Survivors at public hearings, the Royal Commission ensured that thousands of people who wanted to tell their stories were able to do so. Peoples' stories were heard and attended to. The Message to Australia shared with Australian libraries at the concluding hearing of the Royal Commission was a tangible demonstration of the seriousness with which the commissioners and the Royal Commission took the words of victims.[24]

Chapter 11's processes are designed for its more typical case of business-related insolvency, and this underlying economic and social purpose contributes to the form these processes take. The debtor in Chapter 11 is required to provide

[23] Robert Bullard, 'Addressing Environmental Racism' (2019) 73 *Journal of International Affairs* 237, 239.

[24] Nour Haydar and staff, 'Child sexual abuse royal commission hands over stories of survivors in book "too heavy to lift"' ABC News (13 December, 2017), www.abc.net.au/news/2017-12-14/child-sex-abuse-royal-commission-final-hearing/9257944.

notification of the bankruptcy case to any parties that might hold a claim of any sort against it. In larger cases, this means that a claims agent will be appointed, and stakeholders including creditors, shareholders, employees, tort victims and customers may be routinely included in communications about the process and provided with information about how they can participate and advocate for their interests. Unsecured creditors, and sometimes other stakeholder groups, are represented through the appointment of statutory committees made up of representatives of those groups. Statutory committees' legal counsel is paid for by the debtor. Chapter 11, while not creating opportunities to contribute to a narrative of truth, does provide victims with opportunities to contribute to decision-making processes. This limits reliance on the competence of particular judges in understanding stakeholder needs and interests. Its processes are not designed to produce or collect knowledge about the wrongdoing underlying the claims Survivors hold against dioceses, but they do set out specific guidance about how potential claimants should be made aware of the bankruptcy and provided with information about how to participate in the process. Unsecured creditors, including victims of corporate wrongdoing, then have the means for collective action through a statutory committee that represents their interests in the process of negotiating and voting on a plan of reorganization.

C. Participation and Leverage Make a System Responsive

Where Nonet and Selznick see risks of responsive law in having to trust in the competence of judges and legal systems, my view of responsive law would argue for stepping back from the idea of juries and judges being final decision-makers, which relieves the riskiness of a responsive system because it no longer depends on the competence of legal authorities. Stakeholders, especially victims of wrongdoing, holding positions of influence and having roles in decision-making is an embodiment of republican ideals of justice.[25] Chapter 11 demonstrates a practical way that victims of corporate wrongdoing who might not otherwise have the resources to advocate for themselves can be empowered to participate, not as a witness to their own victimisation, but as a participant in a negotiated decision-making process. Rather than relying on an authoritative purpose to control and restrain judges and juries, a responsive system would restrain the role of judges and juries to fact-finding and procedure, and turn to stakeholders themselves for resolutions.

Deliberative democrats point to the benefits of having representative groups of citizens participate in decision-making processes.[26] The shifts in leverage that

[25] John Braithwaite and Philip Pettit, 'Republicanism and Restorative Justice: An Explanatory and Normative Connection' in Heather Strang and John Braithwaite (eds), *Restorative Justice: Philosophy to Practice* (Taylor & Francis Group, 2000) ch 9.

[26] Ron Levy and Graeme Orr, *The Law of Deliberative Democracy* (Routledge, 2017).

accompany the shift from a dual-party adversarial system to a multi-party negotiation allow for the interests of various stakeholder groups and judicial oversight to prevent any one constituency from dominating the decision-making process. The unique positioning of a debtor-funded committee of creditors and the importance of fulcrum securities in a prototypical Chapter 11 case creates space for a deliberative process that may be Chapter 11's most responsive feature. When participating in consensus-building processes at my Quaker college, it became clear that the consensus process gives those with the strongest interest in the outcome of the process the most leverage in decision-making. Parties who cared the most would be the most likely to hold out for what they want. By contrast, a feature of autonomous systems is that the parties with resources and connections to power tend to have leverage to protect their interests and further their agendas. Chapter 11 demonstrates a way that leverage can be afforded according to how much a victim of corporate wrongdoing is owed, rather than by what they have, and provides victims with the opportunity to negotiate for their own preferred outcome, including non-monetary agreements or, with respect to for-profit corporations, equity interests in the reorganized corporation.

Chapter seven explained how procedural rules facilitating informed and productive negotiation among all relevant stakeholders, and the bankruptcy judge's broad discretion to fit procedural rules to accommodate practical realities of individual cases, may have facilitated better settlement terms in the Diocesan Debtor cases than have been negotiated in other legal proceedings involving dioceses. Bankruptcy does little to amplify the voices of victims who want to tell their stories, to have those stories validated and be vindicated. But it does not silence them. Bankruptcy courts are very unlikely to hold evidentiary hearings or make findings about the facts or truth of allegations of tortious action underlying a claim against the bankruptcy estate. They do not have the authority to make final determinations in causes of action not directly related to the bankruptcy case without consent. In the Diocesan Debtor cases, however, a procedural system adept at responding to unique problems in business or industry has been able to listen to Survivor voices and adjust procedure to accommodate their needs and interests. Bankruptcy judges provide opportunities to allow victims to speak, almost all confirmed bankruptcy plans included provisions requiring the diocese or order to provide forums for people to tell their stories, and lawyers representing victims issued releases telling the stories their clients wanted told publicly. Through their representative members on the committee of unsecured creditors, Survivors' preferences were heard and they had leverage in decision-making despite the kind of resource gap that frequently undermines plaintiff power in tort cases, even as the experience for Survivors of the Diocese of Gallup suggests that vindication may not necessarily accompany the achievement of other litigation goals.

The process results in a counterbalance to what is typically a gap in resources between a Survivor and the Church. Survivors' participation in a bankruptcy case does not require them to have significant resources. Because the counsel for the committee of unsecured debtors is paid through the bankruptcy estate, by the debtor, all parties have an incentive to negotiate, but an inability to pay for a lawyer or sudden emergency does not impact a decision about what kind of settlement is acceptable in the way it does for a claim brought in tort. The debtor who hopes to preserve its resources and reorganize rather than liquidate is incentivised to settle disputes with the committee quickly because the debtor pays for the committee's counsel. Victims in mass tort cases also benefit from the kind of insider knowledge, relationships and strategy that repeat players in large bankruptcy cases develop in a system that is designed to facilitate a negotiated settlement among multiple parties with divergent interests.

This is not to say that the process is entirely healing or attentive to Survivors. In Gallup, the Committee of Unsecured Creditors (led by five Survivors and advised by both local plaintiffs' attorneys and experienced bankruptcy counsel) effectively negotiated a settlement with the Diocese and its insurers that left them with a plan for a trustee to administer significant financial settlements, apologies and other symbolic measures of apology – much, but not all, of what they wanted. One member of the creditors' committee in Gallup told me in an interview about feeling as if lawyers (plaintiffs' lawyers and bankruptcy counsel) dominated conversations, which may have had a silencing impact or influenced the committee's decision-making process. Survivors spoke at the confirmation hearing about accepting the plan even though it did not provide for the transparency they wanted from the diocese. They wanted the diocese to release its records, but decided to accept the plan despite that, because they wanted to put the case to an end.[27] Those speaking out were satisfied that they had been able to get concessions from both the diocese and its insurers, although disappointed that they did not get the vindication and transparency they wanted. The process did not provide them with a means of having their stories credited publicly, except in the ways they were able to negotiate through the plan process.

If Chapter 11 has the effect of empowering victims, this effect is, as discussed in chapter seven, not the purpose of system. While equitable treatment of creditors is one of the goals of bankruptcy, it was designed with the assumption that most creditors would be lenders, suppliers, employees, bondholders, shareholders or others engaging with a for-profit business. The Diocesan Debtor cases placed Survivors in a position to advocate for their own interests in negotiating a plan of reorganization, while denying them the opportunity to witness and participate in a trial or have their claims vindicated through a formal determination. Chapter 11 is not the right forum for addressing corporate wrongdoing, but it does demonstrate how stakeholder participation can address Nonet and Selznick's concerns with the inherent flexibility of a responsive legal process. Corporations, by their nature, have multiple stakeholder bodies with interests that exist in relationship to each other. In most cases of corporate wrongdoing, stakeholders include employees,

[27] Elizabeth Hardin-Burrola 'Bishop Apologizes; Bankruptcy Judge Confirms Reorganization' *The Gallup Independent* (22 June 2016).

lenders, insurers, business partners and directors, as well as tort victims. While judges or juries can be necessary to ensure a fair process and make findings of fact, each of these stakeholder groups are themselves best placed to understand their own interests. A system that provides victims of corporate wrongdoing with leverage to secure their own interests in a multi-party negotiation involving other corporate stakeholders is more responsive than a system that depends on judges and juries to be competent in determining the correct allocation of defined types of redress.

III. Characteristics of a Responsive Approach to Corporate Wrongdoing

Truly responsive legal systems require: (1) embedded knowledge of social realities in multiple aspects of law; (2) a purposive approach; (3) procedural flexibility; (4) the deliberate and effective inclusion of impacted stakeholders in decision-making; and (5) a normative agenda of countering domination and accounting for social disparities that impact capacity to further litigant interests through legal proceedings. Chapters six and seven discussed how the Royal Commission and Chapter 11 bankruptcy have some but not all of these attributes; enough that they can both be characterised as quasi-responsive law. True responsiveness, however, requires that these attributes be embedded across multiple aspects of law. Both Chapter 11 bankruptcy and the Royal Commission fall short of the ideal for responsive law. Notably, however, the strengths and weaknesses of the two systems complement each other. When considered together, it becomes possible to imagine a more fully responsive system.

Truly responsive law must do more than just make it theoretically possible for ordinary people to access justice, it must actively work to facilitate participation by vulnerable members of society. It should find ways to ensure peoples' leverage in negotiating solutions is relative to their interest in a problem more than to their capacity to pay for legal services. Common law systems use judges or juries as decision-makers. A responsive system would encourage negotiated solutions and consensus-building among stakeholders. A responsive system would recognise the plurality of interests in a social or legal problem and would facilitate the effective participation of all stakeholders in proportion to their interests in the outcome.

Responsive law should seek and encourage stakeholder participation and engage with communities through a process that empowers weaker parties and facilitates a stakeholder-led decision. The role of disinterested judges should be restricted to fact-finding, adjudicating procedural rules, responding to bad faith and acting as decision-makers of last resort when an agreement cannot be reached. Deliberative, relational and flexible proceedings are capable of counteracting forces of domination and fairly governing disputes between individuals and organisations. Such proceedings may have rules that provide parties and officials involved with flexibility and adaptability of process. The freedom to make determinations about how to conduct legal proceedings and having a range of tools from which to choose gives stakeholders the means to reach equitable resolutions are keys to responsiveness. Between the Royal Commission and Chapter 11, it is possible to glimpse how a truly responsive system might operate. A responsive legal system would incorporate the voices and facilitate the participation of impacted parties, not just as evidence for third-party decision-makers, but in the decision-making itself. It would be flexible and purposive, so that rigid rules do not stand in the way of substantive justice. Responsive systems should also be alive to the forces of domination within social orders and intentionally facilitate the effective participation of stakeholders in ways that alleviate or counter the effects of those forces. They would ensure that capacity to finance litigation would not be determinative of capacity to advocate for interests within the system.

The key take-aways from this book are that responsive legal systems are possible; that responsive law embraces *deliberative, relational and flexible* proceedings; and that the responsiveness of a system is a function of its overall character – purpose, theory and logistics are at least as important as doctrine and procedure. A truly responsive legal system would incorporate victims' voices and facilitate meaningful participation of impacted parties, not just as evidence for third-party decision-makers but also in the decision-making itself. Responsiveness and a deep understanding of how corporations function would be embedded not just in doctrine, but in all aspects of a legal system designed to hold corporations accountable. Between the flexible, purposive fact-finding process of the Royal Commission's inquiry process and the stakeholder-led, deliberative process of decision-making in the Chapter 11 process, elements of a truly responsive system to address serious corporate wrongdoing start to become clear.

TABLE OF CASES

Australia

United States

Federal

TABLE OF STATUTES

Holy See

United Kingdom

Australia

United States

BIBLIOGRAPHY

Articles, Books and other Secondary Sources

Adams, DW, *Education for Extinction* (University of Oklahoma Press, 1995).

Albert, TC, 'The Insolvency Law of Ancient Rome' (2006) 28 *California Bankruptcy Journal* 365.

Anatrella, T, 'La relation pastorale, l'équilibre de la vie affective des prêtres et problems de déviances' in *Testimoni Del Risorto: Atti del Corso Annuale di Formazione Per I Nuovo Vescovi* (Libreria Editrice Vaticana, 2015).

Anderson, CC, 'When Magisterium Becomes Imperium: Peter Damian on the Accountability of Bishops for Scandal' (2004) 65 *Theological Studies* 741.

Aroney, N, 'A Power "Singular and Eccentrical": Royal Commissions and Executive Power after Williams' (2014) 25 *Public Law Review* 99.

—— 'The Constitutional First Principles of Royal Commissions' in S Prasser and H Tracey (eds), *Royal Commissions & Public Inquiries: Practice & Potential* (Connor Court Publishing, 2014) ch 2.

Atiyah, P, *Accidents, Compensation and the Law* (Weidenfeld and Nicholson, 1970).

Baca, JM, *Constant Reminder: A Memoir of Priest Abuse and Recovery* (CreateSpace Independent Publishing Platform, 2013).

Badawi, S and Rose, M, 'Considerations for Holders of the Fulcrum Claim in a Chapter 11 Proceeding' (2022) 36 *Insights: The Corporate & Securities Law Advisor* 25.

Baird, DG, 'Bankruptcy's Uncontested Axioms' (1998) 108 *Yale Law Journal* 573.

Balboni, JM, *Clergy Sexual Abuse Litigation: Survivors Seeking Justice* (First Forum Press, 2011).

Banerjee, SB, 'Necrocapitalism' (2008) 29 *Organization Studies* 1541.

Barker, DK, 'Kill the Indian, Save the Child: Cultural Genocide and the Boarding School' in DA Morrison (ed), *American Indian Studies: An Interdisciplinary Approach to Contemporary Issues* (Peter Lang, 1997).

Beal, JP, 'Doing What One Can: Canon Law and Clerical Sexual Misconduct' (1992) 52 *The Jurist* 642.

—— 'The 1962 Instruction *Crimen sollicitationis*: Caught Red-Handed or Handed a Red Herring?' (2007) 41 *Studia Canonica* 199.

Becker, ME, 'The Abuse Excuse and Patriarchal Narratives' (1998) 92 *Northwestern University Law Review* 1459.

Beckett, K, 'Culture and the Politics of Signification: The Case of Child Sexual Abuse' (1996) 43 *Social Problems* 57.

Benkert, M and Doyle, T, 'Clericalism, Religious Duress and Its Psychological Impact on Victims of Clergy Sexual Abuse' (2009) 58 *Pastoral Psychology* 223.

Berman, HJ, *Law and Revolution: The Formation of the Western Legal Tradition* (Harvard University Press, 1983).

Blackstone, W, *Commentaries on the Laws of England*, 21st edn (Sweet, Maxwell, Stevens & Norton, 1844).

Block-Lieb, S, 'The Logic and Limits of Contract Bankruptcy' (2001) 2 *University of Illinois Law Review* 503.

Boswell, J, *Christianity, Social Tolerance, and Homosexuality: Gay People in Western Europe from the Beginning of the Christian Era to the Fourteenth Century* (University of Chicago Press, 1980).

Braithwaite, J, 'Relational Republican Regulation' (2013) 7 *Regulation & Governance* 124.

Braithwaite, J and Pettit, P, *Not Just Deserts: A Republican Theory of Criminal Justice* (Oxford University Press, 1990).

—— 'Republicanism and Restorative Justice: An Explanatory and Normative Connection' in H Strang and J Braithwaite (eds), *Restorative Justice: Philosophy to Practice* (Taylor & Francis Group, 2000) 145–63.

Bryce, I, 'Child Abuse Royal Commission – a Personal Perspective' (2017) 126 *The Australian Humanist* 20.

Boyd, C, 'The Nestlé Infant Formula Controversy and a Strange Web of Subsequent Business Scandals' (2012) 106 *Journal of Business Ethics* 283.

Budiselik, W, Crawford, F and Chung, D, 'The Australian Royal Commission into Institutional Responses to Child Sexual Abuse: Dreaming of Child Safe Organisations?' (2014) 3 *Social Sciences* 565.

Bullard, R, 'Addressing Environmental Racism' (2020) 73 *Journal of International Affairs* 237.

Burns, RI (ed), *Las Siete Partidas*, vol 1, tr Samuel Parsons Scott (University of Pennsylvania Press, 2000).

Cahir, F, *Black Gold: Aboriginal People on the Goldfields of Victoria, 1850–1870* (Australian National University E Press, 2012).

Calabresi, G, *The Cost of Accidents: A Legal and Economic Analysis* (Yale University Press, 1970).

Calavita, K, *Invitation to Law and Society*, 2nd edn (University of Chicago Press, 2016).

Cane, P, 'Distributive Justice and Tort Law' (2001) 4 *New Zealand Law Review* 401.

—— 'Reforming Tort Law in Australia: A Personal Perspective' (2003) 27 *Melbourne University Law Review* 649.

—— 'Searching for United States Tort Law in the Antipodes' (2011) 38 *Pepperdine Law Review* 257.

Cashmore, J, Taylor, A and Parkinson, P, 'The Characteristics of Reports to the Police of Child Sexual Abuse and the Likelihood of Cases Proceeding to Prosecution After Delays in Reporting,' (2017) 74 *Child Abuse & Neglect* 49.

Carroll, SJ et al, *Asbestos Litigation* (RAND Institute for Civil Justice, 2005).

Chezem, LL, 'Public Health Law & Equal Access to Justice in Rural America' (2014) 59 *South Dakota Law Review* 529.

Chiao, V, 'What is the Criminal Law For?' (2016) 35 *Law and Philosophy* 137.

Chopko, ME, 'An Overview on the Parish and the Civil Law' (2007) 67 *The Jurist* 194.

Clark, S and Harris, C, 'The Push to Reform Class Action Procedure in Australia: Evolution or Revolution?' (2008) 32 *Melbourne University Law Review* 775.

Coffee, JC, '"No Soul to Damn: No Body to Kick": An Unscandalized Inquiry into the Problem of Corporate Punishment' (1981) 79 *Michigan Law Review* 386.

Coughlin, JJ, 'The Clergy Sexual Abuse Crisis and the Spirit of Canon Law' (2003) 44 *Boston College Law Review* 977.

Couratin, AH, 'Liturgy' in J Daniélou, AH Couratin and John Kent (eds), *Historical Theology* (Penguin, 1969).

Courtin, JE, 'Sexual Assault and the Catholic Church: Are Victims Finding Justice?' (PhD Thesis Monash University, 2015).

Crenshaw, K, 'Demarginalizing the Intersection of Race and Sex: A Black Feminist Critique of Antidiscrimination Doctrine, Feminist Theory and Antiracist Politics' (1989) 1 *University of Chicago Legal Forum* 139.

Crisp, BR, 'Silence and Silenced: Implications for the Spirituality of Survivors of Sexual Abuse' (2010) 18 *Feminist Theology* 277.

Cross, F and Silver, C, 'In Texas, Life is Cheap' (2006) 59 *Vanderbilt Law Review* 1873.

Dagan, H and Kreitner, R, 'The New Legal Realism and The Realist View of Law' (2018) 43 *Law & Social Inquiry* 528.

Daly, B, 'Priestly Celibacy: The Obligations of Continence and Celibacy for Priests' (2009) 4 *Compass* 20.

Daly, K, *Redressing Institutional Abuse of Children* (Palgrave Macmillan Limited, 2014).

—— 'Inequalities of Redress: Australia's National Redress Scheme for Institutional Abuse of Children' (2018) 42 *Journal of Australian Studies* 204.

Damian, P, *Book of Gomorrah*, tr Pierre J Payer (Wilfrid Laurier University Press, 1982).

Davitt, C, 'Whose Steeple Is It? Defining the Limits of the Debtor's Estate in the Religious Bankruptcy Context' (2005) 29 *Seton Hall Legislative Journal* 531.

Death, J, *Governing Child Abuse, Voices and Victimisation: The Use of Public Inquiry into Child Sexual Abuse in Christian Institutions* (Routledge, 2017).

Delaney, EM, 'Canonical Implications of the Response of the Catholic Church in Australia to Child Sexual Abuse' (PhD Thesis, University of Ottawa, 2004).

Dickens, C, *Little Dorrit* (Ticknor and Fields, 1867).

Dog, MC and Erodes, R, *Lakota Woman* (Harper Perennial, 1991).

Donahue Jr, C, 'A Crisis of Law? Reflections on the Church and the Law over the Centuries' (2005) 65 *The Jurist* 1.

Doyle, TP, 'Clericalism: Enabler of Clergy Sexual Abuse' (2006) 54 *Pastoral Psychology* 189.

Doyle, TP, Sipe, AWR and Wall, PJ, *Sex, Priests, and Secret Codes: The Catholic Church's 2,000-Year Paper Trail of Sexual Abuse* (Volt Press, 2006).

Duff, RA, 'Repairing Harms and Answering for Wrongs' in J Oberdiek (ed), *Philosophical Foundations of the Law of Torts* (Oxford University Press, 2014).

Eburn, M and Dovers, S, 'Learning Lessons from Disasters: Alternatives to Royal Commissions and Other Quasi-Judicial Inquiries' (2015) 74 *Australian Journal of Public Administration* 495.

Edelman, J, 'Direct and Vicarious Liability of Corporations' in E Peel and R Probert (eds), *Shaping the Law of Obligations: Essays in Honour of Professor Ewan McKendrick KC* (Oxford University Press, 2023) 211–26.

Edelman, M, 'Responsive Law and the Problem of Corporate Crime' (2022) 38 *Australian Journal of Corporate Law* 46.

—— 'Corporate Moral Insolvency: Lessons from Purdue Pharma' (2024) *Griffith Law Review* 1.

Engle Merry, S, 'Legal Pluralism' (1988) 22 *Law & Society Review* 869.

Faggioli, M, *A Council for the Global Church: Receiving Vatican II in History* (Augsburg Fortress Publishers, 2015).

Feeley, MM, 'Law, Legitimacy, and Symbols: An Expanded View of Law and Society in Transition' (1979) 77 *Michigan Law Review* 899.

Flatscher-Thöni, M, Leiter, AM and Winner, H, 'Pricing Damages for Pain and Suffering in Court: The Impact of the Valuation Method' (2013) 10 *Journal of Empirical Legal Studies* 104.

Ford, C, 'Commission of Care: The Royal Commission into Institutional Responses to Child Sexual Abuse Brought Innovative Special Measures to Its Five-Year Inquiry' (2018) 92 *Law Institute Journal* 20.

Formicola, JR, 'The Further Legal Consequence of Catholic Clerical Sexual Abuse' (2007) 49 *Journal of Church and State* 445.

Foucault, M, *Power*, tr James D Faubion (Allen Lane, 2001).

Francis, *Pascite Gregem Dei* (Apostolic Constitution, 23 May 2021).

—— *Fidem Servare* (Apostolic Letter issued 'Motu Proprio', 11 February 2022).

Frank, J, 'Mr. Justice Holmes and Non-Euclidian Legal Thinking,' (1932) 17 *Cornell Law Quarterly* 568.

Frantzen, AJ, 'The Penitentials Attributed to Bede' (1983) 58 *Speculum* 573.

Galanter, M, 'Why the "Haves" Come Out Ahead: Speculations on the Limits of Legal Change,' (1974) 9 *Law & Society Review* 95.

Gardner, J, *Offences and Defences: Selected Essays in the Philosophy of Criminal Law* (Oxford University Press, 2007).

Garth, B and Sterling, J, 'From Legal Realism to Law and Society: Reshaping Law for the Last Stages of the Social Activist State' (1998) 32 *Law & Society Review* 409.

Gaunce, NM and Luther R III, 'Deliver Us From Evil: Why Bankruptcy Judges May Properly Rely on the Free Exercise Clause & RFRA to Protect Church Property from the Grasps of Tort-Creditors' (2008) 43 *Valparaiso University Law Review* 641.

Gaustad, ES (ed), *A Documentary History of Religion in America to the Civil War* (Eerdmans Publishing Company, 1993).

Gauthier, A, *Roman Law and its Contribution to the Development of Canon Law* (St Paul University, 1996).

Genestal, R, 'Les Origines du Privilege Clerical' (1908) 32 *Nouvelle Revue Historique de Droit Francais et Etranger* 161.

George, TE, Gulati, M and McGinley, A, 'The New Old Legal Realism' (2011) 105 *Northwestern University Law Review* 689.

Gleeson, K, 'Why the Continuous Failures in Justice for Australian Victims and Survivors of Catholic Clerical Child Sexual Abuse?' (2016) 28 *Current Issues in Criminal Justice* 239.

—— 'Exceptional Sexual Harms: The Catholic Church and Child Sexual Abuse Claims in Australia' (2018) 27 *Social and Legal Studies* 734.

Godden-Rasul, N, 'Tort Law and Feminist Strategy: Lessons from Social Movement and Community Lawyering' (2025) *Social & Legal Studies* 1.

Goldberg, JCP, 'The Constitutional Status of Tort Law: Due Process and the Right to a Law for the Redress of Wrongs' (2005) 115 *Yale Law Journal* 524.

Goldberg, JCP and Zipursky, BC, 'Torts as Wrongs' (2010) 88 *Texas Law Review* 917.

—— 'Civil Recourse Defended: A Reply to Posner, Calabresi, Rustad, Chamallas, and Robinette' (2013) 88 *Indiana Law Journal* 569.

Golding, F, 'Sexual Abuse as the Core Transgression of Childhood Innocence: Unintended Consequences for Care Leavers' (2018) 42 *Journal of Australian Studies* 191.

—— '"Problems with Records and Recordkeeping Practices Are Not Confined to the Past": A Challenge from the Royal Commission into Institutional Responses to Child Sexual Abuse' (2019) *Archival Science* 1.

Gómez, LE, 'Race, Colonialsim, and Criminal Law: Mexicans and the American Criminal Justice System in Territorial New Mexico' (2000) 34 *Law & Society Review* 1129.

—— 'Off-White in an Age of White Supremacy: Mexican Elites and the Rights of Indians and Blacks in Nineteenth-Century New Mexico' (2005) 25 *Chicano-Latino Law Review* 9.

Green, TJ, 'Clerical Sexual Abuse of Minors: Some Canonical Reflections' (2003) 63 *The Jurist* 366.

—— 'CDF Circular Letter on Episcopal Conference Guidelines for Cases of Clerical Sexual Abuse of Minors: Some Initial Observations' (2013) 73 *The Jurist* 151.

Griffin, L and Briffa, G 'Still Awaiting Clarity: Why Victoria's New Civil Liability Laws for Organisational Child Abuse are Less Helpful Than They Appear' (2020) 43(2) *University of New South Wales Law Journal* 452.

Gross, K, 'Finding Some Trees But Missing the Forest' (2004) 12 *American Bankruptcy Institute Law Review* 203.

Guerzoni, MA and Graham, H, 'Catholic Church Responses to Clergy-Child Sexual Abuse and Mandatory Reporting Exemptions in Victoria, Australia: A Discursive Critique.' (2015) 4 *International Journal for Crime, Justice and Social Democracy* 58.

Guido, JJ, 'A Unique Betrayal: Clergy Sexual Abuse in the Context of the Catholic Religious Tradition' (2008) 17 *Journal of Child Sexual Abuse* 255.

Hamilton, MA, *Justice Denied: What America Must Do to Protect Its Children* (Cambridge University Press, 2008).

—— *God vs. the Gavel* (Cambridge University Press, 2014).

—— The Time Has Come for a Restatement of Child Sex Abuse' (2014) *Brooklyn Law Review* 79 *Brooklyn Law School* 397.

Hammond, GP and Rey, A, *Don Juan de Oñate, Colonizer of New Mexico, 1595-1628* (University of New Mexico Press, 1953).

Harding, S, *Objectivity and Diversity: Another Logic of Scientific Research* (University of Chicago Press, 2015).

Harner, MM, 'Trends in Distressed Debt Investing: An Empirical Study of Investors' Objectives' (2008) 16 *American Bankruptcy Institute Law Review* 69.

von Hefele, KJ, Hergenröther, J and Knöpfler, A, *Histoire Des Conciles d'Après Les Documents Originaux* (Ulan Press, 2012).

Hershovitz, S, 'Harry Potter and the Trouble with Tort Theory' (2010) 63 *Stanford Law Review* 67.

Hewamanne, S and South, N, 'Women and the Structural Violence of "Fast-Fashion" Global Production: Victimisation, Poorcide and Environmental Harms' in E Milne, P Davies, J Heydon, K Peggs and T Wyatt (eds), *Gendering Green Criminology* (Bristol University Press, 2023) 148–69.

Holder, R, *Just Interests: Victims, Citizens and the Potential for Justice* (Edward Elgar Publishing, 2018).

Holscher, K, 'The Trouble of an Indian Diocese: Catholic Priests and Sexual Abuse in Colonized Places' in TJ Wenger and SA Johnson (eds), *Religion and US Empire: Critical New Histories* (New York University Press, 2022) 231–52.

Husak, D, 'The Price of Criminal Law Skepticism: Ten Functions of the Criminal Law' (2020) 23 *New Criminal Law Review* 27.

Ison, T, *The Forensic Lottery: A Critique on Tort Liability as a System of Personal Injury Compensation* (Staples Press, 1967).

Jackson, TH, 'Bankruptcy, Non-Bankruptcy Entitlements, and the Creditors' Bargain' (1982) 91 *Yale Law Journal* 857.

Jones, TW, 'Sin, Silence and States of Denial: Canon Law and the "Discovery" of Child Sexual Abuse' (2015) 41 *Australian Feminist Law Journal* 237.

Jones, TW and Wright, C, 'The Goldfields' Sabbath: A Postsecular Analysis of Social Cohesion and Social Control on the Ballarat Goldfields, 1854' (2019) 43 *Journal of Religious History* 447.

Kaufman, KL et al, 'Recommendations for Preventing Child Sexual Abuse in Youth-Serving Organizations: Implications From an Australian Royal Commission Review of the Literature' (2019) 34 *Journal of Interpersonal Violence* 4199.

Keating, GC, 'Is There Really No Liability Without Fault?: A Critique of Goldberg & Zipursky' (2017) 15 *Jerusalem Journal of Legal Studies* 152.

Klug, H and Engle Merry, S, 'Introduction' in S Engle Merry and H Klug (eds), *The New Legal Realism Volume 2: Studying Law Globally* (Cambridge University Press, 2016) 1–10.

Krygier, M, 'Walls and Bridges: A Comment on Philip Selznick's "The Moral Commonwealth"' (1994) 82 *California Law Review* 473.

—— *Philip Selznick Ideals in the World* (Stanford Law Books, 2012).

Kuennen, TL, 'Private Relationships and Public Problems: Applying Principles of Relational Contract Theory to Domestic Violence' (2010) *Brigham Young University Law Review* 515.

Kuney, GW, 'Hijacking Chapter 11' (2004) 21 *Emory Bankruptcy Developments Journal* 19.

Lacey, N, '"Philosophical Foundations of the Common Law": Social not Metaphysical' in J Horder (ed), *Oxford Essays in Jurisprudence: Fourth Series* (Oxford, 2000) 17–39.

Laeuchli, S, *Power and Sexuality: The Emergency of Canon Law at the Synod of Elvira* (Temple University Press, 1972).

Landers, JM, 'Reflections on Loan-to-Own Trends' (2007) 26 *American Bankruptcy Institute Law Review* 44.

Lecompte, J, 'Coronado and Conquest' (1989) 64 *New Mexico Historical Review* 279.

Lee, Harper, *To Kill a Mockingbird* (Lippincott, 1960).

Legg, M, 'The United States Deposition – Time for Adoption in Australian Civil Procedure?' (2007) 31 *Melbourne University Law Review* 146.

Levy, R and Orr, G, *The Law of Deliberative Democracy* (Routledge, 2017).

Leyser, C, 'Cities of the Plain: The Rhetoric of Sodomy in Peter Damian's "Book of Gomorrah"' (1995) 86 *Romanic Review* 191.

Lipson, JC, 'The Shadow Bankruptcy System' (2009) 90 *Boston University Law Review* 1609.

—— 'Governance in the Breach: Controlling Creditor Opportunism' (2010) 84 *Southern California Law Review* 1035.

—— 'Bargaining Bankrupt: A Relational Theory of Contract in Bankruptcy' (2016) 6 *Harvard Business Law Review* 239.

—— 'The Secret Life of Priority: Corporate Reorganization After *Jevic*' (2018) 93 *Washington Law Review* 631.

Liu, S, 'Law's Social Forms: A Powerless Approach to the Sociology of Law' (2015) 40 *Law & Social Inquiry* 1.

Llewellyn, KN, 'A Realistic Jurisprudence-The Next Step' (1930) 30 *Columbia Law Review* 431.

LoPucki, LM, 'The Trouble with Chapter 11' (1993) *Wisconsin Law Review* 729.

Lyndall, R, '"No Right to the Land": The Role of the Wool Industry in the Destruction of Aboriginal Societies in Tasmania (1817–1832) and Victoria (1835–1851) Compared' in M Adhikari (ed). *Genocide on Settler Frontiers: When Hunter-Gatherers and Commercial Stock Farmers Clash* (Oxford University Press, 2015).

Lytton, TD, *Holding Bishops Accountable: How Lawsuits Helped the Catholic Church Confront Clergy Sexual Abuse* (Harvard University Press, 2008).

Macaulay, S, 'A New Legal Realism: Elegant Models and the Messy Law in Action' in E Mertz, S Macaulay and TW Mitchell (eds), *The New Legal Realism Volume I: Translating Law-and-Society for Today's Legal Practice* (Cambridge University Press, 2016) 29–50.

Macaulay, S, Friedman, LM and Mertz, E, *Law in Action: A Socio-Legal Reader* (Foundation Press, 2007).

MacMahon, P, 'Proceduralism, Civil Justice, and American Legal Thought' (2013) 34 *University of Pennsylvania Journal of International Law* 545.

Main, TO, 'The Procedural Foundation of Substantive Law' (2010) 87 *Washington University Law Review* 801.

McAleese, M, *Quo Vadis? Collegiality in the Code of Canon Law* (Columba Press, 2012).

McDonnell, K, 'Feminist Mariologies: Heteronomy/ Subordination and the Scandal of Christology' (2005) 66 *Theological Studies* 527.

McKinnon, J, *Report on a Survey of the Religious Attitudes of the Diocese of Ballarat* (Diocese of Ballarat, 1973).

McPhillips, K, 'Traumatic Isolation: Institutional Stigma and the Australian Royal Commission into Institutional Responses to Child Sexual Abuse,' (2018) 20 *Health and History* 75.

McSweeny, B, 'The Priesthood in Sociological Theory' (1974) 21 *Social Compass* 5.

Merriam, CE, *Political Power: Its Composition and Incidence* (Mc Graw-Hill, 1934).

—— *Colonizing Hawai'i: The Cultural Power of Law* (Princeton University Press, 1999).

—— 'Legal Pluralism and Legal Culture Mapping the Terrain' in BZ Tamanaha, C Sage and M Woolcock (eds), *Legal Pluralism and Development: Scholars and Practitioners in Dialogue*, (Cambridge University Press, 2012).

Michalowski, R, 'The Necropolitics of Regulation' (2020) 1 *Journal of White Collar and Corporate Crime* 83.

Milavec, A, *The Didache: Text, Translation, Analysis, and Commentary* (Liturgical Press, 2003).

Miller, HR and Waisman, SY, 'Is Chapter 11 Bankrupt?' (2005) 47 *Boston College Law Review* 129.

Mohamed, A (ed), *Genocide on Settler Frontiers: When Hunter-Gatherers and Commercial Stock Farmers Clash* (Oxford University Press, 2015).

Molot, JT, 'How US Procedure Skews Tort Law Incentives' (1997) 73 *Indiana Law Journal* 59.

Moreton-Robinson, A, 'Imagining the Good Indigenous Citizen: Race War and the Pathology of Patriarchal White Sovereignty' (2009) 15 *Cultural Studies Review* 61.

Morton, S, 'Getting Evidence into Action to Tackle Institutional Child Abuse' (2017) 74 *Child Abuse & Neglect* 111.

Nonet, P and Selznick, P, *Law and Society in Transition: Toward Responsive Law* (Routledge, 2001).

Noonan, KG, Lipson, JC and Simon, WH, 'Reforming Institutions: The Judicial Function in Bankruptcy and Public Law Litigation' (2019) 94 *Indiana Law Journal* 545.

Nungent, JS, 'A Higher Authority: The Viability of Third Party Tort Actions against a Religious Institution Grounded on Sexual Misconduct by a Member of the Clergy (2002) 30 *Florida State University Law Review* 957.

Oates, K, 'The Royal Commission into Child Sexual Abuse: A Beginning, Not an End' (2018) 54 *Journal of Paediatrics and Child Health* 221.

Olick, JK, *The Politics of Regret: On Collective Memory and Historical Responsibility* (Routledge, 2007).

O'Reilly, JT and Chalmers, MSP, *The Clergy Sex Abuse Crisis and the Legal Responses* (Oxford University Press, 2014).

Palmer, D, and Feldman, V, 'Toward a More Comprehensive Analysis of the Role of Organizational Culture in Child Sexual Abuse in Institutional Contexts' (2017) 74 *Child Abuse & Neglect* 23.

Parker, JF, 'Blaming Eve Alone: Translation, Omission, and Implications of עמה in Genesis 3:6b.' (2013) 132 *Journal of Biblical Literature* 729.

Parkinson, P, 'Child Sexual Abuse and the Churches: A Story of Moral Failure?' (2014) 26 *Current Issues in Criminal Justice* 119.

Pascoe, S, 'The 2009 Victorian Bushfires Royal Commission: Lessons for the Conduct of Inquiries in Australia' (2010) 69 *The Australian Journal of Public Administration* 392.

Peters, MA, 'Child sexual abuse: The final report of the Australian Royal Commission into institutional responses to child sexual abuse' (2019) 51 *Educational Philosophy and Theory* 233.

Pettit, P, *Republicanism: A Theory of Freedom and Government* (Clarendon Press, 1997).

Pike, AM, 'Discovering Records Beneath the Robes: Canonical Protection and Civil Resurrection of the Boston Archdiocese Secret Archives' (2010) 19 *Journal of Information Ethics* 86.

Porter, K and D Thorne, 'The Failure of Bankruptcy's Fresh Start' (2006) 92 *Cornell Law Review* 67.

Posner, R, 'Instrumental and Noninstrumental Theories of Tort Law' (2013) 88 *Indiana Law Journal* 469.

Potts, D, 'Arizona Case Note: *Engler v. Gulf Interstate Engineering, Inc.* and the Role of Control in Vicarious Liability' (2012) 54 *Arizona Law Review* 1157.

Pound, R, *An Introduction to the Philosophy of Law* (Yale University Press, 1922).

—— 'Law in Books and Law in Action' (1940) 44 *American Law Review* 12.

—— *Jurisprudence* (West Publishing, 1959).

Prasser, S, 'When Should Royal Commissions be Appointed?' (2005) *Public Administration Today* 57.

—— 'Royal Commissions in Australia: When Should Governments Appoint Them'? (2006) 65 *Australian Journal of Public Administration* 28.

Prasser, S, and Tracey, H, 'History, Trends and Key Issues – The Story So Far …' in S Prasser and H Tracey (eds), *Royal Commissions & Public Inquiries: Practice & Potential* (Connor Court Publishing, 2014).

Provost, JH, 'Some Canonical Considerations Relative to Clerical Sexual Misconduct' (1992) 52 *Jurist* 615.

Pruitt, LR and Colgan, BA, 'Justice Deserts: Spatial Inequality and Local Funding of Indigent Defense' (2010) 51 *Arizona Law Review* 219.

Pruitt, LR and Showman, BE, 'Law Stretched Thin: Access to Justice in Rural America' (2014) 59 *South Dakota Law Review* 466.

Ransley, J, 'Public Inquiries into Political Wrongdoing' in S Prasser and H Tracey (eds), *Royal Commissions & Public Inquiries: Practice & Potential* (Connor Court Publishing, 2014) ch 4.

Rashid, F and Barron, I, 'The Roman Catholic Church: A Centuries Old History of Awareness of Clerical Child Sexual Abuse (from the First to the 19th Century)' (2018) 27 *Journal of Child Sexual Abuse* 778.

Rasmussen, RK, 'Debtor's Choice: A Menu Approach to Corporate Bankruptcy' (1992) 71 *Texas Law Review* 51.

—— 'An Essay on Optimal Bankruptcy Rules and Social Justice' (1994) 1 *University of Illinois Law Review* 1.

Rasmussen, RK and Skeel, DA, Jr, 'The Economic Analysis of Corporate Bankruptcy Law' (1995) 3 *American Bankruptcy Institute Law Review* 85.

Reid, CJ Jr and Witte, J Jr, 'In the Steps of Gratian: Writing the History of Canon Law in the 1990s' (1999) 48 *Emory Law Journal* 647.

Reilly, MT, 'Catholic Dioceses in Bankruptcy' (2019) 49 *Seton Hall Law Review* 871.

Reitsema, AM and Grietens, H, 'Is Anybody Listening? The Literature on the Dialogical Process of Child Sexual Abuse Disclosure Reviewed' (2016) 17 *Trauma, Violence & Abuse* 330.

Renati, CG, 'Prescription and Derogation from Prescription in Sexual Abuse of Minor Cases' (2007) 67 *The Jurist: Studies in Church Law and Ministry* 503.

Rheinstein, M (ed), *Max Weber on Law in Economy and Society* (Harvard University Press, 1954).

Rivera, ÁE, 'Contested Necrocapitalism: Indigeneity Versus Extractivism in Northern Canada' in A Estévez (ed), *Necropower in North America: The Legal Spatialization of Disposability and Lucrative Death* (Palgrave MacMillan, 2021) 129.

Ruether, RR, *Women and Redemption: A Theological History* (Fortress Press, 1998).
Rustad, ML, 'Twenty-First-Century Tort Theories: The Internalist/Externalist Debate' (2013) 88 *Indiana Law Journal* 419.
Ryan, D, and Hoysted, P, *Unholy Trinity: The Hunt for the Paedophile Priest Monsignor John Day* (Allen & Unwin, 2013).
Salter, M, 'The Transitional Space of Public Inquiries: The Case of the Australian Royal Commission into Institutional Responses to Child Sexual Abuse' (2020) 53 *Australian & NZ Journal of Criminology* 213.
Schwarcz, SL, 'Sovereign Debt Restructuring: A Bankruptcy Reorganization Approach' (2000) 85 *Cornell Law Review* 956.
Selznick, P, *The Moral Commonwealth: Social Theory and the Promise of Community* (University of California Press, 1992).
Sherr, R, 'A Canon, A Choirboy, and Homosexuality in Late Sixteenth-Century Italy,' (1991) 21 *Journal of Homosexuality* 1.
Shiner, RA, 'Corporations and Presumption of Innocence' (2014) 8 *Criminal Law and Philosophy* 485.
Simmons, W and Emanuele, R, 'Male and Female Recoveries in Medical Malpractice Cases' (2004) 62 *Review of Social Economy* 83.
Skeel, DA Jr, 'Vern Countryman and the Path of Progressive (and Populist) Bankruptcy Scholarship' (1999) 113 *Harvard Law Review* 1075.
Silink, A and Stewart, P, 'Tort Law Reform to Improve Access to Compensation for Survivors of Institutional Child Sexual Abuse' (2016) 39 *University of New South Wales Law Journal* 553.
Skolnick, JH, 'Legacies of Legal Realism: The Sociology of Criminal Law and Criminal Justice' (2012) 8 *Annual Review of Law and Social Science* 1.
Southworth, A, Garth, B and Fisk, C, 'Some Realism about Realism in Teaching about the Legal Profession' in S Engle Merry and H Klug (eds), *The New Legal Realism Volume 2: Studying Law Globally* (Cambridge University Press, 2016) 74–94.
Spender, P, 'Blue Asbestos and Golden Eggs: Evaluating Bankruptcy and Class Actions as Just Responses to Mass Tort Liability' (2003) 25 *Sydney Law Review* 223.
Steele, PD, 'Child Sexual Abuse among Socially Marginalized Groups: Cultural and Governmental Influences Perpetuating Maltreatment in American Indian Country' (2009) 1 *Forum on Public Policy*.
Stern, PJ 'The Corporation in History' in G Baars and A Spicer (eds), *The Corporation: A Critical, Multi-Disciplinary Handbook* (Cambridge University Press, 2017) 21–46.
Stewart, P, and Stuhmcke, A, *Australian Principles of Tort Law*, 3rd edn (The Federation Press, 2012).
Stoltenborgh, M, van IJzendoorn, MH, Euser, EM and Bakermans-Kranenburg, MJ, 'A Global Perspective on Child Sexual Abuse: Meta-Analysis of Prevalence Around the World' (2011) 16 *Child Maltreatment* 79.
Strang, H and Sherman, LW, 'The Practice of Restorative Justice: Repairing the Harm: Victims and Restorative Justice' (2003) *Utah Law Review* 15.
Sunstein, CR, 'Incompletely Theorized Agreements' (1995) 108 *Harvard Law Review* 1733.
Sutherland, EH, 'White-Collar Criminality' (1939) 5 *American Sociological Review* 1.
Tamanaha, B, 'Law's Evolving Emergent Phenomena: From Rules of Social Intercourse to Rule of Law Society' (2018) 95 *Washington University Law Review* 1149.
Tamanaha, BZ, 'Legal Realism in Context' in E Mertz, S Macaulay and TW Mitchell (eds), *The New Legal Realism Volume I: Translating Law-and-Society for Today's Legal Practice* (Cambridge University Press, 2016) 147–68.
——'Functions of the Rule of Law' in J Meierhenrich and M Loughlin (eds), *The Cambridge Companion to the Rule of Law* (Cambridge University Press, 2021) 221–36.
Tapsell, K, *Potiphar's Wife: The Vatican's Secret and Child Sexual Abuse* (ATF Press, 2014).
Tishelman, AC and Fontes, LA, 'Religion in Child Sexual Abuse Forensic Interviews' (2017) 63 *Child Abuse and Neglect* 120.

Tucci J, and Blom, M, '"These Were Terrible Years. No Love or Kindness, No Safety or Warmth". Reflections on the Outcomes of the Royal Commission into Institutional Responses to Child Sexual Abuse in Australia' (2019) 20 *Journal of Trauma Dissociation* 373.

Twining, W, 'Legal R/Realism and Jurisprudence: Ten Theses' in E Mertz, S Macaulay and TW Mitchell (eds), *The New Legal Realism Volume I: Translating Law-and-Society for Today's Legal Practice* (Cambridge University Press, 2016) 121–46.

Umphrey, MM, 'Review' (2004) 38 *Law & Society Review* 833.

Unger, RM, *Law in Modern Society* (Free Press, 1976).

Walpole, S, 'Criminal Responsibility as a Distinctive Form of Corporate Regulation' (2020) 35 *Australian Journal of Corporate Law* 235.

Warren, E, 'The Untenable Case for Repeal of Chapter 11' (1992) 102 *Yale Law Journal* 437.

Warren, E and Westbrook, JL, 'The Success of Chapter 11: A Challenge to the Critics' (2009) 107 *Michigan Law Review* 603.

Welch, JR and Brauchli, RC, '"Subject to the Right of the Secretary of the Interior": the White Mountain Apache Reclamation of the Fort Apache and Theodore Roosevelt School Historic District' (2010) 25 *Wicazo Sa Review* 47.

Wells, CP, 'Who Owns the Local Church? A Pressing Issue for Dioceses in Bankruptcy' (2004) 29 *Seton Hall Legislative Journal* 375.

White, MD and Terry, KJ, 'Child Sexual Abuse in the Catholic Church: Revisiting the Rotten Apples Explanation' (2008) 35 *Criminal Justice and Behavior* 65.

Wirenius, JF, '"Command and Coercion": Clerical Immunity, Scandal, and the Sex Abuse Crisis in the Roman Catholic Church' (2012) 27 *The Journal of Law and Religion* 423.

Withers, WB, *History of Ballarat and Some Ballarat Reminiscences* (Ballarat Heritage Services, 1999).

van Wormer, K and Berns, L, 'The Impact of Priest Sexual Abuse: Female Survivors' Narratives' (2004) 19 *Affilia – Journal of Women and Social Work* 53.

Wright, K, 'Remaking Collective Knowledge: An Analysis of the Complex and Multiple Effects of Inquiries into Historical Institutional Child Abuse' (2017) 74 *Child Abuse and Neglect* 10.

Wright, K, and Swain, S, 'Speaking the Unspeakable, Naming the Unnameable: The Royal Commission into Institutional Responses to Child Sexual Abuse' (2018) 42 *Journal of Australian Studies* 139.

Youngdahl, J, *Working on the Railroad, Walking in Beauty: Navajos, Hózhǫ́, and Track Work* (Utah State University Press, 2011).

Zatkin, J, Sitney, M and Kaufman, K, 'The Relationship Between Policy, Media, and Perceptions of Sexual Offenders Between 2007 and 2017: A Review of the Literature' (2022) 23 *Trauma, Violence, and Abuse* 953.

Websites and Archival Sources

www.abuseincare.org.nz

www.BishopAccountability.org

www.Catholicproject.catholic.edu/catholic-church-finances/bankruptcy-information/

www.Childabuseroyalcommission.gov.au/

www.uscourts.gov/court-records/electronic-filing-cm-ecf

INDEX

www.ingramcontent.com/pod-product-compliance
Lightning Source LLC
LaVergne TN
LVHW012313071225
827216LV00003B/114